The Churchill Myths

The Churchill Myths

STEVEN FIELDING
BILL SCHWARZ
RICHARD TOYE

OXFORD
UNIVERSITY PRESS

OXFORD

UNIVERSITY PRESS

Great Clarendon Street, Oxford, OX2 6DP,
United Kingdom

Oxford University Press is a department of the University of Oxford.
It furthers the University's objective of excellence in research, scholarship,
and education by publishing worldwide. Oxford is a registered trade mark of
Oxford University Press in the UK and in certain other countries

First Edition published in 2020

Impression: 3

Published in the United States of America by Oxford University Press
198 Madison Avenue, New York, NY 10016, United States of America

British Library Cataloguing in Publication Data

Data available

Library of Congress Control Number: 2020933790

ISBN 978-0-19-885196-7

Printed and bound by
CPI Group (UK) Ltd, Croydon, CR0 4YY

Contents

List of Figures

Introduction

This is not a book about Winston Churchill. It is not a book about the historical figure of Churchill, who lived from 1874 to 1965 and served as Britain's prime minister during the Second World War and again between 1951 and 1955. It is not about his politics, nor his rhetorical imagination, nor about the man himself.

What the book does explore, however, is how memories of Churchill have been variously deployed, especially since his death. In this respect Churchill has proved in the past, and continues to prove in our own times, that he was and remains 'good to think with' (to use Claude Lévi-Strauss's term). That is to say, he is a highly charged figure through whom many Britons imagine their relationship with their past, present, and future.

If Churchill had been a comparable figure in France, historians and media commentators, following Pierre Nora, would have readily understood 'him', or rather his memory, as a *lieu de mémoire*: that is, as a site where conflicting memories accumulate and carry sufficient weight that they can create a publicly sanctioned shorthand for understanding—and for intervening in—the relations between the past and the present.[1] There is no handy equivalent in the anglophone world. As authors of this book we can say, though, that we are concerned with the place of *symbolic* Churchill in the recasting of history. It should be noted that, although we do not attempt to arbitrate between competing interpretations of the historical Churchill, we do occasionally discuss whether certain given claims about him can be said to have a factual basis.

Why do we, in the pages which follow, present 'remembered Churchill' as a problem which needs to be discussed rather than a figure to be celebrated? Are we 'Churchill bashers', or 'detractors', as his critics are sometimes labelled? Are we amongst those who, it is often claimed, like to run Britain down by carping at its former glories? In truth we sidestep these concerns for what we propose has little to do with Churchill the man, cast as either hero or villain. It is not our mission here to adjudicate on this, apportioning points for or against as in a boxing match. Mythic Churchill calls for our attention because, we argue, it (not 'he') stands as a serious fact of modern life. This mythic strain is never only a quaint, touristy audit of an old country, featured on biscuit tins and in jigsaw puzzles, handy for gifts to distant, ancient aunts or uncles whose emotional investments we find improbable. 'He'—what he has come to represent—has transmogrified into a deeper, more troubling, and darker phenomenon in which the past weighs unforgivingly on the present. He is a constant point of reference in political discussion and popular culture, in which we are all implicated.

We embarked on this book in the conviction that we need to illuminate those aspects of the past which are placed beyond the reach of immediate memory. This occurs *precisely because of* the mythic properties which dominate the elemental Churchill story. We suggest that in the very moment Churchill is remembered a forgetfulness is simultaneously induced, resulting in the elimination or relegation of other competing stories.

We argue, further, that there exists a compulsive current to the persistent resurrections of Churchill. This is a syndrome which traverses, on the one hand, the accredited intellectual world of historians, newspaper commentators, and some politicians and, on the other, the less ordered domain of popular storytelling. The compulsions informing the collective mentalities which gather under the banner of Churchill need to be acknowledged for what they are, in all their strangeness. Why is it that Winston Churchill, the man, is repetitively revived? Would it not be wiser for us to switch attention analytically from the mortal being, and from the temptations to deify him, and to focus instead on the historical predicaments of those who devote themselves to summoning his spirit?

The imagined Churchill explored in this book is a phenomenon that appeals to many Britons but especially to those who speak of 'England'. When the fate of the people is perceived to be in danger, however highly strung these fears may be judged, Churchill is on hand to enter the frame. Those identified as the enemies shape-shift; but the persona of Churchill remains, it seems, implacably resilient. Just when it looks as if he has served his time and all life within him is spent, back he comes, growling and thundering, the principal lead in the national melodrama. In the popular iconography he is reduced to his growl, to his V-for-victory gesture, to his cigar, or to his hat. These signs, working as a code instantly decipherable to those in the know, are familiar features in the nation's mental landscape. Even so: he never goes away; he is always on hand, awaiting his moment. And as things stand, it is overbearingly likely that future generations will remain, unwilled, subject to his memory.

The Meaning of Myths

In order to describe this state of affairs we employ the term myth. The concept itself, for us, carries no intrinsic value judgements. Myth we understand to be an indispensable dimension of our historical world, inside us all. We are influenced here by two dominating approaches.

On the one hand myth can be conceptualized as a system of signs which settles deep in the symbolic foundations of a society, unnoticed but providing the means by which external phenomena are arranged and classified. By this means, it is possible to make sense of the external world. This perspective owes much to Claude Lévi-Strauss and to the popularizations of his methods in Roland Barthes' *Mythologies*.[2] Arbitrary objects, through a teeth-gritting process of social negotiation, become 'good to think with'. As Barthes puts it: 'Every object in the world can pass from a closed, silent existence to an oral state, open to appropriation by society, for there is no law, whether natural or not, which forbids talking about things.' He continues: 'it is human history which converts reality into speech, and it alone rules the life and death of mythical language.'[3] For both Lévi-Strauss and Barthes the key lies in the ways that formal systems of classification become socially agreed, leading to a method of working committed to prising open the organization of mental life, in its deep, invariant forms over the long duration.

Critics of this approach habitually condemn it as inimical to history, pointing to its formalism and lack of interest in temporal change. While true, it was also the case that the virtue of studying myth, for Barthes if not for Lévi-Strauss, was that the unutterable task of myth was to *divest the world of its historicalness.* 'It transforms history into nature' and, in doing so, it becomes a crucial means by which 'common sense' is organized. This raises the political stakes. Myth for Barthes naturalizes what requires to be historicized. In a concluding flourish he defined myth as '*depoliticized* speech'.[4]

An alternative perspective, on the other hand, takes myth to be malleable, contingent, and the active consequence of human agency. This analysis is concerned with content rather than with internal, unseen structures. As manifest in anglophone historiography, in tone it is empirically minded, drawn to that which is observable on the surface of social life, and tenaciously respectful of the play of historical movement.

A single example will illustrate this. In 1954 the great historian of seventeenth-century England, Christopher Hill, published a renowned essay with the title 'The Norman Yoke', at the same time that Barthes was writing his *Mythologies*.[5] He argued that from the early modern period it was usual in popular life to imagine the Norman Conquest to have uprooted the ancient liberties of Anglo-Saxon England, imposing a foreign tyranny under the rule of Norman barons, or *banditti*, as Tom Paine was fond of impugning them. This, as Hill demonstrated, only weakly conformed to any discernible historical record. But it nonetheless provided a rich resource in vernacular life for articulating the experience of social exploitation. The name Alfred—after the Saxon figurehead, Alfred the Great—henceforth itself became an intoxicating sign for liberty. The myth of the Norman Yoke continued to function in a substratum of popular life, Hill contends, until the onset of the Industrial Revolution when a new politics emerged in the recast field of class relations, evident later in Chartism. In Hill's interpretation, this allowed the exploited to look forward to emancipation in the future, rather than looking back to an illusory untarnished past. As these new historical circumstances took hold, affiliations to the imperatives of the Norman Yoke dissipated, having had a long run, present now only in the occasional ghostly remnant.

In contrast to Barthes, Hill's reading is organized by his faith in the potential vitality of mythic thought as a vernacular form of collective historical consciousness. He was at pains to emphasize the historical conditions which explain the making, and the unmaking, of the long duration of the mythic Norman Yoke. Myth, in Hill's reading, is exactly *not* depoliticized thought. It is how politics is fought out in the symbolic world.

In the human sciences these two approaches have conventionally been understood, in terms of their respective methods, as divergent or as necessary alternatives. However, there is a case to view them as illuminating contradictory aspects of the same phenomena, that can coexist—in tension—together. They alert us to the simultaneous presence of the foundational structures of a myth (*langue*, in Ferdinand Saussure's terms) and its more mobile, historically variable manifestations (*parole*), where history impinges more immediately.

Similarly, we might also understand the realm of myth as itself contradictory, with the potential both to empty the historical world (negatively) of its historicalness and (positively, perhaps) to function as a live theatre for popular feeling, creating new ways in which the past is lived in the present.[6] Mythic imaginings, in the abstract, are neither, essentially, positive; nor are they, essentially, negative. We, therefore, examine the 'Churchill myths' in the plural. Although there is a powerful core myth, which focuses on the 'Finest Hour' of 1940, even this has not been static over the decades. This myth has been internationalized and domesticated in the United States, playing an important role in presidential rhetoric from the Vietnam War onwards. It can be used instrumentally as well by groups within Britain and Europe who might not be thought to be natural Churchill admirers, notably those who have invoked his memory in aid of Britain's membership of the EU. There are also anti-Churchill myths, whereby the Great Man theory of history is inverted, to turn him into the ultimate embodiment of the evils of capitalism and imperialism.

History and the Churchill Myths

The Churchill myths, like all myths, are historically particular, and they are taken up by different people for different reasons. They are not programmed to follow a destined path. Mythic Churchill signals for some an uncanny, fraught mode of remembering. It carries a profound melancholic timbre animated by the idea that, confronted by the depredations of the present, our 'Finest Hour' operates only in the past, working as a vanishing memory. For others however, it is an inspiration to future action: that which we did in the past we can do again. But when Churchill is summoned in the present, often he arrives at the call of an unspecified 'we' or 'us', or as 'ours'. Who, we ask, is this collective first person, and who is excluded?

The very weight and grandeur of *these* pasts can imperceptibly turn into a mechanism for divesting the present of its history. In an awkward, uncomfortable contortion, the future is locked in 'our' collective backward glance. Mythic Churchill takes command. When we glimpse 'him' looming on the horizon, 'he' commonly acts as an invitation for us to stop *thinking* about ourselves. We know the story even before the first syllables are uttered. Providence descends and thought evaporates.

We have, however, reached a new phase in the history of the Churchill myths. Views of Churchill the man are today probably more polarized than they have ever been. His popularity, although contested, is undeniable. In 2002 nearly half a million television viewers voted him the 'Greatest Briton' in a BBC poll. This is not to say that he is or has been universally applauded. The social confidence in the authority of mythic Churchill is marked by the fact that, in one of its very heartlands, the contrariness of the Great Man has been prominently institutionalized. In the exhibition attached to the Churchill War Rooms visitors are invited, in the name of pluralism, to vote on whether they consider him to have been a 'Radical or reactionary?' Yet it is curious that the outcome of the poll—whatever it may be, day by day—is less material than the fact that the queues for the exhibition are always long and that visitors (or some of them) choose to cast a vote. This suggests perhaps that *mythic* Churchill operates in a different domain of social practice from a simple allegiance to a pro- or anti- stance: to good or bad, to hero or villain. The myths of Winston Churchill, it seems, depend on an order of meaning in which particular political preferences are largely rendered secondary. The person who advocated Churchill's case in the 2002 BBC poll was, it should be recalled, the former Labour cabinet minister Mo Mowlam.

Even so, there are plenty of instances when public hostility to Churchill is evident. In 2019, when a tweet from the official

Conservative Party feed declared that its former leader was 'For many, the greatest Briton to have ever lived', it generated the riposte that he was, on the contrary, 'For many, the greatest genocidal butcher to have ever lived.'[7] This was undoubtedly a minority sentiment. But examples from Britain and around the world can be multiplied. Nor are such negative interpretations only retrospective. During his lifetime, the terminology may have differed—'warmonger', or even 'more blood on his hands than Hitler', rather than *genocidal* butcher'—but the criticisms were none-theless voiced.[8] During the 1951 election, for example, at the height of the Cold War, the Labour Party cast Churchill as a formidable enemy of peace, leading the *Daily Mirror* to carry on its front page, on the day of the vote, an image of a cocked revolver alongside the menacing question: 'Whose Finger?'[9]

That there is an undertow of antagonism to the historical figure may not be surprising. Yet what is striking is the degree to which dissident voices do little to impede the continued unrolling of mythic Churchill. It's startling how even tempered criticisms, based on a deal of justifica-tion in the historical record, are received as a way of thinking akin to sacrilege. To challenge the prevailing Churchill stories risks blowback. For example, in an essentially celebratory BBC documentary broadcast five decades after Churchill's funeral, the usually acerbic presenter, Jeremy Paxman, concluded:

> Sure, he was a chancer, an egotist, a workaholic and sometimes a bit of a charlatan, but in this age of political miniatures, there is no one who can hold a candle to him. For the sake of the nation, we must hope that the old cliché about never seeing his like again isn't true because, one day, we may need his like, but in the fifty years since his death, there has been no sign of such a figure.[10]

Even this, however, was regarded by Churchill's descendants as defama-tory; the family, as Paxman put it, went 'nuts'.[11] Churchill's great-grandson Randolph fumed at what he regarded as the presenter's impertinence:

> I am lucky enough to know what the truth is—that to this day, the Churchill name carries with it a lustre that makes everyone's eyes light

up. You can see the image that his very name paints for people. It brings a smile to their faces. In times of difficulty people delve deep and reach out to his story and remind themselves that things are by no means as hard as the crises that he faced.[12]

In contemporary Britain, Churchill himself may be long dead. But his myths are seemingly immortal.

Brexit and the Churchill Myths

When Geri Horner (aka Ginger Spice) claimed in 2019 that Churchill was 'the original Spice Girl' because he 'won a war for us and he got fired' it was not possible to discern any given politics. Yet even if Horner's comment represented no more than a means to publicize her upcoming tour, its very banality is revealing of wider currents.[13] For she spoke in the aftermath of the 2016 Brexit referendum campaign, one which saw Churchill reanimated and conscripted to fight for two diametrically opposed causes. Echoes of May 1940, when Britain 'stood alone' free from European entanglements, punctuate Brexiteer sensibilities. Remainers, however, challenge this perspective, and invoke their own Churchill. As the former Conservative cabinet minister Michael Heseltine told a demonstration against Brexit in March 2019: 'Alone was never Churchill's hope or wish: it was his fear.' To the likes of Heseltine, Churchill was a man of international engagement, not one seeking isolationism.

Some Brexiteers argue that isolation is not their aim, insisting that they intend to restore Britain's greatness by recapturing the dynamism of their Victorian forebears, 'to go back out into the world', in the words of Boris Johnson, 'to find friends, to open markets, to promote our culture and our values'.[14] Again, Churchill serves a useful function. While it is now common for his modern-day cheerleaders to acknowledge his imperial and racial views to be anachronistic in today's world, in the same breath they insist that during Churchill's life such thinking was wholly of its time and thus excusable. If the imperial dimensions can be stripped away as merely tangential to his core Britishness, we are left with a bulldog Churchill who comes to personify a post-imperial national spirit. By such means old-school chauvinism is reconciled with the claim to be outward-looking and 'global'.

Even so, underpinning Brexit has been a long-standing mistrust on the British right of European federalism, which some have viewed as a Trojan Horse for German domination. In 1990 one of Margaret Thatcher's favourite ministers, Nicholas Ridley, spoke for many in the Conservative Party when describing plans for European Monetary Union as 'a German racket designed to take over the whole of Europe', concluding that if it was not prevented, 'You might just as well give it up to Adolf Hitler, frankly.'[15] Ridley was forced to resign when his comments became public. But since then such instincts have become more confidently voiced. During the referendum Johnson claimed the EU shared with Hitler the same ambition to unite Europe, establishing parallels between the choice that confronted Britain in 1940— Churchill's historic moment—and the decision then facing voters. By choosing to Leave, he argued, once again Britons would be 'the heroes of Europe' by stopping the expansion of untrammelled power.[16] Some have gone further. Building on Johnson's comments, the UKIP MEP and future (albeit short-lived) party leader, Gerard Batten, claimed that the European Economic Community 'was planned [and] created by the kind of people who would have run Europe's economies if Germany had won the war, and their plans followed a very similar pattern'.[17]

If history demonstrated to the satisfaction of militant Leavers the Nazi roots of the EU, it also legitimized the conviction that Britons possessed the fortitude to again oppose this traditional threat to their liberty. This was likely the meaning behind the future Brexit Party leader Nigel Farage's tweet that 'I urge every youngster to go out and watch #Dunkirk' after the latest dramatization of the 'miraculous' evacuation of 400,000 Allied soldiers under heavy German fire.[18] Ann Widdecombe, a former Conservative minister and successful Brexit Party candidate in the 2018 European Parliamentary elections, declared a No Deal Brexit would be 'as nothing compared to the sacrifice we asked a previous generation to make in order to ensure Britain's freedom ... People lost sons and husbands and fathers and they did this because they wanted freedom.'[19] If some, like Johnson, appear to have exploited this sentiment for their own purposes, others give every impression of being its willing prisoner. When Farage visited Shoreham Aircraft Museum, dedicated to the memory of the Battle of Britain, he regarded the remains dug up from crash sites scattered about the fields of Kent with a solemnity more usually associated with a pilgrim inspecting religious relics.[20] However, Farage's expression of respect exists side by side with his desire to profit from the visceral thrill of reliving the war, safe from the personal need of sacrifice. Most blatantly his arrival at a packed 2019 Brexit Party rally in Birmingham was preceded by wailing Second World War sirens and a blackout.[21]

Wartime nostalgia continues to work in conjunction with the fashioning of new instalments of the Churchill myths, each acting upon the other. At the beginning of the twenty-first century, memories of the war continue to provide rich seams in the remakings of popular culture. Clearly, it is important not to overstate the importance such factors have in driving political outcomes. Most obviously, the impact of the post-2007 banking crisis should certainly be taken into account when considering what led to the result of the EU referendum. But it may well be that economic distress and a sense of crisis meant that nostalgic appeals fell on fertile soil. In 2009 Dame Vera Lynn—known during the war as the Forces Sweetheart, and best known for her rendition of 'We'll Meet Again'—became, aged ninety-three, the oldest living artist to score a Number 1 album, with her 'Very Best Of' collection.[22] The year before Premier Foods sought to revive the fortunes of its long-established Hovis brand of breads by producing a commercial that deftly narrated the social history of twentieth-century Britain through the story of a single—impossibly long-lived—loaf of bread. As one might have predicted, the Blitz and the soundtrack of Churchill declaring that he would 'fight on the beaches' both featured. In this the copywriters knowingly addressed the TV nostalgia with which the Hovis brand had been indelibly associated.[23] In a different sector of the national culture the British National Party employed the image of a Spitfire in its election propaganda.[24] These are instances which suggest, paradoxically, that nostalgia isn't what it used to be. But the more knowing it becomes, the greater it seems its hold.

The Principles of the Book

This book is the work of three pairs of hands. Yet while our chapters employ contrasting approaches to the Churchill myths, they are all guided by the following principles.

First, mythic Churchill is ordered around no organizational centre. While the influence of the Churchill family and the legal authority of the Estate remain of material significance, there is no HQ directing operations, with sufficient reach and authority to police what is said or not said. The phenomenon is amorphous rather than externally regulated, arising from a plurality, or mixed economy, of cultural and political sources. Philanthropy, legal regimes concerning archival material, copyright restrictions, and even the National Lottery, have all had their parts to play. Many of the figures who have helped shape Britons' understanding of Churchill have been American. It is precisely the plurality of social institutions which commit themselves to mythic Churchill that is most in need of historical explanation.

Second, recognizing this diversity, we place in a single analytical frame both the many, contrary manifestations of the various Churchill legends *and* the common, invariant properties which make the range of individual stories recognizably instalments in a common process of codification, resulting in Churchill *as* myth. We endeavour to attend both to the structures and forms of the mythic dimension, on the one hand, and on the other, to the contingency and plurality of the swirl of competing manifestations in their particular historical moments.

Third, we are alive to the fact that Churchill, as self-styled man of destiny, was throughout his political career peculiarly self-conscious of his own rendezvous with history. He was assiduous in establishing his own historic—or mythic—credentials, much as Charles de Gaulle, his *bête noir*, was in the France of the same period. Both believed themselves to be the incarnations of their respective nations, each in an age when the nation state was beginning to lose its political authority. In this regard, the emphasis on Churchill as a dedicated rhetorician constitutes a crucial element in our argument.

Fourth, in developing our argument we give historical shape to the dominating trajectories of the Churchill myths. We supply a history to what otherwise can too easily be perceived as an invariant feature of Britain's political landscape. We are attentive to the conjunctural shifts and turns in the fortunes of Churchill's reputation. In this way, through the prism of the figure of Churchill, we aim to map the predominating ideological shifts in post-war Britain.

We listen in particular to those occasions when the 'death' of the mythic Churchill has been foretold. It is noteworthy that in 1973 the historian J.H. Plumb declared that the great Churchillian theme of 'England's providential destiny...no longer holds credence either for the governing elite or the nation at large'.[25] And yet it was in the 1970s— a time when Britain endured severe economic and political difficulties that some saw as constituting a national crisis comparable with 1940— that dramatized film and TV representations of Churchill began to proliferate, which promulgated his heroic status to a watching public of millions. The ebb and flow the Churchill myths are shaped by the contexts in which they are articulated.

Although we heed what we understand to be the compelling shifts in the formal historiographies, our book does not represent an exercise in historiographical reconstruction. We broaden our analysis to encompass the Churchill phenomenon as it is registered across the media, in a field more expansive and capacious (and more unwieldy) than that which marks the established corpus of recognized historians. It is precisely the interactions between professional and popular, or 'high' and 'low', or culture and politics, which we believe to be significant.

As we concluded the writing of this volume, Boris Johnson achieved his ambition of taking up residence in Downing Street. We had sent our proposal to Oxford University Press in July 2018 and delivered the (almost) final manuscript a year later, on 25 July 2019, the day after Johnson became Prime Minister. At this dramatic juncture, our historical narrative is obliged to close. We reviewed the book's proofs in March 2020, by which time Johnson had won a substantial election victory and Brexit had taken place, albeit a few months later than the prime minister had originally hoped. At this point Britain was engaged in negotiations as to its future relationship with the EU but the default to a No Deal scenario at the end of the transition period remained a distinct possibility. We resisted the temptation to revise the substance of our text in the light of these developments; in fact they did not require us to alter our essential argument.

Boris Johnson is Britain's first prime minister—aside from Churchill himself—to have published a study of Churchill. Although he might well have succeeded in grasping the keys to No. 10 even if he had never written the book, we suggest that his publishing *The Churchill Factor* signaled a significant moment in Johnson's political journey. It offers a way of understanding Brexit Britain and of the man who has chosen to position himself as its leader.

*   *

From its inception, our book has been collaborative. It was conceived as a joint venture, and it was executed in this spirit. The various drafts changed hands many times. Having said that, we each took responsibility for the initial drafting of the separate chapters: Bill Schwarz (Chapter 1); Richard Toye (Chapter 2); and Steven Fielding (Chapter 3).

We would like to thank Richard Batten, who made the index. In addition to the staff at Oxford University Press, particularly Cathryn Steele, we wish to acknowledge:

Steven Fielding: Thanks to Ben Holland, Phil Tinline, and Alex von Tunzlemann for their help and comments on earlier drafts of my chapter. I also wish to thank Churchill College for permission to quote from papers held in its Archives Centre.

Bill Schwarz: My contribution to the volume first came to life as the Ward Lecture of September 2018 in the History Department at the University of Sydney. With great thanks to Barbara Caine, Larry Boyd, and to all those who participated on the occasion of the lecture. Thanks as well, in the longer run, to Neil Belton, Mary Chamberlain, David Feldman, Henry Chapman, Jamie Chapman, Ray Kiely, Kat Ochynski, Fintan O'Toole, Stein Ringen, and Stuart Ward. I'm particularly grateful to Caroline Knowles, who has lived with Churchill for longer than she ever imagined or wished. It was never part of the bargain.

Richard Toye: I would like to thank Hao Gao, Glen O'Hara and Robert Saunders for useful discussions and points of information.

1

Brexit May 1940

> The orator is the embodiment of the passions of the multitude.
> (Winston Churchill, 'The Scaffolding of Rhetoric',
> November 1897)[1]

> We want no megalomaniac dreamers, no paranoics with their
> stars of destiny, no avatars of Alexander, Caesar, Napoleon, no
> romantic tragedians who use Europe as their repertory theatre.
> (J.B. Priestley, *Out of the People*, 1941)[2]

> The problem is not that we were once in charge, but that we are
> not in charge any more.
> (Boris Johnson, 'Cancel the Guilt Trip', 2 February 2002)[3]

Digital Pasts

Imagine, then, that you're a Londoner on the afternoon of Tuesday 28
May 1940. You're on the underground stopping at St James's, heading
east towards Westminster. It's wartime and London is a city of sirens,
sentries, and sandbags. Mortal time presses in. 'The wall between the
living and the living', wrote Elizabeth Bowen when recollecting the home
front in the Second World War, 'became less solid as the wall between
the living and the dead thinned'.[4]

The carriage doors clatter open and Winston Churchill, the prime
minister, enters wearing his voluminous three-piece suit, spotted bow tie,
and Homburg hat, a large Havana cigar in hand. While he maintains his
class authority it's readily apparent he's ignorant of the customs required
for travelling on the underground. At the outset, he's like an unknown
species-being, barely even a Londoner. Yet in the very act of undertaking

the journey we witness his *becoming* so, becoming a citizen of the capital. At first the other passengers are nonplussed. They're unaccustomed to sharing public transport with so exalted a figure. After Churchill exchanges good-willed banter, obtains a light, and starts puffing on his cigar, he settles down to business. However, he doesn't directly address what's uppermost in his mind.

His predicament could not have been more serious, nor his need to arrive at a conclusion more urgent. He had only recently become prime minister, having replaced Neville Chamberlain less than three weeks earlier. Large numbers in his own party are openly hostile; those who aren't, are doubtful about his judgement.[5] At this very moment the appeasers are plotting to open negotiations with the enemy. His allies, and those he can trust, are few. The previous night George VI, breaking formalities, had paid an unannounced nocturnal visit in a bid to give him succour. Initially, at the time of Churchill's appointment, the king had not at all welcomed the prospect of his forming a government. Now, Churchill has to confess that without the support of his party there is little he can do to halt those pressing the government to sue for peace. But three weeks into the new government the king had learned to understand and appreciate Churchill's virtues, and offers his unequivocal support. 'Beat the buggers', he tells his first minister. He goes on to counsel him: 'Go to the people. Let them instruct you. Quite silently, they usually do. Tell them the truth unvarnished.'

Clementine, Churchill's wife, urges him to maintain his resolve. Otherwise, aside from his monarch and his wife, he is alone.

He is a man burdened by the enormity of the historic task confronting him, faltering. History weighs heavily. The choice before him is whether to strike a deal with Germany, in the hope of salvaging something of nation and empire, or whether to struggle on against a mighty enemy. A vast component of the British army is stranded at Dunkirk, numbering some quarter of a million British personnel and half that number again of Allied soldiers, awaiting annihilation. The threat of Nazi invasion moves inexorably closer. Given the fate of Britain's forces in northern Belgium, if Germany chose to advance across the Channel there would be no army to call upon. Defeat and occupation loom. At this juncture it appears that momentarily Churchill wavers. Should he capitulate to his foes in the party?

'You are the British people', he announces to the hapless travellers in his carriage. 'What is your mood?' They gather in close. Churchill quizzes a number of them, taking in their names and viewpoints. Oliver Wilson; Jessie Sutton; Abigail Walker; Marcus Peters; Agnes Dillon; Maurice Baker; Alice Simpson; and Margaret Jerome. To a person his new companions vow that were they to face invasion they would fight. One declares that if necessary she would set about the invaders with a broom handle. Another insists that the job would be to 'Fight the fascists!' 'Would you give up?', enquires Churchill. 'Never!' comes the reply, the individual passengers transmuting into a collective wartime chorus as 'Never!' turns into a crescendo. A young girl, appearing for all the world as if she's just stepped out of Humphrey Jennings' wartime documentary *Listen to Britain*, looks him in the eye and speaks softly but firmly: 'Never! Never! Never!'

Churchill, visibly moved, begins to recite a passage from Lord Macaulay's epic poem 'Horatius', familiar to English men, women, and children of his generation.

> Then out spake brave Horatius
> Captain of the gate:
> 'To every man upon this earth
> Death cometh soon or late.
> And how can man die better
> Than facing fearful odds
> For the ashes . . .

At which point a passenger close to Churchill, Marcus Peters, interrupts the soliloquy. He is the lone non-white person in the carriage. He's young and most likely West Indian, stylish but certainly not *loud*. 'They will never take Piccadilly' had been his resounding intervention in the earlier chorus, said with a broad, man-about-town smile. He—the black colonial—completes the verses from Macaulay:

> For the ashes of his fathers
> And the temples of his Gods.'

As his recitation ends the train slows. The prime minister silently weeps, apologizing to his new intimates as he does so. 'Westminster. It's my stop.' He alights and heads for the House of Commons, his resilience fortified by his encounter with 'the British people'. He's ready to attend to the quislings within his own ranks and ready, too, for the larger battle. He speaks these words, generating uncontained applause:

> We shall go on to the end. We shall fight in France, we shall fight on the seas and oceans, we shall fight with growing confidence and growing strength in the air, we shall defend our island, whatever the cost may be. We shall fight on the beaches, we shall fight on the landing grounds, we shall fight in the fields and in the streets, we shall fight in the hills; we shall never surrender . . . .[6]

This is history in dramatic, heroic mode.

Yet readers won't be surprised to learn that none of it happened. Or if it did, not as portrayed here, nor on this day, nor in this sequence. Churchill's lack of acquaintance with the underground was legendary (he first dialled a telephone himself, we should recall, when he was seventy-three), while the 'British people' only exists in this rendition as a contrived, cinematic representation.[7] It comprises a brief scene in a recent film about Churchill in May 1940, *Darkest Hour*, released in the UK in 2018. It's a twenty-first century memory, carefully fabricated, of an old story.[8]

But where does it come from? And what does it mean?

Men of Destiny

Some while before the film was released the journalist and Conservative MP Boris Johnson, having edited the *Spectator* from 1999 to 2005 and completing his second term as London mayor (2008–16 in all), was on the lookout for further opportunities to advance his political and financial assets. Boris Johnson, we should recall, is one persona, often shortened in the vernacular to 'Boris'; alongside this figure there exists the more formal, more exalted, Alexander Boris de Pfeffel Johnson, attesting to a distinct social heritage. Given the currency of 'Boris', it's wise to keep in mind this doubling of Johnson's person, taking him first this way, then that.[9]

The term Brexit, on which he was later to stake his claim, was not yet current. His commitments to Europe and to the European Union were characteristically wayward, but not yet honed into a politics. In questions of ethics and principle he already had form.[10] He had been fired by *The Times* in 1989 for playing fast and loose with the truth; and then later—in the future—he was to be jettisoned from the shadow cabinet for the same offence. But his class bonhomie came to his rescue. After the first sacking he was appointed the Brussels correspondent for the *Telegraph*, in the aftermath of Mrs Thatcher's Bruges speech of September 1988. There he passed his time concocting reports on the irrationalities of the EU, some of which conformed to fact, others which were invention.[11] He was never content with being simply a jobbing journalist. As Johnson himself recalls these years:

> everything I wrote from Brussels I found was sort of chucking these rocks over the garden wall and I listened to this amazing crash from the greenhouse next door over in England, as everything I wrote from Brussels was having this amazing, explosive effect on the Tory Party, and it really gave me this I suppose rather weird sense of power.[12]

In this he followed a long line of upper-class men drawn to the erotics of taking apart the social system they'd long been tutored to preserve, allying themselves to the perversities of power.

At some point he was invited to write a book on Winston Churchill. This has been a conventional hobby for public men in England, to use an old term, when time hung heavily. But this wasn't Johnson's situation. He was, putatively at least, running London; he was on the lookout for returning to the House of Commons—for his last twelve months in office he was to be established as MP for Uxbridge and South Ruislip; and he laboured to keep his hand in as a journalist. Yet as a diversion, the book on Churchill came to be written.

The Churchill Factor: How One Man Made History appeared in 2014 to predictable fanfares from the conservative press.[13] Its publication preceded Johnson's formal allegiance to the Brexit camp. For a long while there seemed every reason to ignore it; but then, as history turned, the moment arrived when it seemed impossible *not* to read it.[14] It became too important a document in the emergent mental hinterland of Brexit Britain. The persona of Churchill projected in the biography is not so far from the author's alter-ego. Churchill is presented as boisterously, bloke-ishly irreverent (in the first pages Johnson is impatient to supply graphic evidence of his subject's irreverence supplied to him in the Savoy Grill by Nicholas Soames, Churchill's grandson); unique in his populist regard for the instincts of the common people; and—supremely—possesses the will to turn history to his own ends. Johnson makes an early declaration:

> He [Churchill] is the resounding human rebuttal to all Marxist histor-ians who think history is the story of vast and impersonal economic forces. The point of the Churchill Factor is that one man can make all the difference.[15]

Which provides the cue for him to clamber up on the historical stage.

Johnson writes the book as an episodic love letter to the man he wished to be. His is a prose composed from the dated argot of public school life of a generation or two ago, driven—not by piety to the official values of the nation—but by a cocksure, Bullingdon, damn-it-all con-ception of the rights which accrue to the privileged, in the spirit of the young protagonists of Kipling's *Stalky and Co*; from a welter of contem-porary clichés, on one occasion alongside an invocation of Jeremy Clarkson; and from classical allusion and a vocabulary which you're only likely to hear from a classically educated (Eton and Balliol) toff. His is a high-speed style which rocks along, the author zipping past out of reach of the reader and disappearing in a blur. Yet the consistency of the story he tells lies in the fact that, notwithstanding that he is ostensibly writing about Churchill, it's transparently shaped by Johnson's own dreams and desires.

The book doesn't conceal the hostile views toward Churchill of his rivals, active in the political world prior to May 1940, who condemned him for being a cad and a turncoat, a man whom couldn't be trusted in any department of his life and who was without bottle. Johnson chooses to designate these critics as the 'Respectable Tories', time-servers all.[16] In this rendition Churchill's wayward human attributes, so far as he gives them credence, were part and parcel of the qualities which made him the Great Man he was, acting out his allotted role on the stage of History. Building a political career by behaving like a cad has, for Johnson, its own virtue.

Some of the story he tells is sound enough, recycled with panache; much, however, is misinformed.[17] Overall, in this account Churchill's every motive was unsullied by anything base or profane. Yet every so often, tiring of the responsibilities imposed by the discipline of writing history, Johnson hams it up, interposing provocations for the hell of it.

He opens with the events of 28 May 1940, consecrating the 28th as the day when history turned. He takes the reader by the hand:

> If you are looking for one of the decisive moments in the last world war, and a turning-point in the history of the world, then come with me. Let us go to a dingy room in the House of Commons—up some steps, through a creaky old door, down a dimply lit corridor; and here it is.

This room, the destination of this shadowy quest for world history, is where Churchill had met with his war cabinet at four o'clock on the 28th.[18] Churchill aside, the war cabinet comprised Lord Halifax, the foreign secretary and the staunchest proponent in the government for overtures to Germany; Neville Chamberlain, prime minister until his replacement by Churchill, who was broadly in accord with Halifax's positions but differed sharply on tactics and timing, and through the day edged closer to Churchill; Archibald Sinclair, the leader of the Liberal Party who, whilst not nominally a member of the war cabinet, could attend by invitation, as he did on this occasion, and whose sympathies were with the prime minister; and from Labour, Clement Attlee, and Arthur Greenwood, who by and large favoured the Churchill line. In Johnson's opinion the role of Labour was inconsequential, a view not universally shared by historians who conventionally regard the Labour Party in the spring of 1940 to have been a significant agent in the realignment of the nation's political forces.[19] On paper, the majority was Churchill's.[20] When they met, Halifax reported that he'd recently received word from Mussolini—Britain and Italy were not at war until 10 June—which couldn't have occurred without promptings from Germany. Halifax, as foreign secretary and as Churchill's principal rival just a few days beforehand, remained an authoritative political figure with a significant following. Or at least this was so as the 28th dawned.[21]

At this point there is lack of clarity in the historical record. It's evident that a further, larger meeting of the cabinet followed immediately. It's not certain whether Churchill had decided that the discussion should be adjourned in order to allow a meeting of the full cabinet or whether the meeting had already been planned. Churchill's most assiduous chronicler, Martin Gilbert, simply conveys the fact that once the war cabinet had been adjourned 'the room was filled with all those Ministers who were not members of the War Cabinet, some twenty-five in all.'[22] It's undoubtedly the case that the personnel excluded from the war cabinet had been milling around the Westminster corridors; that they were keen to be apprised of what was going on; and that they welcomed the opportunity to make their views known.[23]

In this second meeting, which Churchill alone of the war cabinet attended, he was in his element as he had not been earlier. No official record was taken. Most accounts, including the words ascribed to him, depend on the version written up by Hugh Dalton in his diary. In Dalton's recounting, Churchill declared that were the Nazi invasion to take place, '"We should become a slave state"'. He continued with these much quoted words: '"If this long island story of ours is to end at last, let it end when each one of us lies choking in his own blood upon the ground"'.[24] In his biography of Churchill, Roy Jenkins reminds the reader of the mediations in play, suggesting it's 'impossible now to tell whether this last somewhat melodramatic phrase was Churchill's own or whether it was a Dalton pastiche of his style', although, actually, the latter seems the more likely.[25] Yet although Dalton does nothing to diminish the extraordinary temper of the meeting, his interpretation is relatively measured. He suggests that although there was no dissent, nor was there any great outpouring of transcendent enthusiasm. Churchill's own subsequent recollection differed dramatically: 'There was a white glow, overpowering, sublime, which ran through our Island from end to end.'[26]

We can't be sure why the adjournment of the war cabinet was insti-
gated: whether Churchill decided it on the spot or whether it had been
planned earlier; or, in the first case, if this occurred on the practical
grounds that the meeting was deadlocked or as a result of greater tactical
initiative. Johnson concludes, sure in his own mind, that it was a matter
of decisive political calculation. He calls it Churchill's 'masterstroke',
adding this gloss:

> The appeal to reason had failed. But the bigger the audience the more
> fervid the atmosphere; and now he [Churchill] made an appeal to the
> emotions. Before the full cabinet he made a quite astonishing speech—
> without any hint of the intellectual restraint he had been obliged to
> display in the smaller meeting. It was time for 'frightful rot' on steroids.

The reference to 'frightful rot' comes from Halifax's diary from the
previous day, conveying his estimation of Churchill's political perform-
ance. The 'masterstroke', if that's what it was, won the day, and in
Johnson's version Churchill secured 'the clear and noisy backing of the
cabinet'.[27]

The contemporary resonance of Johnson's account stands out in relief.
For him the meaning of 1940 spans both past and present. The past
comes to inhabit the present. A political stalemate prevails, abetted by
party foot soldiers who lack fire in their bellies. The man of destiny
intervenes, realizing that to abide by the norms of political conduct
would do nothing to break the crisis. He discovers, further, that reasoned
argument can't do the job. Salvation lies in abandoning 'reason' and
'intellectual restraint', and in recourse to rhetorical flights of fancy 'on
steroids'. Political 'masterstrokes' are the product of 'frightful rot'.

In Johnson's telling Churchill indisputably becomes the man of 1940.
As Johnson rewrites the story for the present, looking out over his bijou
canal-side vista in Islington, it isn't difficult to determine who, if such a
crisis were to recur, he has in mind as the saviour.

There can be no doubt that the occasion he describes—May 1940—is
of great historical significance. But the man-of-destiny imperative, to
which Johnson is drawn, casts a spell he can't resist, and which orches-
trates a heavy-handed telling of the story.

We have no quarrel with the idea that human agency, individual human agency included, can change the course of history. It happens all the time, or at least much of the time. Of this Churchill is emphatically an example. Like Johnson we're, too, unreservedly thankful that things turned out as they did. On these grounds we should credit Churchill's political will, largeness of spirit, and tactical intelligence. A great man? Why on earth not?

Yet it is quite another matter to travel from historical interpretation in this tenor to the inflated supposition that a single individual saved Britain, shape-shifting from one world-historical crisis to the next until history lay in his grasp. Or that he saved the Empire. Or the free world. Or democracy. History is indeed in part, *pace* Johnson, 'the story of vast and impersonal economic forces'. Yet although he arrived at what the great majority regard as the right decision in May 1940, his politics was never driven by an allegiance to universal freedom or liberty. He remained wedded to his caste. His deepest motivation, as he proclaimed often enough, was to maintain Britain's standing in the world. During the war every major strategic decision was judged in terms of its geopolitical impact on the Empire. This required no discussion, for it functioned—for Conservatives of every stripe, and for the vast bulk of the Labour Party—as the premise for everything. There was nothing mythic about this state of affairs, notwithstanding Churchill's own rhetoric. It was how politics worked: realpolitik. The determination of Churchill to maintain the integrity of the British world overrode, when necessary, the immediate practicalities of destroying the Axis powers: similarly Roosevelt, Stalin, and (to Churchill's perpetual exasperation) de Gaulle insisted on pursuing their own national interests.[28]

Churchill never, personally, won the war. Gawping at a musty room in the Palace of Westminster in the company of Boris Johnson does nothing to reveal the stupendous resources that Britain commandeered from the Empire, nor the power of its fleet, let alone the presence of the big guns and massive human power of the Red Army, nor of the seemingly limitless resources of the United States. Britain's victory in 1945 required such enormous investments that it broke the conditions—'the vast and impersonal forces'—which sustained the Empire. As he strove to defend the Empire, Churchill unwittingly, in the very same moment he triumphed, contributed greatly to its dissolution. Each success proved also to be his failure. Such outcomes are not particular to Churchill. They're the stuff of history, with which we're required to live. When everything appears to be going as hoped, events turn out to diverge from cherished expectations. New contingencies open up, leaving historical actors dazed, unsure how they'd arrived in the circumstances where later they find themselves. Unwilled histories take command.

The only politics which can follow the reverie that 'one man makes history' is to surrender to those self-same men of destiny. In Britain in the early twentieth century there was a name for this phenomenon. It was known in political circles as Caesarism, in which the appointed men of destiny veered between embracing a populism, from below, and at the same time seeking to install a hard authority, from above.[29] To be conscripted into such a politics, then as now, is to mortgage the collective destinies of the people to the ambitions of men who swoon at the prospect that, one day, they may be masters of their own rhetorical intemperance.

In the period from 1914 to 1945 there were a number of self-perceived, and commonly distrusted, men of destiny—pre-eminently David Lloyd George ('less a Liberal than a Welshman on the loose'), Oswald Mosley, Winston Churchill—who regarded the primacy of party allegiance as an open matter, never as an abiding absolute.[30] They boasted an early radicalism before settling in on the right. It wasn't clear, in any single moment, where and in alliance with whom each would next appear.[31] Nor was there any knowing where they would eventually end up. In 1917 the energetically conservative *Morning Post* had identified Churchill as 'a floating kidney in the body politic'.[32] There were numerous others—the returning proconsuls; the fleeting 'little Caesars' of the moment—whose day never arrived, and whose hours were spent in the clubland shadows, a whisky and soda to hand, plotting dizzying constellations of political intrigue.

These were the years in Britain of the installation of the two-party system in the historic conditions of universal democracy. The transition from Whig and Tory, and from Liberal and Conservative, to the dominating two-party system of the twentieth century, was far from a harmonious evolution. Despite the many and various invocations of the genius of British politics, there was no prescribed destination. The contingencies at work were certainly more apparent at the time than in retrospect. One means for stabilizing the political field, in times of flux, was by overriding the two-party arrangement, as in the improvised solutions 'from above' which dominated the organization of the state from 1915 to 1945. Such occasions, suspending the putatively 'normal' procedures of parliamentary bargaining, Antonio Gramsci—following the conventions of the time—termed as Caesarist, manifest, in what he identified as its various 'gradations'.[33] Coalitions and national governments marked the first step in the recourse to Caesarism.

Although this term is not Johnson's, these same preoccupations underwrite his interpretation of Churchill. Churchill, in this scenario, was propelled by the belief in his own greatness, forever endeavouring to transcend the humdrum business of daily political brokerage. In Johnson's vision, strategic and ethical objectives were secondary in Churchill's political make-up. He was, for sure, reluctant to accept party allegiance and political principle as absolutes. Yet Johnson's interpretation is particular. For him—following his reading of Churchill—if allegiance and principle are deficient in explaining the deepest motivations for politics then, he decides, the defining criterion for understanding political practice must be *rhetoric*.[34] This, for Johnson, is largely what politics *is* or what, in the eyes of those who seek destiny, it becomes. It is above all the means by which the multitude is bound to the leader.

He quotes Churchill: 'I do not care so much for the principles I advocate as for the impression my words produce & the reputation they give me.'[35] You can imagine Johnson's eyes opening wide and his pulse racing when he spotted this. So *this* is Churchill! This is what most distinguishes Churchill's political life. He was in thrall to the power, not of political principle, but of rhetoric. He was at full reach when word and deed converged.[36] And sometimes, when things didn't quite mesh as he'd wished, his words took off, untethered, rising to the sky but signifying nothing. But never mind. Rhetoric—capturing the imagination of the masses—is all. Principle be damned.

In May 1940 historical time underwent a periodic shift of gear. History accelerated. In Johnson's words the 'events themselves had reached their own pitch of hyperbole' and Churchill's rhetoric, he argues, matched the pace of history. At this moment he articulated—according to Johnson, his sensibility untroubled by an association with an unedifying mysticism—the 'ancient instincts' of the nation.[37] This estimation of Churchill's rhetoric, overriding principle, reimagines what politics is. A politician is to be rated by his (predominantly, his) rhetorical prowess. The command of rhetoric, in Johnson's vision, becomes the means by which the command of history is realized. As he tells his tale of Winston Churchill we are obliged to ask the extent to which the facsimile man of destiny—'Boris'—glimpses on the horizon his own political future.[38]

Brexit May 1940

In the closing shots of *Darkest Hour*, when Churchill reaches the climax of his invocation of 'Their Finest Hour', the MPs go wild with euphoria. (No matter that it occurred the following week.) Halifax, in the gallery of the House of Commons, is asked by a puzzled spectator what on earth he's just witnessed. Knowing it signals his defeat, Halifax's reply is terse. Churchill's triumph, he explains, occurred because he had 'mobilized the English language and sent it into battle'.[39]

The scene functions as a riposte to determinist philosophies of history which preclude human intervention, as Johnson claims. It conveys the prospect that, with requisite willpower, individuals—or more precisely, men of destiny with the power to mobilize the multitude—can overcome history, take charge of it, and bend it to their purposes. It's an intoxicating possibility, gliding over the accumulated political differences of the past and relegating their significance to little more than passing squabbles, of no concern to the men who set their sights on higher things.

Something akin to this is evident, today, in the collective mentalities of the cadres who actively embrace the intransigent dreams of breaking free from the incubus of 'Europe', imagining that forty or fifty years of history can—in a single blow, in the blink of an eye, while having their cake and eating it—be jettisoned, and a new/old dispensation be heralded. Nor should it be surprising if in the current phase of the Brexit impasse, when politicians flounder in their desperation to alight upon a way through deadlock, the determination to leap over the practicalities of mundane Westminster politicking spawn new and unsettling political attachments.

The prolonged and continuing disputes about Britain's relations to the European Union have generated charged reflections on where England is to be located and what it means. In the referendum of 2016, these questions, for long active in the life of the nation, moved sharply to the core of immediate state concern. As we write, England, the geopolitical conductor for Brexit, is in slow-motion disintegration. The governing class acts as a captive of the very drama it unleashed, mesmerized by the consequences of its own decisions. As political life spirals out of control, those charged with governing the nation find the institutions of Westminster accentuate the political logjam.

Theresa May's premiership provided a grievous reflection on the larger situation. When she took office in the immediate aftermath of the referendum she appeared a safe pair of hands, a woman who knew where the COBRA room (Cabinet Office Briefing Room) was and what to do when she got there. But her image of competence proved illusory as, over the next three years, she stumbled from one crisis to the next, in part as the consequence of her declaration to the Tory Party conference of 2016 that she would pursue an uncompromisingly militant Brexit. The *Daily Mail* approved. Yet the further she followed this line the more she found herself enmeshed in her own declarations. As if in a macabre game of pass-the-parcel in which she had never learned what she was meant to do, she held tight to the poisoned cup, vainly looking about her for colleagues to help her out. She proved unable to relinquish that which she most treasured and that which, simultaneously, was rapidly becoming the source of unending grief. In the general election of the following year the precipice deepened, her political calculations subsumed to the ill-judged whisperings of Nick Timothy, her chief of staff, urging his boss to stick to a portfolio bristling with redlines. From that point on, her career continued repetitiously to hang by a thread. The pack of Conservative pretenders circled, awaiting their moment. While she embodied a politics characterized by dogged psychic dissociation, day by day the public world unravelled. No one in authority had a notion what practically could be done. In this collapse we were all, as citizens, demeaned.

In this crisis of the state the memory of Winston Churchill has had a role to play. It is (loosely) a postcolonial phenomenon, illuminating a United Kingdom after Empire, whose contraction—in fits and starts—continues apace. Britons are becoming accustomed to seeing themselves through the eyes of their neighbours as the newly diagnosed sick man of Europe. It's little wonder, in these circumstances, that the restaging of the drama of the House of Commons in May 1940 functions as a magical release from history, affirming the genius of what once was. Symbolic Churchill still has much work to do, for those on both sides of the Brexit divide.[40]

At this point let's step back for a moment. In 1993 John Charmley published *Churchill. The End of Glory*, a book discussed in more detail in Chapter 2. Charmley is an energetic investigator of modern British politics. His histories are organized by his deep attachments to a conservative order. Notable was his early study charting the political career of Lord Lloyd, a Tory who held extravagantly regressive views on everything and about whom Charmely was courteously 'balanced'.[41] Even so, his dedication to historiographical 'balance' doesn't preclude a penchant for an iconoclasm of the right, as he finds it hard to resist having a pop at reigning liberal nostrums. This has included, amongst other things, the reputation of Churchill.[42] Although he concedes Churchill's leadership to have been 'inspiring' he decides finally that it was 'barren' because 'it led nowhere, and there were no heirs to his tradition.' After copious pages his concluding sentences read:

> Churchill stood for the British Empire, for Britain independent and for an 'anti-Socialist' vision of Britain. By July 1945 the first of these was on the skids, the second was dependent solely upon America and the third had just vanished in a Labour election victory. An appropriate moment to stop, for it was indeed the end of glory.[43]

In the immediacy of the short term this may be right. However in the larger perspective it's myopically too literal. Naturally in July 1945 Churchill felt despondent, acutely so. Awaiting the results of the election, he was shaken by a dreadful presentiment. As he informed his surgeon-in-waiting, Charles Moran:

I dreamed that life was over. I saw—it was very vivid—my dead body
under a white sheet on a table in an empty room. I recognized my bare
feet projecting from under the sheet. It was very life-like.

Perhaps, Churchill mused, 'this is the end.'[44]

But Churchill's political time was far from terminated in 1945.
Although it is indeed the case that, in the decades which followed,
Britain's Empire was largely broken beyond repair, Churchill himself
nonetheless strove to prolong Britain's global greatness by creating a
nation, as he famously proposed at the Conservative Party conference in
Llandudno in 1948 (with the aid of his blackboard), positioned at the
centre of three defining concentric circles: the Empire, the anglophone
Atlantic, and Europe. Conviction in Britain's greatness was not extinguished. Hopes for a great Britain after Empire for long prevailed as the
common sense of the governing class, outliving the person of Churchill
and continuing, perhaps, into the Brexit years.[45] His heirs, whatever their
party allegiances, were many. Whether these commitments were wise or
rational or good for democracy is a question of judgement; the fact that
they underwrote British geopolitical strategy for a generation or more is
another matter entirely. He was also, a matter of the first importance in
the making of his mythic self, an architect of the Cold War. It's not that
Churchill's legacy was nowhere. On the contrary it was everywhere, so
deeply naturalized a feature of the political landscape that even professional historians can fail to identify it. On domestic matters, notwithstanding Churchill's personal impatience with the minutiae of party-
political dispute, as the two-party system of universal democracy settled
after 1945 he came to personify the constitutional imperative of the
Crown-in-Parliament, his early Whiggish allegiances persisting into a
new age. Again notwithstanding his own beliefs, as a veteran of the
wartime coalition he came to represent a political settlement in which
labour was accorded its role in the social organization of the nation.[46]
This is not a modest legacy nor, whatever one makes of it, can it easily be
construed as 'barren'.

Yet in an acute observation Charmley notes that after Empire, as
Britain's global 'decline' proceeded, 'so did the need for Churchill
grow.'[47] This formulation is important for the presiding arguments we

assemble here. In this reading Churchill, or more properly the memory of Churchill, is presented not as an unadorned relic of Empire, lifeless and locked in is time like his waxwork persona in Madame Tussauds, but as a protean phenomenon which is the product of our times. Mythic Churchill, in this sense, tells us as much about 'us' as it does about 'him'.[48] 'He' becomes more deeply indecipherable and harder to reach.

However, Charmley discounts his own analytical insight. His argument is skewed by choosing to organize his interpretation through the prism of 'glory', of a 'glory' once 'ours' but now forever lost. In a tautological collapse, his category of glory comes to be equated with the person of Winston Churchill. Empire, Churchill, glory: each stands in for the other. Once one goes, so must the other. So too the existence of the past-in-the-present disappears as well. The avenues of enquiry which he'd opened up close down. All that's left is to mourn the loss of bygone glories.

In the twenty-first century there are many ways of reckoning with Churchill-as-the-past. Notwithstanding the plurality of stories in contention, the weight of the narrative carries the gravity of myth. It's difficult to circumvent. In the present moment it works as a fantasized, mirror image of the disparagement of the nation's actually existing rulers which day after day fills the news reports in Britain and on the Continent.

It's instructive that Johnson explains that he was first prompted to embark on the biography by his worry that the memory of Churchill was close to vanishing. Yet the matter is more complex than this suggests. For sure, there is a younger generation unconcerned with the stories of the nation's past. And yet simultaneously the authority of mythic Churchill deepens as the idea of England becomes more precarious: these two phenomena are interconnected, as Charmley suggests. 'He', Winston Churchill, has become a potent symbol in the times of Brexit. When he enters the story we can generally be sure that faith in English exceptionalism will preside. When we hear his name uttered in public, chances are that what follows will be underwritten by faith in the Empire as the unilateral medium for the benediction of others. Repetition of Churchill *as* the nation's story runs deep. In its mainstream, popular variations it's impervious to critique. It's not that contrary voices don't exist. They do, and frequently they're heard. It is, rather, that the Ur-story reproduces itself regardless of whatever manifestations of dissidence cross its path. The more repetitious it becomes, the more impregnable it is, and the further it departs from historical realities. In its telling, thought is eviscerated. The past is acted out, with no need for reflection. The story—the myth—obliterates history. *The story tells itself.* Churchill becomes as much a feature of England's memory as the M25 or the seaside in winter.[49] It's how it is.

Active in Churchill's current renaissance, as can be seen in Johnson's telling, is the notion that in the past—particularly in the imperial past—indigenous Britons, wherever they happened to be located, managed their own destinies. As legend has it, there once existed a time when ordinary British, or English, men and women commanded their own history. (Let's not press when this could have been.) They were never subject to the capricious forces beyond their control. The greatest iniquity is that 'Brussels' has usurped England's providential history, whose premier totem is Churchill himself. The people, so the frequently heard injunction now demands, have to be true to the spirit of Winston Churchill. They have to *take back* control.[50]

During the finale of the referendum on the European Union, Nigel Farage, at the time the leader of the United Kingdom Independence Party (UKIP), knew his moment had come. In the very early hours of 24 June 2016 he couldn't help but ventriloquize Shakespeare's *Henry V* on the eve of Agincourt and Churchill on 4 June 1940. As much as Farage was speaking, equally the words spoke him.

> We have fought against the multinationals, we have fought against the big merchant banks, we have fought against big politics, we have fought against lies, corruption and deceit. And today honesty, decency and belief in nation . . . is going to win. Let June 23 go down in our history as our independence day.[51]

Today's Churchill is mobilized from the grave by those who feel that—somewhere, sometime—they surrendered their historical patrimony. The symbolic antidote to this social apprehension takes the phantasmatic form of Churchill. This is the work with which post-mortem Churchill is designed to undertake. We need to listen once again to Johnson:

That was why he was associated with so many epic cock-ups—because he dared to try and change the entire shape of history. He was the man who burst the cabin door and tried to wrestle the controls of the stricken plane. He was the large protruding nail on which destiny snagged her coat.[52]

Notwithstanding the collapse of his prose, it's clear that the higher his hero levitates the more destiny takes command.

In Johnson's book we witness the fusion of historic Churchill, the man of destiny, with the emergent time of Brexit—the jamming together of two historical durations which 'Brexit May 1940' endeavours to signify.

Since his book appeared Johnson has chosen to defect from his milieu of patrician Conservatism and to refashion himself as a political *jefe*, sending up into the night sky volleys of tracer bullets to test his new-found allegiance to a populist xenophobia.[53] Whether he believes what he says no one, including we suspect Johnson himself, can be sure. It's difficult to decide which is the more grievous: whether he truly believes what he says, or whether he lives with his own mendacity without a blush. But this isn't, here, the issue. In his latest incarnation he has become a key provocateur in the unhinging of the political class. He is—as we write; the situation changes fast—drawing the force of the populist right into the field of state power. He has crossed the river of fire, from old-school Burkean Tory to militant Jacobin populist. This unlikely transition may be reason enough to attend to *The Churchill Factor*. But more than that. On the journey Churchill functioned as a significant vehicle which drew Johnson—step by step, appropriately or not—toward his chosen destination.

Mythic Churchill

Through his life mythic Churchill coexisted with his flesh-and-blood version, each playing off the other, and each driven by an unstated faith in the transcendent power of the masculine hero. From early on Churchill possessed an unwavering disposition to locate his life in a greater history—as the embodiment of his long line of ancestors, from the Duke of Marlborough to his father, Randolph—and to project his own persona onto the larger screen. 'An endless moving picture in which one was an actor' was how he described this split from his own being.[54] This is a captivating modernist manoeuvre, by which he created himself as the spectator of his own life. Looking back, he imagined himself to exist separately from the grandiloquent projections which he himself had cultivated. He laboured hard to shape his every move as if for posterity.

Distinguishing a life from its myriad narrations is never possible, as a life is largely given form by narrative. That's what biography seeks to do: to give narrative form to a life. Inevitably there is friction between language and a life. But with Churchill the problem is excessively convoluted. This may account for the continuing fascination which his story exerts. It's probably a factor in the mind-bending inflation in the contemporary historiography, which recycles title after title of Churchilliana in a system of manic overproduction. There's no sign of it letting up.

Notwithstanding the intensity of Churchill's own impulsive attractions to the mythic qualities of his life—that is in the first place, to *his own* creations—there occurs, as often it does, a qualitative break once the person in question dies and when the memory of others supervenes. The task of remembering becomes more promiscuous, detached from the wishes of those appointed, or who appoint themselves, custodians of the legacy.[55] A free-for-all slowly results, in which the life becomes a public, unmonitored possession. In post-mortem Churchill we witness a multiplicity of continuing, contrary resurrections. Telling are those occasions when we can hear and feel—when we catch—history *becoming myth*: when formal histories nestle up close to mythic thought and surreptitiously borrow its mental modes of operation.

Funerals, the formal commemoration of a life, are weighty occasions. Emotions are raw. They mark the time when, in a choreographed setting, competing stories of a life jostle for primacy, and begin to take on an unanchored existence of their own. Churchill's funeral in January 1965 signalled a spectacle of state theatre, his monumentalization rising steeply. The theatricality couldn't easily accommodate the private grief of those closest to him. In the first instance, his death was a matter of state. But the authority of the state can't ensure what develops.

We can take a single response, private rather than public. This concerns John Lukacs, a prolific historian who from the 1990s, late in life, established himself as a formidable Churchill scholar. Lukacs had been born in Budapest in 1924. He was Jewish, insofar as he was the son of a Jewish mother, although through his adult life he affiliated to the Church of Rome; in his schooldays he had spells in England which touched him greatly, creating an early spark which was to transport him to a quietly zealous Anglophilia; in 1944 he was conscripted into an army labour battalion and was fortunate, mainly thanks to his desertion, to have survived. At some point during the war's end his youthful affinity for socialism shattered and in 1946, fearing the arrival of Communist rule, he emigrated to the United States, where in May 2019 he died.

He was, in the Continental rather than in the English sense, a conservative, not averse to thinking of himself as a reactionary. He was unapologetic in the esteem he accorded aristocratic elites, holding in disdain anything which smacked of populism, which he regarded as the antidote to the principle of *authority*. Churchill, whose own commitments and affections didn't easily conform to Lukacs's variant of highminded conservatism, nonetheless operated in his mind at full voltage.[56]

When Churchill died, Lukacs happened to be teaching in France. He seized the opportunity to travel to London, in the company of his eight-year-old son, to bear witness to the departure of a man whom he regarded as his hero. He kept a private diary which he later came to consider 'perhaps unduly sentimental'.[57] At this stage in his career he'd published no book on Churchill. Nor did he until 1990, when there appeared *The Duel. Hitler vs Churchill: 10 May–31 July 1940.*[58] Soon after the monograph had entered the world, he decided to submit his record of the funeral for publication, which for some thirty years had lain dormant, unacknowledged, a private memoir with no claim to be a public document. By this time Lukacs believed history to be turning. 'In these years...', he declared a little later, when the diary was reprinted, 'Winston Churchill's reputation is at a peak.'[59]

The story—elegiac in its every note—is as much preoccupied with England as it is with Churchill. It takes the form of a masculine romance, structured around two pairings. First there's Churchill, the man to be honoured, and Lukacs himself, who speaks for the anonymous multitude keen to pay their respects. Second there's father and son, the latter obliged to be tutored by the former, his mentor. The diary works as a pedagogic handbook for mastering the curriculum of England. Quintessentially it's a view from outside, and bears its marks. Having been brought up elsewhere, but as a man driven by the force of his desire for an England of the mind, he imagined he'd come to inhabit the deepest mainsprings of the nation he loved. The self-consciousness of the diary reads like a peculiarly 'migrant'—outside, tangential—estimation of the Great Man. In the story, Lukacs is positioned as the medium, bringing Churchill and his own unnamed son, the neophyte, into dialogue. The son is gently encouraged to learn how he can experience, appreciate, and identify with the English, while the father is emotionally conscious of the degree to which, in 1965, 'Nineteen-forty is close now.'[60]

The Labour cabinet minister, Richard Crossman, observed of Churchill's funeral that 'It felt like the end of an epoch, possibly even the end of a nation.'[61] It was a common feeling. This is the melancholy, lyrically enunciated, which the Lukacs memoir enacts. As with Charmley, nation and leader metamorphose the one into the other. Yet as this conflation happens, reason is confounded. Thought slips away. It's clear from the opening pages that we're faced with a distinctive sensibility: 'England has the finest public lettering'; the English possess 'love for the Word'; England is a 'Shakespearian nation'; Churchill's London house, Queen Anne architecture, and Churchill himself 'are, all three, a monument of decency'; 'it is a good queue because it is an English queue'; the English 'are shy because they are kind'... and so on.[62] Affiliations such as these may or may not have foundation. But the possibility for the reader to decide which it is to be remains out of reach, for the rhetorical power of the prose lies precisely in its abstraction. It's a way of depicting the world untouched by any regard, even formally, for the value of Popperian falsifiability.

Lukacs proclaims his attachments to hierarchy with no subterfuge. Churchill, he concludes,

> was a monarchist not merely out of sentiment but because of his deep historical reason. In a fatherless world they [the monarchs] are sources of a certain strength and of a certain inspiration. May they live and reign long! May their presidency over the Sunday afternoons of Western Europe be prolonged![63]

He adores—respectfully, not passionately—the lack of ostentation of England's middle class:

> Now, in his [Churchill's] death, the pomp means less to them than to the others; it is not the might and the parade, the flags and the bands, that impress them, but they, perhaps for the first time, have an inner comprehension of the magnanimity of this man now dead. Now, in his death, he belongs to them perhaps even more to anyone else in England.[64]

Toward the end he leaves himself and the reader with an enigmatic, perplexing cameo, which may, perhaps, be anticipating things to come. He drops into a Wimpy Bar. This was, in 1965, on the frontline of London's commercialized popular modernity. A 'fortyish man' who, he surmises, 'may have been a teacher in a poor school in the Midlands', orders a Wimpy—the prototype of an English MacDonald's. '"A Wimpy, please." As he said that, there passed a shadow of embarrassment, a flicker of resigned disturbance across his face.'[65] A hamburger? 'Resigned disturbance'? What sacrilege looms?

When his narrative draws to its close, all hints of ambiguity are dispelled. He's back on track. The language heightens. 'Farewell Churchill. Farewell British Empire. Farewell, spiritual father. Of many. Including myself.'[66]

Passages like this don't read well in our more quizzical age, reminiscent of the poetic talents of E.J. Thribb, lampooned in *Private Eye*, and no doubt didn't read well at the time. Nevertheless the text is revealing. It provides an insight into the reveries of an admirer of Churchill at the very moment of his death. Legitimately, it's a historical document. But it can't be judged itself as a formal history. Lukacs never conceived it to be so. It stands as a personal story, propelled by an outsider who sought recognition as an insider. The author himself was conscious of what was in play. Later, he was conscious too of the vulnerabilities of the record he'd composed so many years before.

Yet psychic attachments of this intensity don't simply come and go. In Lukacs's case they infiltrate the formal histories where they don't—according to the disciplinary protocols, properly—belong. The genre shifts and the abstractions are curbed. But the sentiments can't be appeased. Mythic Churchill, and all that this represents, aren't absent from the formal histories. Echoes of his 1965 sanctification of England recur.[67] The histories represent less departures from Churchill-as-myth than its reiteration. The tone changes; the premise remains immovable.

Lukacs, as historian, has been a notable influence on the historiography of England, May 1940. He—the displaced Hungarian Jew—sketched a template from which later, native, historians work, and from which others draw succour. This instalment of the myth opened in 1990 with the arrival of Lukacs's *The Duel. Hitler vs Churchill: 10 May–31 July 1940*, with its North American title of *The Duel. 10 May–31 July 1940: The Eighty Day Struggle between Churchill and Hitler*. This was followed in 1999 with his *Five Days in London. May 1940*. In turn, *Churchill. Visionary, Statesman, Historian*, appeared five year later, comprising in part his 1965 diary. And finally, as the culmination, we were presented in 2008 with his *Blood, Toil, Tears and Sweat. The Dire Warning*. These are highly regarded within sections of the academy. Some are published by a leading university press. It's difficult to think of any comparable historian who has laboured as diligently to elevate the minutiae of Westminster in May 1940 in order to refocus the historical spotlight.

Even so, Lukacs's is a peculiar historical project. In the guise of history, mythic Churchill lives.[68] And when it transpires that he served as the named 'historical adviser' to *Darkest Hour*, the movie, it must make us wonder what his duties could possibly have entailed. What was going on?

In one respect, however, Lukacs was not alone. This opens an unexpected lineage. It enters the light of day in 1949 when Isaiah Berlin, the lauded Oxford philosopher, published a tribute to Churchill in the United States which stands as an early codification of the May 1940 story, carrying the spare but evocative, democratic title, 'Mr Churchill'.[69] It made an immediate impact, alive to the ideological stakes imposed by the Cold War. Such was its influence that, shortly after, it was published in the UK as a stand-alone book. Berlin set out to defend the integrity of Churchill the man and—above all—to insist on the virtue of his political rhetoric. It was significant in its emphatic reverence for the Churchill of

May 1940. And so too in its determination to address a North American readership, anticipating a potential new audience for future dispatches on Churchill, reaching beyond his home nation.[70] From the start, transnational Churchill was crucial in the making of mythic Churchill.

Berlin, like Lukacs, originated from East European Jewry. He'd been born in Riga and later—before his swift assimilation into the apex of England's (emigré) intellectual caste—he identified as a Russian Jew.[71]

We should note in this context, as well, the later role which Martin Gilbert was to play. Gilbert is the historian who was—all but singlehandedly—responsible for monumentalizing Churchill in print and in the historiography. He was born in North London. His four grandparents were Jews from the Russian Empire (contemporary Poland and Lithuania), and Gilbert himself remained a lifelong observant Jew and Zionist choosing, when his end arrived, he be buried in Israel. In 1962, two years after he'd graduated from Oxford, he was invited by Churchill's son, Randolph, to join him as a researcher on his father's biography. This was a colossal work which, after Randolph's own early death, fell to Gilbert to take on. He completed volumes III to VIII (the last published in 1988), each longer than its predecessor, and set in train the publication of some twenty additional, weighty 'companion' volumes of documents.[72] His dedication to nurturing the memory of Churchill remains supreme.

Berlin, though, remains the most intriguing of the three.[73] From his All Souls vantage in Oxford through the thirties he had initially exhibited little patience for Churchill. He, and his fellow dons at All Souls, the putative apex of Oxford's collective intellect, found that when Churchill visited the college in 1936 he appeared (in Berlin's words) as a 'sacred monster'.[74] His identification with politics, with *the world*, appeared to the votaries of analytical philosophy, predominant at the time, to be unbalanced. Over the coming years, however, the political differences which had divided Churchill and Berlin—appeasement, Zionism, the Middle East—began gradually to diminish. The opinions of each began to converge. In Berlin's case this was manifest in the loosening of his own ties to an uncompromising Zionism. From 1940, as he took up a succession of diplomatic posts in the United States, and later significantly in Moscow, he was persuaded that Churchill would return England to its 'true spirit' which, at this time for Berlin, meant an accommodation with *the idea of* Zionism.[75]

His experience in Moscow, coinciding with the intensification of the Cold War, redoubled his sympathies for Churchill. In 1947, through the intermediary of William (Bill) Deakin, an old colleague from Oxford and a prominent member of Churchill's loyal band of literary subalterns, Berlin was asked to vet *The Gathering Storm*, the first volume of Churchill's history of the Second World War. For this, he was offered the handy sum of two hundred guineas. (Initial hardback sales exceeded half a million; investments of this order, though hardly modest, were handsomely recouped.) Berlin's influence nourished the configurations of mythic—popular—Churchill. Yet his evocation of Churchill, in its *form*, didn't make any concessions to a popular readership. It remained instinctively highbrow. 'Suppose', he suggests at one point, 'that Shelley had met with Voltaire.'[76] Where would this have left the majority of his readers? In voice, All Souls had not budged. Even while Berlin allied intellectually with the popular mood, he was a million miles away from inhabiting anything but the Oxford clerisy.

Berlin's 'Mr Churchill' engaged with *The Gathering Storm*, notwithstanding his own role in the book's production. His intellectual trajectory, as he was drafting the book, was moving from a habitual appreciation of the higher reaches of academic abstraction to a new-found respect for thought as 'worldly'. His enthusiasm for Churchill, in 1949, represented an oblique testament to *his own* new-found allegiances. What he most valued in Churchill was his capacity to create a voice able to convey the urgent imperatives of a human life. The war, the Holocaust, and the Cold War concentrated the mind. He was aware that prevalent in the earlier generation of intellectuals had been the idea that Churchill's high-blown speeches worked to eliminate intellectual and moral discrimination. It was this interpretation of Churchill—an interpretation which had once been his—that Berlin sought to dispatch. By 1949 he had no time for Churchill's highbrow critics, sure that they were subject to 'an inner life of absorbing complexity and delicacy' and deaf to the larger circumstances. Berlin proposed that, in order to communicate anything of value, qualification and equivocation needed to be eliminated. A mode of address needed to be fashioned which would deliver the 'vision of experience': 'to give shape and character, colour and direction and coherence, to the stream of events'. Rhetoric for Berlin was far from superfluous. Indeed he believed that how thought happened was by means of narrative itself, through the strategic ordering of stories. 'To interpret, to relate, to classify, to symbolise are those natural and unavoidable human activities which we loosely and conveniently describe as thinking.' In our own times this is commonly described, simply, as 'narrative'. Through the creation of narratives we comprehend the external world. In Berlin's time, much the same precept sailed under the flag of 'myth'. Berlin was unique in giving life to the myth of Churchill as, simultaneously, he reflected on the properties of myth itself. In Churchill's hands, rhetorical excess wasn't something which needed to be disowned, nor was it the cause for embarrassment. In the time of mass democracy it provided the essential dimension for popular politics. Such ways of thought, for Berlin at the end of the forties, made democracy work.

For Berlin, the power of Churchill's political imagination lay in his capacity to translate an ethical position into a popular syntax. Or to put this in other terms, into myth. Churchill, from this perspective, was legitimately the 'epic poet' of his time. To the unease of those who prided themselves on their mastery of intellectual discrimination, the purpose of *democratic* speech, Berlin insisted, was to create stories 'simpler and larger than life... with no half tone, nothing impalpable, nothing half hinted, nothing half spoken or hinted or whispered'. 'Fantasy', Berlin went on, can 'transform the outlook of an entire people or generation'. The power to create and communicate a nation's myth was, for Berlin, where Churchill's public—human—virtue lay.[77]

This reflective encomium to Churchill led Berlin to become, in the words of his most insightful biographer, 'one of the biggest contributors to the inflation of the postwar Churchill myth'.[78] Yet as this happened Berlin was, in the same breath, championing the virtue of mythic thought itself.

What, though, of more recent manifestations of mythic Churchill in May 1940?

Recently, there has been a glut of formal histories, in which the divisions between history and myth continually slip and slide. These include Robin Prior, *When Britain Saved the West. The Story of 1940* (2015); John Kelly, *Never Surrender: Winston Churchill and Britain's Decision to Fight Nazi Germany in the Fateful Summer of 1940* (2016); Anthony McCarten, *Darkest Hour. How Churchill Brought Us Back from the Brink* (2017); with some variation, David Owen, *Cabinet's Finest Hour. The Hidden Agenda of May 1940* (2017);[79] Nicholas Shakespeare, *Six Minutes in May* (2017); and Tim Bouverie, *Appeasing Hitler: Chamberlain, Churchill and the Road to War* (2019). The opening pages of Roger Hermiston's *All Behind You, Winston: Churchill's Great Coalition, 1940–45* (2017) rehearse the same story; tributaries in the greater flow include Kenneth Weisbrode, *Churchill and the King* (2015) and David Cohen, *Churchill and Attlee. The Unlikely Allies Who Won the War* (2018).

A variation on the theme, substituting an aeroplane for the prime minister, occurs in John Nicol's *Spitfire: A Very British Love Story* (2018). And in case we missed the significance of such memorialization, Liam Fox, then secretary of state for the Department for International Trade, tweeted on the occasion of a rebuilding of an old Spitfire: 'Liam Fox and the Great Britain Campaign are delighted to be supporting [the] restoration of one of [Britain]'s iconic Spitfires. Once restored the plane will embark on an around the world flight in summer 2019 #ExportingisGREAT'.[80] Either way, the protagonist, person or plane, becomes the vehicle for delivering the nation from extinction. A while later the BBC was required to blame 'human error' for the announcement on a news bulletin that Mrs May's return to Brussels for further negotiations with the EU would be by Spitfire. In Brexit times even the crazily fanciful carries the aura of plausibility.[81] The elements of the story vary. Its deeper organizing structure, in which its meaning is located, remains repetitively the same.

The resurrections of Churchill and May 1940—the line dividing the two is continually blurred—are not restricted to print: we come to the cinematic and other manifestations in the final chapter.[82] But as we've emphasized in the prominence we give to *Darkest Hour*, the popular dimensions of mythic Churchill are of the first importance. The professional histories don't operate in a vacuum.

There's one final intervention to be noted, from 2018, the same year as *Darkest Hour*, which set out to turn the tables and radically re-vision the story of May 1940. Andrew Roberts' thumping, thousand-page biography, *Churchill. Walking With Destiny*, was received in a high pitch of critical acclaim. The book is self-consciously styled as Roberts' *magnum opus*, its scope and ambition seeking to match the enormity of its subject. As the title indicates, the conceptual organization of *Churchill* is not complicated. It works to endorse Churchill's own self-evaluation in which he acts out the role of the supreme 'man of destiny'.[83] A moment's never missed to take the reader out for a stroll with providence, and to bask in its glow.

As we'll see in Chapter 2, there was a time when Roberts had been vilified by those on the right as one of the rowdies who took it upon themselves to indulge in 'Churchill bashing'.[84] The cause for this was his acknowledgement of Churchill's racist predispositions. Yet Roberts' detractors failed to heed that this was presented, not as a human or political flaw, but as an indispensable ingredient of his very greatness. In the new book, this line of argument is pursued with gusto.

In a gruelling pursuit of historical objectivity, Roberts unveils an entire roster of Churchill's misdemeanours, which escalate into a higher order of human and political error. But in litanies of earnest breathlessness, one by one these failures are discharged in the longer run as of little consequence. Indeed each is transformed into an act of redemption due simply to the fact that in their sum, in May 1940, they made Churchill *who he was*. They prepared him for the providential occasion when his life transubstantiated into History, en route to his becoming the saviour of 'Liberty'.[85]

Even so, on occasion Roberts' tone in his new appraisal is oddly defensive. Empire, he declares, was Churchill's 'creed'.[86] Roberts, too, has been renowned for his enthusiasm for Britain's imperial past, always ready to depict Empire in its most favourable light. So the reader is brought up short to confront the unanticipated, unadorned statement that: 'Today, of course, we know imperialism and colonialism to be evil and exploitative concepts, but Churchill's first-hand experience of the British Raj did not strike him in that way.' This is followed by a long list of the features which Churchill himself admired about Britain's imperial rule in the Indian subcontinent, which silently works to draw into question the accusation which just precedes it. In closing this passage, however,

Roberts closes the circle by repeating his hostile reckoning of Empire. 'For Churchill this was not the sinister paternal oppression that we now know it to have been.'[87] These are curious formulations. There are few historians who designate imperialism as 'evil' or 'sinister', leaving it at that, with no further word. Fewer still would hazard the idea that imperialism and colonialism are 'exploitative concepts', as it's not the concepts which undertake the material work of exploitation. Most of all, who on earth is this 'we', so certain ('of course') of the fundamental depredations of Empire? What is it that we know 'now' that we didn't before? The reader is invited to accept that the first person plural must embrace the author. Yet is there anything in the book, or indeed in any of Roberts' writings, which leads a reader to conclude that, in itself, Empire was a nefarious business? Does Roberts believe what he says? Or is his use of 'we' perversely ironic?

But for all his effort to present himself as a man of reason, judiciously even-handed, a concluding observation raises the stakes. Roberts returns to the question of Churchill's commitments to white dominion and to his belief in the racial superiority of the British people. It was *precisely* these qualities, Roberts contends, which enabled Churchill to triumph in May 1940. As we show in Chapter 2, by such means, May 1940 is recast as the providential vindication of Britain's—England's—long history of racial supremacy.

As the story—of Churchill; of May 1940; of Churchill in May 1940—evolves, in book and film, the tempo of national salvation heightens.[88] The more historical time is reduced—from eighty days; to six days; to five days; to six minutes—the more England's history comes to be ordained by providence. The overarching form of the generic narrative is precisely that: generic. May 1940, when the nation stood 'alone' against dictatorial Europe, comes alive in contemporary times, redeployed anew. A familiar history is emerging again *as* national memory. In this lies the significance of the new biographies—by Johnson and Roberts—of Churchill: they're representative of a strategic bid to reorder the historical landscape. Nineteen-forty is more than the sum of the various individual stories. Each new telling seeks to revive the political currency of the nation's past for the present. And each works, in varying degrees, to shift the dispositions of the historical present.

*   *

When social memory crystallizes it acquires the status of myth. It rarely ever functions as the simple antidote to formal, professional history. 'Myth' and 'history' feed off each other, coexisting in shared locations. For much of the time, acknowledged or not, historians make unseen pacts with modes of thinking which unsettle the inherited codifications of formal history: with *bricolage*, in Claude Lévi-Strauss's terms, or more generally with the unruly domains of memory and fantasy. In recognizing this it's clear that the job for the historian is not unequivocally to banish mythic stories from the repertoire of the social agenda, but to comprehend their historical provenance and their meaning. They need to be understood as a means for 'ordering of historical consciousness' which possess their own syntactical logic; which commonly rely on heightened modes of narration; and which privilege the subjective investments of reader or viewer.[89] Myth reaches the parts which conventional histories seldom do.

In our discussion of May 1940 up to this point in our chapter, our emphasis has fallen on mythic Churchill as a symbolic system in which the story culminates in the capacity *to tell itself*. This is when myth works against history. When this happens the past is repetitiously—pathologically—acted out; in so doing, the mythic properties of the story tighten and the space for collective human agency diminishes. This, we've suggested, underwrites the Churchill projected in *Darkest Hour*, as well as informing the set-piece histories of Boris Johnson, John Lukacs, and Andrew Roberts.

In this reading, mythic Churchill catches something of an otherwise inexplicable persistence of social, half-formed memories, dormant for long periods but never quite extinguished. Their compulsive repetition suggests an unwilled acting out. The narrative takes command over the author. In contemporary recuperations of Churchill, England's exceptionalism exerts its authority. There persists a puzzling faith in the notion that England, providentially, has been peculiarly immune to the existential darkness which shadows modern selfhood. Whether anyone actually believes this or not, as a literal truth, may be unlikely. But its echoes nonetheless persist. This is a voice heard at different volumes and in different frequencies. It's not restricted to self-evidently ideological evocations of the nation's past. Its sensibilities infiltrate the accredited historiography, where we might least expect them to surface.[90] These voices recur in political life. They constitute a barely conscious substratum of popular experience, flaring into the light of day in tabloid headlines. They turn on an attachment to the protocols of an English fundamentalism. When critics point to the dark matter in the nation's past—to the violence of colonialism, to enslavement, to the racialization of others—a reflex is triggered as if even to *say* such things the lifeblood of English selfhood is carried to the precipice of destruction. It's a refrain in national life which occasionally dips out of sight but never entirely disappears. A repertoire of melancholic associations does indeed infiltrate contemporary political sensibilities.[91] English fundamentalism confronts us, even as it militantly disavows its very existence.

In our view it's impossible to understand these mentalities of contemporary England—the reflexes, the sensibilities, the disavowals—without heeding its vanished imperial core, bequeathing governing instincts which carry into the present a peculiarly postcolonial imperiousness.[92] The vanished Empire continues to be, irrepressibly, a material and historical reality. Nor should we suppose that these sentiments, these days, are the exclusive preserve of those dedicated to engineering a maximalist Brexit.

We've proposed that Churchill on the underground in *Darkest Hour* is a faultless re-enactment of the old story of mythic May 1940, dressed up for our own times, in which the 'depoliticizing' qualities of the myth are evident. It doesn't miss a trick. In crucial respects the film shares its founding presumptions with Boris Johnson's portrayal of Churchill. It evokes an imaginary England (alone) and—in the slipstream of a charismatic Churchill—a depoliticized people who are consonant with the reveries of the conservative nation. They possess no agency except that exercised through the totemic powers of their leader.

This is not to say that the political affiliations of those who made the film are *the same* as those espoused by Johnson, or by the cadres pressing for Britain to leave the EU. When shooting of *Darkest Hour* started, neither Brexit nor Trump was on the political agenda; by the time of its release both were prominent. Joe Wright, the film's director, speaks of his movie as a testament to anti-fascism, all the more necessary, he warns, as the populist right gathers force in the historic anglophone democracies.[93]

Wright is an unlikely proponent for an idealized, old-school England. He directed *Atonement*, based on the Ian McEwan novel, as well as a funky rendition of *Anna Karenina*. He was tutored at the Anna Scher Theatre School—a popular community institution in a fashionable North London locality, suitably iconoclastic—leaving his formal education with few qualifications but ending up at a forcing-ground for the avant-garde, Central St Martins. In the 1990s he found himself at Oil Factory, a music video production company on the Caledonian Road. He's married to a daughter of the globally celebrated sitar player, Ravi Shankar. There's nothing blimpish in this biography; on the contrary, it's twenty-first century, metropolitan cool. The same probably holds for the scriptwriter, Anthony McCarten, a New Zealander whose previous film was the biopic of Stephen Hawking, *The Theory of Everything* (2014). Unlike Johnson, there's no reason to suppose that the pair set out with an ideological agenda, scheming to win viewers to this position or that. Their overriding aim was, we expect, to make what they took to be good cinema, fashioning a charged story with a capacity to move audiences.

Yet that's exactly our point. Notwithstanding their personal investments, or their hip credentials, the moment they embarked on the retelling of May 1940 the inherited narrative generates its own momentum. It takes over, doing their work for them. Ineluctably the story begins to tell itself. From the first shots the cinema audience knows the script. Churchill growls and huffs and puffs, taking his put-upon wife, 'Clemmie', to the lip of distraction.[94] By sheer bloody-mindedness, ninety minutes or so later, he triumphs. The House of Commons breaks into relieved uproar. The tub of popcorn's finished. And the film comes to its end, reassuring its viewers that, with the appropriate will, history will be ours.

In fact the entire endeavour is built on an invisible paradox. If these days a desire to reanimate May 1940 is propelled, insistently, by the wish to recuperate the efficacy of individual human agency in shaping the collective fate of a people, the telling of the actual story attests to its precise contrary: to the power of the past in organizing the meaning of the stories we choose to tell. Not even the national colossus, Winston Churchill, can be emancipated from the gravity of history. He's mortal after all.

However, notwithstanding the significance of this mythic summoning of May 1940, this isn't the whole story. When mythic Churchill is resurrected, no matter how systematized the story, he's necessarily brought back in history. The story may follow a familiar pattern, but the historical circumstances in which it's received have altered. How Churchill is viewed or read is open-ended and contingent.[95] The organizing structure of the myth may be overpoweringly present; but readers and spectators nonetheless possess the discrimination to interpret for themselves what passes before them. The raw material of mythic Churchill—the speeches, the writings, the interminable volume of work devoted to charting his luminous role in realizing the nation's true destiny, the movies, the plastic schlock of mass-produced icons (bulldogs, cigars)—provides an immediate, inescapable symbolic frame of reference. Churchill becomes a means for the English to think about— or, in those instances when depoliticization is heavily accentuated, to stop thinking about—who they are. The inherited narrative logic frames what we're writing now. We are subject to the myth as much as anyone. But that's all it does: frame the intellectual landscape of what we say. It doesn't legislate what is said. In order to prevent the story from possessing us we need ceaselessly, self-consciously, to listen for the subtextual, unspoken undertow.

These reflections are necessary for engaging with the political world we inhabit. The contemporary Eurosceptic-inspired national pasts, which intervene in the present, now carry a sharp, immediate, and material force.[96] In these circumstances the old stories—while still on the familiar narrative treadmill—generate new resonances.

Churchill is now part of a broader current: that of the larger Brexit imbroglio. Too often Brexit has been explained in terms of the desire for returning to the past. Or more particularly, in terms of a nostalgia for past greatness, in which the memory of the Empire plays a prominent role. Since the referendum this has become an intellectual reflex.[97] This isn't the position we follow. It may not be wrong. But it's too abstract, accounting at once for everything and nothing. Although it may carry an element of truth, it short-circuits too many imponderables. Can it, really, stand as the overriding causal factor for a volcanic political rupture?

Memory doesn't work by prescriptions which are either this literal or specific. Nostalgia itself is constituted by multiple levels of displacement, a single sign—empire—containing within it an array of mobile, collateral meanings. Memory, in any case, always represents a tricky, ambivalent, encounter between past and present. It's lived as a way of being which is neither quite at home in the present nor the past. That is the dominating, uncanny property of memory. Translating this psychic disposition into an explanation for how the mass of the population voted, or for determining their institutional loyalties, is an awkward way to proceed. Remembering is not only a question of retrogression. The process of animating the past is always, also, a means to fashion new futures. Memory, in the very moment it latches on to a past, simultaneously ordains a mode of *becoming*.

Mythic Churchill, it follows, carries contrary resonances. When the old story is repeated, as if by rote, the world is divested of its historicalness, and the political is itself depoliticized. Yet at the same time the very bid to resurrect the past also conjures up contending new futures yet to be made. This presents us with the conundrum of how the political future is to be imagined on the back of a depoliticized past.

England's Populism: 1940

'Walk where history happened.'
(Churchill War Rooms, London, 2019)

As May 1940 unfolded, and as the fallout from a haphazard, rickety grandeur periodically touched the routines of daily life, the designation 'May 1940' itself assumed a mythic quality. The events were experienced—perhaps uniquely in modern Britain—consciously *as* history. Indeed, history-in-the-making was commonly spoken as if mythic time prevailed. J.B. Priestley saw nothing strange in describing a young pre-war friend, by 1940 a pilot officer in the RAF, as 'a figure from some epic—a cheerful young giant out of a saga'.[98] Myth entered the language of the everyday, giving meaning to the disorientating events across the globe.

Prominent in the articulation of the nation was the discursive author-ity of 'the people', working as the arbiter of historical change. In this, the institutions of the mass media were crucial. From the outset, memories of May 1940, and of Churchill within this history, were densely mediated through the wireless, the printed word, and the moving image. When the events of May 1940 first entered memory, 'the people' were dominant (if precariously so) and by comparison Churchill, the political leader, was relatively understated. When he did appear in the popular media, he did so commonly as the expression of 'the people' who, at this juncture, were projected—whatever the realities of the matter—in a radical, democratic spotlight, as masters of their own agency.[99]

In modern Britain the concept of the people, and its correlate, popu-lism, have always been disturbing categories, never quite conforming to the stipulations of the Westminster way of doing things. This was so in the 1940s, and it is true for now as well.[100] In his quest to plot how Churchill the man mutated into 'the greatest living Englishman', John Ramsden, a scrupulous scholar of the myriad of legends enveloping Churchill, comments that:

> the ideological atmosphere of the 'people's war' militated against the building up of a personal leadership mystique while it lasted, and the 1945 General Election demonstrated that many voters did not want Churchill as leader for the postwar world of welfare either.[101]

War radicalism, or war populism, represented a collective mentality, expressing a strain of vernacular aspiration, and given form—that is, *becoming* politics—through the work of its own accredited 'intellectuals', to draw from Gramsci's generous use of the term.

Ramsden outlines the presence of two dominating, contrary national narratives in contention, playing off each other. On the one hand he cites the imperatives of the 'people's war'; and on the other, the 'personal leadership mystique' of Churchill. The collective task of waging total war—in which the domestic population found itself on a frontline of hostilities—propelled in the public sphere a heightened recognition of the political presence of the population as a whole. The dispositions of a radical populism, articulated by the overriding idea of the citizen, were distinct from the sensibilities which animated the cult of Churchill as the nation's providential leader.

Ramsden requires us to consider also the temporalities of the Churchill myths. Until the end of 1941, Churchill could not rely with certainty on the support of even those in his own party. The mythic 'man of destiny' took off only as the war was coming to its end, and in the years which followed. The memory of Churchill-in-1940 which now dominates cohered as myth *after the event*. It came into being after his political authority had diminished, after his heroic days were spent, after the electoral defeat of 1945, and during the build-up of the Cold War. Churchill-as-myth was retrospective, a creation conjured up in the irregular domains of memory.

The transition in collective memory from 'people's war' to 'man of destiny'—that is, the organizing principle of the foundational Churchill myth—signified a material, historical transformation.[102] In social memory the story of the 'people's war' story gradually ceded its integrity to Churchill as titan. Unsurprisingly, remnants of the 'old' were reproduced in the 'new'. The shift was complex, uneven, and never fully accomplished. Yet the more securely Churchill became established as the principal vector by which May 1940 shaped collective memory, the more the radicalism of 'the people' was displaced. While never being eliminated, it was diluted, marginalized, and divested of its historical consequence.

In supplanting 1940 as the story of the people, the emergent myth of epic Churchill was premised on an unspoken core of forgetfulness. As the Churchill story came to encapsulate the many histories which composed May 1940, the authority of the people diminished. The more the single narrative—Churchill's story—prevailed, the further its mythic properties were amplified. Where Churchill was present, history happened; where he was absent, it didn't. The relations between past and present assumed a new timbre. In our own times when, in the cinema or in our reading, we encounter the stream of contemporary Churchilliana we can feel the materiality of this forgetfulness. As mythic Churchill is resurrected, we're invited to forget something of ourselves, vaporizing the pasts which have made us. Far from Churchill supplying the means by which we can reimagine our own historical agency, as Boris Johnson dreams, the contrary occurs. When mythic Churchill unrolls, the agency of the people dwindles.

This is not strictly, however, an instance of amnesia. In some ways it's the opposite. Public memories of May 1940 proliferate. Yet, as collective memories continue to be refracted through the person of Churchill, other historic possibilities slide out of reach. In the very proliferation of memory, forgetfulness is sustained. The people, as a collective historical actor, is divested of its historical gravity. All is subsumed in the deeds of the Great Man.

In order to recover the historical significance of the people it may be instructive to reflect on an episode from the time when Churchill, as the embodiment of the nation, *doesn't* appear. That is, when we—as inheritors of mythic Churchill—might expect to find him heavily accentuated, only to discover in its place a conspicuous absence. If we can *see* this absence perhaps—paradoxically—we might more immediately grasp what has been forgotten.

We can turn to a vignette from J.B. Priestley's *Postscripts*. Priestley was one of the 'intellectuals' of the radical populism of the time, giving it voice and form and, through his access to the mass media, attesting to its reality.

Priestley's *Postscripts* were short, informal, conversational chats—heavily contrived—broadcast on BBC radio. The first was aired on Wednesday 5 June 1940; they followed on successive Sunday evenings until 20 October, almost but not quite spanning the first phase of Churchill's premiership, comprising Dunkirk and the Battle of Britain. The talks were almost completely devoid of the high rhetoric which came to be known as 'Churchillian'. Priestley seldom mentioned the nation's military prowess, the Empire, the Church, or the monarchy. The tone was civic, domestic, feminine, and provincial, understated throughout. He contrived to identify his own voice as that of 'a comfortable pipe-and-slippers man' who would never be counted as one of 'your heroes'.[103]

Churchill himself featured just once, and barely even then. On 4 July Priestley visited the House of Commons. What struck him was neither Churchill's speech nor the elaborate rituals of Westminster. When Churchill entered the chamber he headed toward Ernest Bevin, his Labour colleague in the war cabinet, a man whose girth, sense of self, and expansive being could compete with Churchill's. As he sat down, he delivered to Bevin 'a little dig in the ribs', and broke into an impish smile.[104] This human touch was precisely what Priestley admired. At that very point his sympathies were all for Churchill. In the run of the *Postscript* broadcasts, this joviality—the dig in the ribs—was the single occasion when Churchill was accorded a role in the unfolding drama of the nation in 1940. It signalled a time, furthermore, when the image of Churchill existed independently from his voice. His rhetorical powers were not Priestley's concern. His Churchill was a man *who did not speak*. For us, today, historic demotion of Churchill in this vein is startling, so inured are we to his mythic presence. How could May 1940 be told *without* Churchill the giant brooding over it? We live in a different historical world.

Priestley was content to name the events of 1940 'epic'. The paddle-steamers conscripted to cross the Channel to Dunkirk (in truth, a miniscule component of the flotilla which was principally mobilized by the state) 'seemed to belong to the same ridiculous holiday world as pierrots and piers, sand castles, ham-and-eggs teas, palmists, automatic machines, and crowded sweating promenades'. In their prior incarnation the passengers on the steamers comprised 'gents full of high spirits and bottled beer, the ladies eating pork pies, the children sticky with pepper-mint rock'.[105] Priestley presented to his listeners an epic of the common people, poised to enter the annals of history. 'Already the future histor-ians are fastening their gaze upon us, seeing us all in that clear and searching light of the great moments of history.'[106] 'History was being made, and as I suspect is usual when history is being made, the practice reeked of weary humanity.'[107]

The following year, in a collection entitled *Out of the People*, he returned to these themes. By this stage Priestley had come to be recog-nized as one of the chief ideologues of England's emergent populism. The sequel is more abstract and reflective—less chatty in tone—struggling to pin down the idea of the people. To do this he called upon a breezy, voluntarist conception, which was neither unattractive nor ill-judged: '*We are all the people so long as we are willing to consider ourselves the people.*'[108]

From the Munich crisis of September 1938 through to the mobilization following the declaration of war a year later, the idea of the people
appeared in many manifestations. Despite the plurality of its enunci-
ations, the people assumed a sharper definition. New political identifi-
cations were released. Partly the war radicalism was an effect of official
attempts to win the population to the prerequisites of undertaking total
war; partly it was also due to the fact that Neville Chamberlain's admin-
istrations had conducted a politics of unnerving dissociation, deaf to the
aspirations of the mass of the population. Official society appeared
unable to hear, and unconcerned about, popular sentiment. In response,
a mosaic of liberal, radical, leftish, and patriotic bids to represent the
people were accorded a new-found gravity across a variety of institutions
in civil society, driven by the pressing desire that the people's voice be
heard.

We can only gesture to this here. It's well-worn ground. The political
correlate to *Postscripts* can be found in Victor Gollancz's publication,
Guilty Men, co-authored by Michael Foot, Frank Owen, and Peter
Howard, the latter a Tory, under the collective name of Cato. The
book, published in July 1940, was written in four days. It carried the
temper of its moment, the prose vibrating with its own urgency. It incited
its readers to seize their ('our') time.[109]

Mass Observation's extraordinary determination to archive, from
below, an 'anthropology of ourselves' was in its way archetypal: in its
tantalizing founding volume—the Penguin Special, *Britain by Mass
Observation*, published in 1939—the authors, Charles Madge and Tom
Harrison, vowed 'to give both ear and voice to what the millions are
feeling and doing under the shadow of these terrific events'.[110] Penguin
Books itself formed a generation, as did the Left Book Club. (The political
crisis of May 1940 saw Penguin launch its endeavour to publish selections from *Hansard* in cheap, paperback editions.)[111] In the longer
duration the *Daily Mirror*, *Picture Post*, and *Lilliput* did much to shape
the imagined communities of those who felt they identified—militantly
or carelessly, determinedly or fleetingly—as 'the people'. The photojour-
nalism of Bert Hardy and Bill Brandt sought to illuminate the hidden
lives of those who for long had faced public neglect. Corners of the BBC
(including sections of its Empire Service) were redoubts of radical

sympathies. Alongside the diet of propaganda and newsreels, in the cinema radical iconoclasts—Michael Powell and Emeric Pressburger; Alberto Cavalcanti; Humphrey Jennings; and plenty more—nurtured an independent vision of how 'people' and 'nation' could be lived creatively.[112] We could go on. But the artefacts generated in this maelstrom of activity, for all their differences, shared the conviction that the authority of the people needed to be asserted.[113]

However, striking about the popular sensibilities of the war years was their fluidity. For much of the time there was no iron wall separating those harbouring affinities for a generalized radicalism from those invigorated by Churchill. Paul Addison's account of Churchill demonstrates the influence of these cross-currents. He draws from Mass Observation to show that (in 1941) alongside evident popular hostility to Churchill, plenty of working men and women, while broadly subscribing to the protocols of an orthodox radicalism, supported—or were enthusiastic for—him. This leads Addison to speculate that, in this period, 'There was much truth in the Churchillian myth.'[114]

In similar mode, Priestley himself, although at this time habitually reluctant to condemn Churchill personally, proposed that in reality there existed two Churchills. There was the orator who voiced 'the mood of the people'. And alongside the man of the people there was his double: the man of the state. In Priestley's words, 'when Churchill was not on his feet but back again with his maps, the official mind took charge again.'[115] Churchill, in this reading, inhabited the official mind (the state) while rhetorically identifying with the people.

As Ramsden suggests, this radical populism of the Second World War represented an identifiable current in an inchoate politics 'from below' during the war years. Churchill's coalition formally placed a freeze on the conflicts between Conservative and Labour, allowing geysers of dissent to bubble away outside the usual Westminster institutions. In 1945, once Labour pulled out of its pact with the Conservatives, winning back its political autonomy, the populism which had characterized the wartime political scene attenuated and Labour—with its great electoral majority—established itself as the unrivalled vehicle for radical change. Populism largely ceased to be a factor in British politics, as political conventions returned.

In a collateral shift, the myths associated with 'the people's war' gradually morphed into the story of Churchill as destiny. It's not that the people were expunged from the nation's stories. But in the post-war world, as the Cold War started to act as an axiomatic point of reference, symbolically the people were demoted to the adjunct of one, superior individual destiny. The work of the Churchill myths, in their founding instance, sought to *unify* two principal historical actors—the state and the people—affirming their harmony.[116] This arrangement of mythic Churchill was to have a long, continuing, undisturbed history. Largely it held—in our terms, from Isaiah Berlin to John Lukacs—until roughly the turn of the new century. This was less a matter of who did or didn't do what. It turned on how history itself was to be conceived.

Yet as we approach our own times, a new, contrasting, configuration of the people has been summoned. The historic curriculum has been revised, and—long, long after his death—Churchill has been called upon, once more, to perform further labours for his nation.

England's Populism: Brexit

There's a revealing coda to this story of May 1940. It concerns the work of the inimitable Max Hastings. Hasting is an erstwhile editor of the *Telegraph* and the *Evening Standard*, and the author of an entire library of books which puts the common-or-garden British academic to shame. Some of his writings are serious journalistic assignments, the remainder admirably researched histories. He's iconoclastic but not so much as to loosen his conservative instincts.

We turned to his *Finest Years. Churchill as Warlord, 1940–45*, first published in 2009. The opening sentence wasn't, though, what we'd expected: 'Winston Churchill was the greatest Englishman and one of the greatest human beings of the twentieth century, indeed of all time.' A little while later, when he claims that 'the British people at war ... served as a supporting cast, seeking honourably but sometimes inadequately to play their own parts in the wake of a titan', it seems that we've entered an unexpected mental universe.[117] This signals precisely the situation when the people—popular life, everyday life, ordinary life:

a crucial dimension in which history works—are written out of the story, relegated merely to a 'supporting cast' of the state, dispossessed of all life.

An important historical lineage operates here. Hastings is a distinguished journalist. He's also the son of distinguished journalists, Macdonald Hastings and Anne Scott-James. Indeed, his parents were both apprenticed in the radical populist climate of the forties, working on *Picture Post*, a lively organizer for translating social-democratic precepts into a lived common sense and open to sympathetic card-carrying Tories.[118] They were both indebted to the ethics of *Picture Post*; they themselves were responsible, in part, for creating the magazine's social reputation.[119] Within this single family story an intellectual declension is evident, in which good thinking is usurped by ready-to-hand hyperbole. Churchill deserves plaudits. But 'one of the greatest human beings...of all time'? On what grounds can such a judgement be made? Within what field of vision?[120]

There's nothing populist about Max Hastings' metropolitan urbanity. No strain of populism enters either his historical narrative or his politics.[121] His Churchill is indicative of the evolution of a social memory in which the radicalization of the 1940s has been supplanted by the less supple story which derives from the authority of the man of destiny.[122] A larger politics later impinges: the history of Thatcherism, pre-eminently, or in this context perhaps—more particularly—the continuing aftershocks of the Malvinas/Falklands war of 1982, which did much to redefine the inherited memories of May 1940.[123] As the national politics swung to the right, so in time did the historiography.

In 1973, long before Mrs Thatcher had fully lodged herself in the national consciousness, the historian J.H. Plumb, a man whose sympathies for any variety of leftish radicalism remained perpetually below zero, had this to say of Churchill:

> He is, perhaps, the last great historic practitioner of the historic theme of England's providential destiny...It [this historic theme] no longer holds credence either for the governing elite or the nation at large. There are pockets of believers who comfort themselves with the works of Sir Arthur Bryant, but they know in their bones that their past is dead.[124]

To read these words today is a shock. What Plumb had declared deservedly dead in 1973 now, nearly half a century on, has come alive again, a post-mortem body of writing publicly well received for its intelligence and vigour. The faith in Churchill's wisdom, confined for Plumb in 1973 to 'pockets of believers', is today largely established as the nation's common sense. This is evident in Hastings, and in pretty much the bulk of contemporary writings on Churchill. The titles addressing May 1940 we indicated earlier commonly defer, with no sense of apology, to what Plumb many years ago had derided as faith in 'England's providential destiny'.

This occurs not only in the formal historiography. We can return for the last time to *Darkest Hour*. The film plays on the tensions between state and people, resolving them to leave no room for ambiguity.

At the start of the movie Churchill, although prime minister, has only a precarious hold on the state. His authority in his party is weak and his speedy ejection from office threatens. We encounter him on the afternoon of 28 May in his chauffeur-driven limousine on his way to Parliament. His drive to the Commons is intercut with (digitally contrived) shots of the civilian craft sailing to Dunkirk in order to rescue the British Expeditionary Force, the visual association anticipating what's coming by linking Churchill, shunned by the political establishment, with the pluck of the English people. When the car halts at a traffic light Churchill makes a none-too sprightly dash for freedom and before too long is lost in the city crowd. His escape is reported back to his minders in Whitehall. Consternation follows. 'We've lost the PM.' As he enters the underground station, the cinema audience is witness to the fact that he has momentarily freed himself from the trappings of state and is on the point of crossing the line to pass as a private citizen. This is the necessary prelude to his underground encounter with 'the British people'. The rendezvous is staged on their territory, not his. Just as earlier in the film the king had travelled from Buckingham Palace to Churchill's private apartments, so Churchill himself travels to the people. The class perspective shifts. His entry into the darkened, subterranean world of the people, abandoning the luminosity of life above, is heavy with mythic association.

The episode provides the pretext for the magical resolution which results, in the course of the journey, when Churchill and the people become one. By the time he enters the Commons, Churchill has within him the resolve of the people. In overcoming Halifax and his band of self-serving courtiers the prospect opens for the providential unification of state and people, orchestrated through the person of Churchill.

The film, however, registers an important shift in emphasis. In this regard Boris Johnson's interpretation, possibly, proves material. The figuration of Churchill as a lone figure in the power bloc, surrounded by treacherous colleagues who desire nothing more than to see him dispatched, adds a new dimension. The upper reaches of the state have capitulated to the enemies of the nation. Halifax & Co. *are* the enemies within. The old war-radical narratives, in which the state is deaf to the people, are revived. But as this populism is revived it's reinflected. In order for the enemies within, at the very apex of the state, to be defeated the compact between Churchill and the people becomes the only means by which this can be achieved. Churchill needs the people in order to destroy the enemy within. This is a populism which pays heed to the man of destiny—a man both inside and outside the governing class—who is transfigured into the agent for cleansing the state of its traitors. In so doing, 'he' single-handedly seizes hold of history.

The film rehearses a number of tropes which are now becoming common themes in contemporary tellings of the Churchill story, acknowledging (if timidly) the presence of a twenty-first-century politics of gender: 'Clemmie' as feisty but long-suffering helpmeet; Churchill's thoughtless bullying of his young female stenographers who, when they discover the inner man, learn to adore him; the lachrymose disposition of the Great Man himself.

However, a pronounced new element readjusts these refrains. In *Darkest Hour*, in the midst of this drama of May 1940, as we've already noted, the esteemed nineteenth-century figure of Lord Macaulay unexpectedly and momentarily pops up on the screen: not in person, but through Churchill's recitation of his verse while he travelled on the tube. Though his presence is brief, it's pivotal to the story of the Great Man readying himself for his ascension to serve as saviour of the nation. We know Churchill's escapade on the underground never happened. *But if it had*—in the circumstances adduced in the film—it's not improbable to have him reciting Macaulay. This marks a singular moment when the movie demonstrates a measure of historical plausibility.[125] When France fell in 1940, at exactly the same point in history as Churchill's imagined adventure on the underground, the new minister of information—the high-life socialite Duff Cooper, too worldly to be given to popular sentimentality—took it upon himself to broadcast on the wireless Macaulay's 'The Armada'.[126] At school Churchill himself had learned by heart the entire compendium of the *Lays of Ancient Rome*, and Macaulay remained part of him throughout his life. In 1946 he confessed to an acquaintance, 'I should have to own that I owe more to Macaulay than to any other English writer.'[127]

From the middle of the nineteenth century to the middle of the twentieth century Macaulay existed as a naturalized feature in the mental landscape of Britain's political class.[128] Yet it wasn't only amongst the elite that he was acclaimed. His writings were once an integral component of Britain's popular heritage, amongst high and low, in both metropole and colony. Churchill's recital of 'brave Horatius, Captain of the gate'—were the event ever to have occurred—would have been recognized by his travelling companions.[129]

However, to stage the duet of Churchill, zealot for white supremacy, and Marcus Peters, the black West Indian, reciting 'Horatius' is an act of overwhelming bad faith. In paying their shared obeisance to Macaulay, blackness is effaced, inventing in the self-same moment an unwelcome, peculiarly English minstrelsy. It's an instance of high-speed disavowal, a rare occasion when one can actually *see* and *hear* the past—war radicalism; colonial rule—in the business of being forgotten, made invisible by the camera's devotion to an oversized, weepy Churchill.[130]

Macaulay was an icon in England's pantheon. Yet his appearance in a film of *2018*, as the means to signal the democratic commitments of the people in the *1940s* wipes out from history its very historicalness. Macaulay, as a figure of war radicalism? Macaulay, in the time of Stalin and Roosevelt? This is an index of the degree to which the complexion of England is undergoing renovation. The film proceeds as if the Churchill–Macaulay constitution of the people is the most natural—the most benign—thing ever. It's self-evident, in no need of explanation. Obvs.

Yet Churchill's excursion into the underworld also introduces a higher gradation of populism to the mythic repertoire. The cinematic rendez-vous he has with the people isn't innocent. It's the single moment when Churchill ceases to be identified with the apparatus of the state. 'We've lost the PM.' His departure from the state is the precondition for his communing with 'the British people'. Before he learns from the people, he must relinquish his hold on the state. He has to descend to the level of the citizenry. Indeed Macaulay becomes the medium by which Churchill's identification with the people—the British people and the colonized—can be accomplished. In a double move, the people are cast (first) as the film-makers' idea of what they assume to be the projection (secondly) of Churchill's own imaginary inner life. It's a configuration sealed by the intervention of Macaulay. The ghost of John Lukacs looms, while the mediations accumulate.

Churchill's encounter with the people in the film, however, is a brief detour, giving succour to his deepest instincts. Once his train arrives at Westminster he returns to his commanding role in the state. He has been given faith by his compact with the people. But from this point on—notwithstanding his dalliance with the people—he is more securely *of* the state.

Yet this harmonious articulation of people and state, for long hege-monic, is today losing its ideological authority. This explains the short-lived flurry of 'Churchill wars' which broke out in the media in February 2019, when mythic Churchill had publicly to be defended from its supposedly brutish, rowdy antagonists. Even though the moment quickly evaporated, with other matters pressing in, an emergent sensibility was coalescing in which Churchill has come to assume a bolder populist disposition.[131]

In the interpretations of Andrew Roberts and Boris Johnson a new Churchill is being assembled. No longer does he stand for the idealized *harmony* between state and people. On the contrary, he's now located as the political outsider whose primary sympathies lie with the people, and who harbours a distrust toward the state. In this emergent dispensation, it seems his political career was never—truly—of the state at all. His oligarchic formation (Blenheim Palace, and all stations beyond) carries no material political imprint. In this incarnation Churchill now enters the world as a freelance Caesarist, moving in and out of the field of state power as circumstance demands. He nurtures no given, natural affinity to the state, common to men of his class and generation. It's a view which invites us to conclude, given his providential access to the sentiments of the people, that he can—if obliged—join the people in rallying *against* the state.

This opens a qualitatively new scenario. No longer is it, or 'he', propelled by the desire that people and state become one. In its place arrives a reverie in which the state is reconceived to be—potentially—the enemy of the people.[132] The Halifaxes are all about us. The mythic properties of Churchill are no less emphatic. But the relation between state and people is significantly rearranged.

If the making of the myths of Churchill started life, at the outset of the Cold War, by purging the dominating populist excrescence, in our own times Churchill is reimagined as a new-found populist. He is only weakly deployed as the nation's consensual leader. On the contrary, he is unambiguously a partisan for the people, seeking the destruction of the enemies inside the state.

Ideologues of Brexit have been tireless in conjugating *faux* histories: eccentric, wayward, and for the most part short of any persuasive meaning. Telling has been the appeal arising from the Johnson/Rees-Mogg fraction of the Brexit cadres to the calamities of 'vassalage'. This portrays a melodramatic tableau in which Eton/Oxford/England (one is all, all is one) is on the point of being dispossessed of its historic responsibilities and surrendering its traditions to an imposition of a modern species of serfdom. This evokes an England after Empire subjected to the indignities of a reimposed Norman Yoke, masterminded from overseas.[133] For the Eton/Oxford caste, governing was what they were born to do. It's in their DNA. How could their historic privilege be usurped by alien, overseas 'bureaucrats' stationed in, of all places, Brussels?[134]

Recourse to myth-making in this way works as a screen memory, camouflaging the past and placing it further beyond the reach of the present. In its highly strung manifestations, driven by the more assured populist inflections of Nigel Farage, these putatively historical investments are to be lauded as irrefutable proof that 'Europe' is robbing England of what has uniquely been its own: its providential past.

In its long historical duration Euroscepticism has shifted from its early, instinctive, unmonitored forms, testament to a collective psychic anxiety, raw and unprocessed, to becoming a fully-fledged politics, albeit a 'new' (populist) politics.[135] Day by day, it seems, it seeks to colonize new regions of the state.

The journey from Sir James Goldsmith's Referendum Party in 1995 (boasting as its leading personnel Edward Fox, Carla Powell, and Petronella Wyatt: unknown for their political nous, and not exactly likely or desirable founders of a new state) to the electoral triumphs of the Brexit Party in 2019, only weeks after its founding, has been astonishing.[136] The crystallization of the populist right from the fringes of national life to its deepening gravitational hold on state power can be summarily plotted: from the sacking of Enoch Powell from Edward Heath's shadow cabinet in April 1968, when Powell was claimed by his followers as the people's martyr, shabbily treated by the political class, race traitors all; the founding of the Democratic Unionist Party in September 1971, the repressed past of Orange populism returning reinvigorated to the mainland; Mrs Thatcher's Bruges speech of September 1988, widely interpreted by her followers as a call to arms against 'Europe'; the arrival of UKIP and later, under the generalship of Farage, its capacity to present itself as legitimate competitor to Conservative and Labour; to David Cameron's fateful announcement in January 2016 that he was about to introduce the referendum, turned inside-out the following month by the electrifying announcement that his two senior lieutenants, Boris Johnson and Michael Gove, were jumping ship and allying themselves to the populist ultras. These populist currents of the right have a long, discontinuous, uneven, and largely subterranean history which representatives of the governing class are reluctant to acknowledge.[137]

Each step in this mobilization of popular life has generated a closer link between the populists, on the ground, and those habituated to rule, from 'above'. In doing so it sanctions a new form of governmentality, as is evident from Johnson's daily practice of what he believes 'politics' to entail. As we write, the single most powerful influence on the Conservative Party comes from outside its ranks, in the person of Farage.

In this political upheaval, where no one knows what the following week will bring, the story of May 1940 offers a means—a mythic means—to comprehend what is happening. The inherited dramaturgy is operative, even while its apportioning of moral worth is new. The enemy shape-shifts. The current hue and cry for traitors and quislings is never far away. High officers of state find themselves, from one day to the next, in the media danger zone.

In a hard-to-reach substratum of England's collective consciousness, the prospects of Germany's perceived wish to dominate Europe works as the fantasized sequel to the Nazi past. This represents a deep stratum sedimented in popular experience.[138] A generation ago, Edward Heath and Roy Jenkins, old-school proselytizers for the UK in Europe, were outed as Neville Chamberlain and Lord Halifax resurrected.[139] From the 1980s, extravagant sentiments of this order began to cut into public life. The veteran Thatcherite Nicholas Ridley comes to mind: he unwisely chose to speak out loud what others conveyed with greater circumspection, proposing that German ambitions for domination of Europe at the end of the century were a continuation of Hitlerism, even if conducted with greater guile. May 1940 continues to cast long shadows. What was once considered to be outlandish now exerts a tighter hold on the ruling caste.

Powerful in this organization of new populist attachments has been the press. Since the beginnings of mass democracy in Britain the popular press has played a defining role in its workings, for good and ill. The long succession of press barons has contributed an active element to the makings of modern politics, supplying the institutional infrastructure which those who'd fashioned themselves as men of destiny required. Notwithstanding their own self-projections, seemingly abject and shunned, the aspirant Ceasarists were never as abandoned as they liked to imagine themselves. The press served as the decisive medium by which they could realize their dreams, offering a principal means by which they could call upon 'the people'. As a fledgling Caesar, Churchill was never alone, despite his wayward allegiance to party politics. When out of office he could always rely on the press—in Caesarist manner—to supply a direct line of communication with 'the people'.

Readers will know of the centrality of the *Daily Mail*, under the editorship of Paul Dacre, to the organization of Brexit. As history has proceeded this has had less to do with any particular decision about trade agreements with the EU than a charged sign offering the chimera of a new—fantastic—world. Addressed to the 'left behind', the entire theatre has been stage-managed by those very far themselves from immiseration.

Dacre, a man apparently of unexceptional talents, had been appointed editor of the *Mail* in 1992. He'd boasted an (unexceptional) reputation as a student leftist in the late sixties, before migrating to the right and to a militant espousal of the values of Arnos Grove respectability, which he continued to inhabit from his childhood. He arrived at the *Mail* a couple of months before the financial crisis triggered by Britain's membership of the Exchange Rate Mechanism, in which the value of sterling was dependent on the German mark. This was formative for Dacre, instilling in him an immovable distrust of John Major, the Conservative prime minister, and took him down the road of an unquenchable Euroscepticism.[140]

Notorious was the 'Enemies of the People' headline in the *Mail* of 4 November 2016. This indicted the senior judges of the High Court who'd declared it would be Parliament, not the executive, which had the right to trigger Article 50, formally opening the process of the UK secession from the EU. The enemies were in the state. Some six months later the *Mail* led with its proclamation 'Crush the Saboteurs' (19 April 2017). In the wake of May's announcement of a snap election, the enemy on this occasion were the Lords, who according to the *Mail* were intent on overturning the will of the people. The enemies were not only 'within'. They operated in the highest echelons of the state.

Earlier, on 4 February 2016, just prior to the Johnson–Gove defection from Cameron, the *Mail* in a front-page editorial returned to the eve of the Second World War and asked 'Who Will Speak for England?' It took its readers back to 2 September 1939: to the time when Chamberlain's National Government was equivocating in its confrontation with the Nazi danger. As the Labour MP Arthur Greenwood stood up to speak, the pugnacious Tory Leo Amery, in the face of Chamberlain's political paralysis, urged Greenwood to 'Speak for England.' Such a critical moment, the *Mail* explained, was upon England again—although it was careful to insist, quietly, that the threat presented by Nazi Germany was not of the same magnitude as that emanating from the EU. The editorial signified a critical moment in the delineation of a new incarnation of the English people, determining also to establish its historical credentials as the moral descendant of Churchill in 1939–40.

This was prompted by the apparent failure of Cameron's negotiations with the EU, and by the knowledge that the referendum was about to happen. The extremity of the situation the *Mail* located in the 'tsunami of migrants flooding across Europe'. The paper, true to its popular instincts, was forceful in identifying its antagonists, drawing its net widely: the Conservative Party, the civil service, and the BBC. It nominated as the Brexit backsliders Theresa May, Michael Gove, Philip Hammond, William Hague, Sajid Javid, and John Whittingdale. Boris Johnson the paper believed was doing no more than playing 'flirtatious footsie' with the Brexiteers. Iain Duncan Smith and Chris Grayling avoided expulsion to the ninth circle, although neither was complimented on their competence. Who escaped censure? Lord Lawson, although he was declared to be past it. And Nigel Farage, but in his case, the *Mail* insisted, he was commonly perceived to be too clownish to be considered. Heroes in the cause there were none, although we were yet to learn that the clowns were to carry the future.

Shortly after, however, Johnson broke ranks and stepped into the breach.[141] He did so on the back of Churchill. Introducing his book on Churchill, Johnson warmly acknowledged his boozy discussions about the Great Man with Andrew Roberts, convened at the discreetly plutocratic locale of 5 Hertford Street in Mayfair, where Churchill would have felt himself comfortably at home.

Johnson quotes from a youthful Churchill:

Of all the talents bestowed upon men, none is so precious as the gift of oratory. He who enjoys it wields a power more durable than that of a great king. He is an independent force in the world. Abandoned by his party, betrayed by his friends, stripped of his offices, whoever can command this power is still formidable.[142]

This is Churchill as a precocious Caesar—imagining what it would be like to be abandoned by party; betrayed by friends; stripped of office: a man of destiny alone and divested of all authority—espying on the distant horizon his singular destiny. In this scenario there are no given institutional means that allow him to connect with the people. All he possesses is the power of his rhetoric: through this means alone the people can be delivered to him.

Against the man who embodies destiny, Johnson and Roberts both identify in twentieth-century Britain what they label the 'Respectable Tendency'. This they regard as forming the current against which Churchill defined his very political being. The term was first coined by Roberts in order to understand Churchill's antagonists in his own party in the first phase of his premiership in 1940.[143] These were the place-holders who held Churchill—the chaotic adventurer—in contempt, and whom Churchill himself was eventually to vanquish. Johnson's Churchill is similarly preoccupied by the travails required to dislodge to the dominance of the 'Respectable Tories', although even here he can't resist hamming it up.[144]

Yet Roberts is the more revealing. He is emphatic in presenting the 'Respectable Tendency' as marking the fundamental co-ordinates of the British state itself. Reviving the reflexes of Enoch Powell, he concludes that the traditional governing class itself to be corrupt. At the close of his enormous life of Churchill, Roberts claims that his protagonist

> didn't abide by what was known as 'form', an instinctively respectful behaviour inculcated by the public schools, Oxford and Cambridge, the BBC, the Civil Service, the Court, the City of London, the Church of England, the gentlemen's clubs and the political parties.[145]

Old England and its state are in the firing line. This marks a historically consequent rupture when, in the name of Conservatism, the people are called upon to tear down all that historic Conservatism has sought to preserve. As Tom Nairn argued long ago, with Powell in his sights, 'the English conservative Establishment has begun to destroy itself.'[146] In our day, those who command the state have made such reveries their own.

In this, the man conscripted to deliver old England its *coup de grâce* is none other than Winston Churchill. He's again alive in contemporary public life. The fate of Brexit will take a generation or more to resolve. But the Brexitization of the past is already underway.

2

The Churchill Syndrome

'Winston Churchill—hero or villain?' This was one of a series of quick-fire questions posed to Labour's Shadow Chancellor John McDonnell at the close of an 'in conversation' event organized by the website Politico in February 2019. McDonnell thought for a moment before replying 'Tonypandy—villain.'[1] The reference was, of course, to Churchill's decision, as Home Secretary in 1910, to send troops to assist police in their efforts to deal with riots by striking miners in the Rhondda Valley. In a subsequent interview, McDonnell stated that Churchill 'sent the troops into Tonypandy to shoot the miners, a miner died'. He was speaking the literal truth, but what he said was misleading: one man died from a blow to the head, probably from a police truncheon, prior to the arrival of the soldiers, but nobody was shot. During similar events in Llanelli the following year two men *were* shot dead. 'Churchill was obviously a hero during the Second World War', McDonnell said, but he stuck by his original words nonetheless.[2]

The media storm-in-a-teacup that followed the remark was predictable enough. Little more than two weeks earlier the Green MSP Ross Greer had gained a similar amount of coverage when he had branded Churchill 'a white supremacist mass murderer.'[3] It was no surprise either that Boris Johnson should weigh in. Not only had Churchill saved Britain from fascist tyranny: 'If John McDonnell had the slightest knowledge of history he would be aware that Churchill also had an extraordinary record as a social reformer who cared deeply for working people and their lives.' Comments from an anonymous Labour figure quoted by the *Daily Telegraph* were more revealing, insofar as they laid bare the fratricidal nature of the party's internal politics in the Corbyn era. 'The hard-left just can't help themselves', the MP said. 'It shows the huge gap between their values and what the vast majority of decent people think.'[4]

It was interesting that a Labour MP stuck up for Churchill in this way. Within his lifetime he had been the object of much left-wing hostility, not least on account of his support for British intervention in the Russian civil war and for his hardline stance during the 1926 General Strike. The criticism diminished during the Second World War, but did certainly not evaporate; Churchill was a significantly more controversial figure during these years than legend would suggest.[5] McDonnell had grounds for his statement that 'many working-class people, at the time and well into the forties and fifties, were angry at his behaviour.'[6] During the 1950 general election Churchill was forced to refute the claim that he had been responsible for the shooting of miners at Tonypandy, thus getting lured into a dispute 'which, from the strictly electioneering point of view, can have done Conservatism in Wales little but harm'.[7] In 1978, the Labour Prime Minister James Callaghan, who was on the right of the party, attacked Churchill's grandson and namesake for suggesting in the Commons that the miners' recent 36.5 per cent pay rise was excessive. 'I hope that the hon. Gentleman will not pursue the vendetta of his family against the miners—[Interruption.]—at Tonypandy for the third generation.'[8]

Of course, there was plenty of genuine admiration for Churchill on the left as well. In 1945, it was quite possible for voters to respect him as a war leader even as they concluded that he was not the right man to 'win the peace'. Clement Attlee's eightieth birthday tribute, in 1954, was elegant and sincere.[9] And it was the much-loved Mo Mowlam, formerly a minister in Tony Blair's government, who was the presenter-advocate who helped ensure that Churchill was voted 'Greatest Briton' by the British public in 2002. In words that might easily be voiced by Boris Johnson today, she argued that through victory in the Second World War, Churchill had fulfilled his destiny. In the final sequence of the programme, shot in Bladon churchyard where Churchill is buried, she concluded: 'If Britain, with its eccentricities, its big-heartedness, and its strength of character, has to be summed up in one person, it just has to be Winston Churchill.'[10] Her advocacy appears to have swung opinions—Churchill had been pipped at the post by Shakespeare in a similar poll organized by Radio 4's *Today* programme three years earlier.[11]

The long-term divisions within the Labour Party over Churchill, brought into sharp relief by McDonnell's comments, were just one instance of the complexity of reactions to him. Boris Johnson's portrayal of him as the nation's saviour may represent the dominant response to Churchill within Great Britain and Northern Ireland, yet it has always sat alongside more negative interpretations. (Indeed, the hero-worship of the many may have aggravated the desire by a vocal minority to show that Churchill actually had feet of clay.) Move beyond the United Kingdom—to India, Ireland, or South Africa, for example—and the level of scepticism increases. Of course, there are many places where his name sparks ambivalence or indifference rather than antagonism; and certainly there are people in numerous lands who actively celebrate it. Nowhere is this more the case than in the United States where since his retirement and death, and with even greater intensity since the terrorist attacks of 9/11, many politicians have deployed the memory of Churchill in support of their own goals. The Churchill they invoke is a man who embodies an idealized form of moral steadfastness, unencumbered by the memory of Tonypandy and other inconvenient domestic baggage. Depoliticizing the historical Churchill turns him into a symbol which can be used for highly political ends.

The Battle for Churchill's Reputation

In order to understand the ways in which Churchill's memory has been debated during the 'Brexit moment', it is necessary to step back and consider the prior decades of battling over his legacy. It is equally crucial to observe that historians and archivists, as well as politicians and family members, have played their part in such processes. There is no fixed line where history stops and political argument begins. In this chapter we focus on the way in which, in particular, British and American politicians have used the idea of Churchill as a means of self-validation, sometimes in dialogue with popular and academic history. They have done this, in part, by deploying Churchill as an icon of idealized leadership. This has involved the use of the three rhetorical appeals, or modes of persuasion, identified by Aristotle in his *Art of Rhetoric*: *ēthos* (character), *pathos* (emotion), and *logos* (reasoned or logical discourse). By presenting Churchill's character in a certain way, a speaker can imply that they themselves share his *ēthos* of steadfastness and determination. By evoking his, and the nation's, 'Finest Hour', patriotic and nostalgic emotion can be summoned up. These appeals can be reinforced and complemented by *logos*. Just as Churchill stood resolute against the Nazis in the 1930s and 1940s, it can be argued, so we today should show the same tenacity against our current enemy (as defined by whoever happens to be speaking).

In looking at how the past has been deployed for current purposes, we do not ask (primarily) if politicians' analogies with Churchill have been correct, but rather, why, and in what ways Churchill has been seemingly so useful to them. We also ask why attempts to make different uses of Churchill, in particular the presentation of him as an enthusiastic pro-European, have also become pervasive, even if they have apparently been less successful. Our aim, then, is not to examine politicians' and campaigners' inner feelings about Churchill, but instead to encourage critical awareness of the rhetorical uses to which his memory has been put. To analyse the symbolism of Churchill is to investigate why the man himself continues to hold such power over the collective imagination in Britain, America, and beyond. Understanding why he inspires many helps explain why he causes equal and opposite reactions from those who wish to condemn him.

The concept of 'reputational entrepreneurship' provides a useful framework for examining these questions. Gary Alan Fine has argued convincingly that even negative reputations can serve 'as a rhetorical resource in a contested environment'. Heroic reputations can help build up the solidarity of the community; villainous reputations, or reputations for weakness (such as that of Neville Chamberlain) serve a similar function by helping define what society is against. However, multiple interpretations of the reputation of a given individual, in our case that of Churchill, are always possible. Therefore, as Fine argues, 'The maintenance of reputations requires self-interested custodians', or 'reputational entrepreneurs'. These people seek to shape the reputations of others because they see it as being to their own advantage, and to the advantage of their own community, political party, or nation, to do so. This does not imply that reputations have no connection to 'real' historical events, that they are infinitely malleable, or that they are always the product of cynical manipulation. But in order to understand why certain reputations 'stick' we need to trace the historical processes whereby they are shaped, and how they are employed in public speech and imagery. Yet, although Churchill has (to use Fine's phrase) a 'resonant core image' which appears to have been consistent over time, closer examination shows that actually it has evolved significantly over the decades.[12] It remains recognizable but has nonetheless shifted, partly on account of the actions of reputational entrepreneurs, but also in response to new revelations and changes in society's concerns. Churchill's symbolic meaning has changed significantly, even though modern arguments about him to some extent involve the playing out of debates that started before 1914.

In order to explain how this has worked in practice, it is important for us to note that different reputational entrepreneurs working on behalf of the same figure may have competing agendas. For instance, Violet Bonham Carter, author of *Winston Churchill as I Knew Him* (1965), was at least as sensitive about the reputation of her father, H.H. Asquith, as she was about that of her friend Churchill.[13] Institutions, such as archives and museums, have their part to play too. The UK does not have an exact equivalent of the US Presidential Libraries system, and has thus avoided many of the problems (notably that of partisan exploitation) associated with it.[14] Yet even the impeccably neutral Churchill Archives Centre (CAC) has to contend with the fact that those who have donated materials, or may do so in the future, often have their own agendas. These may concern, for example, the release of sensitive documents.[15] Whereas the CAC has successfully balanced the interests of researchers with those of the Churchill family and other interested parties, the National Trust's presentation of Chartwell (Churchill's house in Kent) and the Imperial War Museum's presentation of the 'Churchill War Rooms' have a more celebratory air. This is not to suggest that the history that they present is inaccurate, merely that the tourist who visits those venues in order to indulge in a bit of hero-worship will find little to trouble her preconceptions. The same could be said of the US National Churchill Museum in Fulton, Missouri; meanwhile the

International Churchill Society caters to a wide body of enthusiasts, with annual conferences and the magazine *Finest Hour*.

Churchill's reputation as an effective leader has proved highly resilient, critical accounts by some historians notwithstanding. Moreover, this reputation has been highly stereotyped—more complex accounts encounter resistance and are found *disturbing* even when they reflect well on Churchill.[16] (Criticisms are often stereotyped too: after all, 'Llanelli' does not have the same resonance as 'Tonypandy'.) Yet it is not our purpose to suggest that Churchill's positive reputation is ill deserved—much as it is the case that the public is frequently presented with an oversimplified picture of the historical reality. The point is that even if it is merited, we still need to explain why he has achieved iconic status—and has thus formed a component of other politicians' rhetoric—when other, perhaps similarly deserving, figures have not. For example, David Lloyd George was widely seen as a courageous leader, hailed in 1918 as 'The Man Who Won the War', but it is a long time since he has been a familiar point of reference in either Britain or the United States.[17] Of course, Lloyd George was a highly controversial figure. But as Dingle Foot MP observed in 1970:

> The same was true of Winston Churchill. But Churchill has been canonised. To recall the distrust with which he was regarded over a large part of his career now ranks almost as heresy. Lloyd George, whose achievement by any standard was not less than Churchill's, is constantly denigrated.[18]

Perhaps Foot overstated Lloyd George's success, but even if so, part of the explanation for the relative status of his reputation and that of Churchill must lie in the comparative effectiveness of those who have sought to advance those reputations. That effectiveness must in turn be explained partly by the fact that Churchill's reputation, for reasons that require explanation, has been the more politically useful of the two.

If Lloyd George has dropped out of public discussion of foreign policy, the same is not true of all of Churchill's contemporaries. Notwithstanding historians' efforts to show a more complex reality, 'appeasers' in general, and Neville Chamberlain in particular, have continued to be portrayed by politicians and journalists as the acme of weakness, and thus as Churchill's opposite.[19] Hence the importance of Fine's point about negative reputations; if politicians have wanted to be viewed as Churchillian, they have at the same time tried to avoid being portrayed as Chamberlainite. Chamberlain offers a point around which even ideological enemies can unite: John McDonnell and Boris Johnson could likely agree to condemn him. The use of Churchill as a rhetorical resource is thus a double-edged strategy. The positive imagery of his resolution, courage, and determination serves as a contrast (which is not always made explicit) to the alleged naivety and irresolution of those who kept him out of office in the 1930s. The positive imagery of 1940, the 'finest hour', is contrasted with the negative lessons of Munich and the notorious 'piece of paper'. Politicians who seek to use Churchill's reputation to their own advantage simultaneously suggest (implicitly or otherwise) that their own domestic political opponents are in favour of appeasement, something which is assumed, axiomatically, to be wholly undesirable. It is notable that Theresa May's negotiations with the EU led to a proliferation of comparisons between her and Chamberlain; the accusation had previously been levelled at David Cameron during the 2016 referendum campaign.

Bulldog

Yet comprehending Churchill's iconic/demonic status in the age of Brexit requires something more than tracing the ebbs and flows of the perceived historical statures of individuals. His significance as a symbol of Britishness has been constructed as part of a much broader phenomenon: the selective remembering and forgetting of empire. And not just the British one, it must be said. America's blindness to its own extensive but deniable empire, as well as the forgotten connections between European empires and the birth of the EU, are important contextual factors.[20] Moreover, if Churchill's racism and imperialism could be overlooked or conveniently explained away, then he could serve a bulldog figure representing pride in a Britain that had supposedly fought 'alone' as an 'island nation'.[21] Equally, it was possible to conjure up a

Churchill whose imperial and racial attitudes had been positively far-sighted, thus validating the Empire itself:

> The massacre of hundreds in Amritsar was indeed 'monstrous', as Churchill said at the time, but it was atypical. [...] Yes, rule by the British had its very real downsides and being massacred by General Dyer was one of them. Compared with alternative imperial regimes, however, it had much to commend it.[22]

In the United States, both Democrats and Republicans could invoke a largely depoliticized and de-imperialized Churchill as an exemplar of resolution and courage. In due course, moreover, pro-Europeans chose to portray him as the godfather of European integration and human rights, thus counterposing a 'virtuous', cosmopolitan Churchill to the narrowly nationalist Churchill of popular myth. He could thus be used as a reproach or a warning to Brexiteers, either on the basis of his actual words or of phrases spuriously attributed to him.[23] But this apparently well-meaning attempt to carve a progressive narrative from Churchillian materials meant obscuring some uncomfortable truths.[24]

Of course, the story of Churchill's reputation cannot be told without reference to his very effective efforts on his own behalf.[25] He acted partly through personal contacts, partly through speeches, and partly through writing his war memoirs—hence his famous remark that history would treat him favourably because he would write the history. He sought, furthermore, to inject his view of contemporary history, and his own role in it, into the Anglo-American collective memory. As he wrote to Clement Attlee, when asking permission to use government documents in his book on the Second World War,

> I think [the memoirs] could win sympathy for our country, particularly in the United States, and make them understand the awful character of the trials through which we passed, especially when we were fighting alone, and the moral debt owed to us by other countries.[26]

Churchill's privileged access to key documents gave him an advantage, but although this helped him influence his reputation, he could not control it completely. For example, his allegation that Gandhi had taken nutrients during his 1943 fast led the *Indian News Chronicle* to launch a scathing attack. 'Mr Churchill has proved to be both a false prophet and a poor historian. He has tried to sub-edit history, over-dramatise events to glorify himself, and presented a perverted version of facts.'[27] Scepticism was also in evidence in West Germany, albeit it was less harshly expressed. A valedictory assessment by the commentator Matthias Zeller described Churchill as a *Gleichgewichtsjongleur* (or 'equilibrium-juggler') whose career had been marked by a fatal error.

> In the end he underestimated the Bolshevist threat. The hatred which he bestowed not only upon 'Prussian militarism' and the 'National Socialist dictatorship', but upon the German Volk itself, blinded him. He realized too late that all the weight of Western and Central Europe had to be placed on one side of the scale to balance out the Russian colossus.[28]

Tellingly, the West German edition of Labour MP Emrys Hughes's highly critical biography was given the title *Churchill: Ein Mann in seinem Widerspruch* (literally: 'a man in his contradictions'). The American edition, by contrast, was subtitled *British Bulldog*.[29]

But even in the United States, where he had a large number of genuine admirers, Churchill was often regarded unenthusiastically. He often spoke sentimentally about Anglo-American relations, although his efforts to romanticize them had a strategic purpose.[30] When President Truman met Churchill at the Potsdam conference in July 1945, he complained of how 'he gave me alot [*sic*] of hooey about how great my country is and how he loved Roosevelt and how he intended to love me etc. etc.'[31] When Dwight Eisenhower became president in 1953, he felt that Churchill's hope that Britain would receive privileged treatment from the United States was inappropriate. 'Winston is trying to relive the days of World War II', the president wrote. Moreover, 'Much as I hold Winston in my personal affection and much as I admire him for his past accomplishments and leadership, I wish that he would turn over leadership of the Conservative Party to younger men'.[32]

Truman and Eisenhower clearly did admire Churchill for his historical achievements, but their political relationship with him was not always comfortable. Churchill returned to power in the autumn of 1951. Reading the press coverage of his trip to Washington early the following year, one is struck by the fact that close Anglo-American relations were by no means taken for granted. 'There is general agreement that these relations can be improved', wrote James Reston of the *New York Times*, 'but to recapture in 1952 the spirit of 1941–45 would be a remarkable achievement even for Mr. Churchill.'[33] Moreover, after the death of Stalin, Churchill's quest for a rapprochement with the Soviet Union proved something of an embarrassment.[34] As the American Embassy in London noted, 'Prime Minister still smarts under "warmonger" charges made by Labor during 1951 election and is at great pains to disprove them at every opportunity.'[35] He did not always have the firmness and consistency of purpose that the stereotyped view of him would suggest.

At the same time, Churchill himself employed that stereotype for his own purposes when it suited him. In 1953, when he felt that Anthony Eden, his Foreign Secretary, was taking an insufficiently tough line in negotiations with Egypt over the future of the Suez Canal base, he became enraged, 'speaking of "appeasement" and saying he never knew before that Munich was situated on the Nile'.[36] After Eden succeeded Churchill as prime minister in 1955, he continued to be sensitive to such accusations of weakness. Much as he resented Churchill, he seems to have been unable to stop comparing himself with him. This may have contributed to his errors of judgement over Suez in 1956. Interestingly, although others did make such claims, Eden did not try to persuade the Americans that Nasser was another Hitler but rather another Mussolini.[37] Although Eisenhower accepted that the comparison was a valid one, it was not enough to persuade him to agree to military action, and the Anglo-French-Israeli invasion of Egypt brought a temporary rupture in British–American relations.[38] Afterwards, though, the 'special relationship' for which Churchill had hoped did come into being, albeit this was only possible because the UK accepted its subordinate status in practice, even if British policymakers continued to hark after a global role.[39] Whereas it is important to treat the rhetoric of Anglo-American

friendship with caution, one can see that in certain respects the relationship actually became deeper and more meaningful than it had been
during the war.[40]

The Special Relationship

Churchill played a part in this, if only a minor one. 'After Suez', according to his wife, he 'specifically set out to mend fences with the United
States', through visits, public statements and discussions with key
American figures.[41] And now that Churchill was no longer in full-time
active politics, it became easier for US policymakers to invoke his image
in support of their own goals. He could be appropriated by both
Republicans and Democrats, in contrast to Roosevelt, who had always
been a divisive figure. Moreover, FDR's standing had suffered during
the early Cold War era, in part due to Churchill's presentation in his
memoirs of the two men's wartime negotiations with the USSR.
'Churchill had indeed been more guarded in his dealings with Stalin,
while FDR appeared at times to be facile, if not cavalier', notes Michael
P. Riccards. 'Churchill's increasing reputation in the United States then
took place, somewhat in the vacuum created by the early disillusion-
ment in the late 1940s and early 1950s with the only major president
most young Americans knew.'[42]

   US politicians of both parties increasingly used the idea of Churchill as
a means of self-validation. They used him as an icon of idealized and
inspirational 'toughness', against which opponents were measured and
found wanting. During the 1960s, the decade of Churchill's death, this
habit became engrained. John F. Kennedy liked to quote Churchill, and it
was he who in 1963 signed the bill conferring honorary US citizenship
upon him. One episode demonstrates the contest for the Churchillian
inheritance. During the 1962 Cuban missile crisis, Kennedy made private
reference to his political opponents' demands that he take a tougher line
against Castro. 'Well, I guess Homer Capehart [Republican Senator for
Indiana] is the Winston Churchill of our generation', he said, with
obvious irony. In a televised address two days later, however, he justified
his own, comparatively moderate blockade policy—regarded by his

critics as 'appeasement'—by invoking the 1930s himself. That decade, he argued, 'taught us a clear lesson. Aggressive conduct, if allowed to grow unchecked and unchallenged, ultimately leads to war.'[43] Thus it was not the case that politicians, by invoking the 'lessons of the interwar years', necessarily locked themselves into foreign policy courses more aggressive than those they might otherwise have taken. They did, however, face strong incentives to find ways to present their own conduct as being as uncompromising as possible.

Lyndon B. Johnson deployed the image of Churchill even more systematically than Kennedy had done. John Ramsden notes how— making reference to the honorary citizenship that he had been given— LBJ referred to Churchill 'routinely and without qualification as "the greatest of all American citizens"'. He also notes how this was part of Johnson's strategy to obtain British and Australian involvement in the Vietnam War.[44] When Prime Minister Harold Wilson visited Washington in the summer of 1966, Johnson publicly compared his leadership to that of Churchill, describing him as 'a man of mettle'.[45] This drew derisive comment in Britain, but, whereas Johnson probably did not really regard Wilson as Churchillian, he does appear to have seen genuine parallels between Churchill's stance in the 1930s and 1940s and what was required to counter global Communism in the 1960s.[46] As the Washington correspondent of *The Times* concluded, 'President Johnson is determined to follow in the footsteps of Churchill and Roosevelt, *or what he sees as their footsteps*.'[47]

This all took place at a time when Britain's ongoing geopolitical reorientation was proving disconcerting to the Americans, even though British participation in European integration had been a long-standing US aim. Popular hostility to the British Empire had been a factor conditioning Washington's approach to Anglo-American relations. But although Roosevelt had used the issue to needle Churchill during the war, much of this was for the purposes of public positioning and display to his own subordinates. Whereas he and post-war presidents were happy that the United States should benefit from Britain's imperial decline, American pressure for decolonization was more symbolic than real and was a relatively minor factor driving the process. Actually, as long as UK policymakers accepted their subordinate role, the Americans were more than happy for Britain to retain a residual global presence where this chimed with US goals. In 1967, the Wilson government announced that British troops were to be withdrawn East of Suez. Secretary of State Dean Rusk decried the shift to a 'Little England' policy. He told his opposite number George Brown: 'For God's sake act like Britain.'[48] The Johnson administration saw the withdrawal as weakening the fight against Communism in South East Asia, and the State Department determined that it would no longer make favourable comparisons between Wilson and Churchill as it had previously.[49] Saying 'be like Churchill' had been the publicly acceptable way of saying 'act like Britain', and saying 'act like Britain' had been the privately acceptable way of advocating the (suitably tempered) imperial spirit.

Towards the end of Churchill's active career, 'Empire' had become an awkward word in Britain, or, as he put it, a 'naughty' one.[50] This was not only because of the problems that it caused with respect to American opinion. After Churchill spoke in Ottawa in 1952, the *Manchester Guardian* noted that 'Canadian nationalists who are bent on the elimination of the words "Empire" and "Dominion" from official terminology feel that there was an implied criticism of this policy in Mr. Churchill's apologies, playful and pointed, for using these words.'[51] In 1964, the year he finally stood down from Parliament, a draft of the Conservative general election manifesto read: 'Unlike our opponents, we make no apologies for the Empire, of whose achievements we are intensely proud.'[52] Yet the published version stressed instead 'the vigour and increased the strength of the modern Commonwealth'—the word 'Empire' was nowhere to be found.[53] In a party political broadcast the same year, the Conservative Prime Minister Sir Alec Douglas-Home sought to exploit Labour's perceived weakness on nuclear defence. 'As reminders from the past to chill or steel the audience there were passages of 1914–18 poetry, Sir Winston Churchill standing like a rock among London's rubble, and Mr. Macmillan working for negotiation out of east-west tensions.'[54] As long as he was firmly located in a Second World War removed from its imperial context, then, Churchill could still serve conveniently as a symbol of British steadfastness and pride.[55]

The Churchill motif, therefore, worked well for both the Americans as well as the British (albeit he was more easily used in the UK on the Tory side than the Labour one). Churchill remained a bipartisan point of reference and his name served as 'memory hook', and his quotations were deployed on public or semi-public occasions almost as catch-phrases.[56] One of these, of course, was the idea of the 'special relation-ship', which could be deployed by the Americans with little cost because it was acknowledged by its nature to be intangible and to confer no specific obligations.[57] The phrases came to have a certain ritualistic air; Richard Nixon deployed the same kind of language to both Wilson and his Conservative successor Edward Heath.[58] The British invoked Churchill in order to tap into (genuine) reserves of US goodwill towards them; the Americans invoked him as a means of displaying that goodwill in non-tangible form.

Between Europe and the Open Sea

Heath was unusual amongst post-war prime ministers in the priority that he placed on Britain's relationship with Europe, even at the expense of that with the United States. He deliberately eschewed the use of the term 'special relationship'. As Britain's chief negotiator during Britain's first, failed bid to join the EEC, Heath had inspired his team by playing them a recording of Churchill's 1946 speech, in which he had advocated 'a kind of United States of Europe'.[59] Now, as prime minister, he was successfully piloting Britain towards membership. In celebration of the twenty-fifth anniversary of Churchill's speech, he himself spoke in Zürich, where it had been delivered. He 'pointed out that the friendship between France and Germany, called for by Sir Winston [...] had become the bedrock of the European Community, which in turn was the core of the wider European unity to whose cause Churchill devoted so much of his energy.' Heath noted that a Commonwealth bloc centred on the UK had failed to materialize and argued that an expanded Community should have a common foreign policy and also make progress towards economic and monetary union.[60] The *Daily Telegraph* cited the French Foreign Minister Maurice Schumann as remarking that it would be Churchill 'whom we are welcoming into the Community'. The paper also com-mented that Heath had spoken 'the day after a television programme which, in recalling the post-war Churchill Government, was a painful reminder of the opportunities which have been lost in Britain's protracted groping towards Europe'.[61]

During the 1975 referendum which confirmed the UK's membership of the EEC, the memory of Churchill was deployed by both sides, although the extent and significance of this should not be exaggerated. Winston Churchill MP contested the No campaign's decision to begin their TV broadcasts with a quotation attributed to his grandfather: 'Each time we must choose between Europe and the open sea, we shall always choose the open sea.' (He pointed out that the quotation, dating from 1944, was about the elder Churchill's preference for Roosevelt over De Gaulle, not about opposition to European integration.)[62] Two days before the vote, the new Conservative leader Margaret Thatcher, appeared at a 'Keep Britain in Europe' rally in Parliament Square. Wearing her famous EEC jumper and carrying a torch, she was photographed in front of the statue of Churchill.[63] It was a classic image-event—or pseudo-event—of the kind to which Churchill's iconography easily lent itself.[64]

In the late sixties, Jock Colville, Churchill's former private secretary, anticipated that once the remaining witnesses had died, a wave of 'debunking, discrediting and disreputing' of his erstwhile boss would begin.[65] On the cultural front, certainly, there were a couple of such attacks, Ralf Hochhuth's play *Soldiers* (1967) and Howard Brenton's *The Churchill Play* (1974). But there were also treatments that fitted well with Churchill's established position as an archetype of idealized leadership, notably the feature film *Young Winston* (1972) and the TV documentary series *The World at War* (1973–4). (TV, film, and theatre will be discussed in detail in Chapter 3). Churchill's historical reputation was now evolving, not least in the light of new archival releases—all of the Second World War Cabinet Papers were available by 1972, and the Ultra Secret was finally disclosed later in the decade. Randolph Churchill and Martin Gilbert's official biography (1966–88) was largely uncritical in its approach, but it (and its documentary companion volumes) had the merit of providing new evidence upon which other historians could draw.

For the most part, Churchill's position as an archetype of idealized leadership was sustained, at least within the United States and what was left of 'the British World'.[66] But his popular image did in some respects become more complex, although not necessarily in ways that were thought to reflect badly on him. Particularly significant was the 1969 essay by the psychiatrist Anthony Storr, which built upon the recent memoirs of Churchill's doctor, Lord Moran.[67] (The Churchill family bitterly resented what they saw as Moran's breaches of confidence and medical ethics.) Storr's picture of Churchill as a manic depressive, afflicted throughout his life by the 'Black Dog' of despair, appears to have caught many people's imaginations, and certainly those of dramatists. This, perhaps, was because it did not challenge the legend of the 'Finest Hour'; rather, it contributed to and reinforced it. 'In that dark time, what England needed was not shrewd, equable, balanced leader', Storr wrote. 'She needed a prophet, a heroic visionary, a man who could dream dreams of victory when all seemed lost.'[68] A dark, troubled hero was a hero all the same.

The more that politicians on both sides of the Atlantic, acting as reputational entrepreneurs, sought to make use of Churchill's iconic status in support of their own agendas, the more they reinforced that status. 'And you know, Prime Minister, that we have a habit of quoting Winston Churchill', joked President Reagan when Thatcher visited him in 1981. 'Tell me, is it possible to get through a public address today in Britain without making reference to him?'[69] Like others before and since, Thatcher and Reagan used Churchill as a means of self-validation. For example, on receiving the Winston Churchill Foundation Award in Washington in 1983, Thatcher stated:

> He [Churchill] was a giant. He saw clearly. He warned clearly. He did what had to be done. His steadfast attachment to fundamental principles, his heroic indifference to the pressures and expediencies of the moment and his unbending determination both saved his own country and helped to save the world.[70]

Although this doubtless reflected her sincere beliefs about the historical Churchill, the implication that she and Reagan shared these virtues cannot have been lost on her listeners. She also used Churchill as an exemplar in private contexts as well as public ones. Her relationship with

Reagan was more complicated than it appeared.[71] She later recalled how she had had to dissuade him from pursuing his vision of a world without nuclear weapons. '*Now look!*' she claimed to have told him, '*The nuclear deterrent is a fundamental part of our philosophy. It has in fact kept the peace for forty years and let me just point out what Winston Churchill said: "Don't you ever give this up until you have got something more powerful!"*'[72]

In 1984, Thatcher made public reference to Churchill in a way that, superficially, appears surprising, given her developing hostility to the EEC. This was in a party political broadcast prior to the elections to the European Parliament. The Conservative campaign was based on a double-edged appeal: that the Community had boosted prosperity and made European war almost inconceivable, and that the Conservatives would fight hard to get Britain the best deal in Europe.[73] The Labour Party had fought the previous year's general election pledging to leave the EEC; this appears to have actually generated a short-term boost to the Community's popularity among the public.[74] Another contextual factor was the 1982 Falklands War, during which the journalist Paul Johnson had suggested that Thatcher's burden was in some ways heavier than that shouldered by Churchill in the Second World War.[75] Whether or not the war itself represented a final gasp of British imperial atavism remains open to question, but the very arguments around that issue that took place at the time were themselves a continued working out of debates about 'Greater Britain' that had been in play since Victorian times. Victory in the South Atlantic emboldened Thatcher to speak openly in praise of Britain's imperial past.[76]

In the broadcast, though, she began by citing Churchill at Zürich. She stated: 'today the structure Churchill foreshadowed nearly forty years ago not only endures, it grows stronger.'[77] She did not choose to make the claim, popular on the 'Yes' side in 1975, that the Commonwealth approved of Britain's EEC membership and would benefit from it—in fact she disliked what she saw as the self-righteous, postcolonial grand-standing of many Commonwealth leaders.[78] Rather, she stressed that 'Two years ago, when the Falklands were invaded, our European friends were not slow to stand up and be counted. We remember the swift support they gave us and the trade sanctions they imposed on the aggressor.' She also emphasized that the EEC still had its problems, raising the question of Britain's budget contribution. However, 'By fighting Britain's corner, this Conservative Government has already won back for Britain refunds of over £2000 million.' Europe, she said, could develop a message for the future, 'which keeps firm our friendship with *the English speaking peoples* across the world, but which builds bridges to the other Europe, beyond the *Iron Curtain*.'[79] (Neither of the phrases we have put in italics had been coined by Churchill, but both had been popularized by him.)[80] This paved the way for her rejection of the conclusion of the Zürich speech, which she herself had quoted at the start, and her depiction of Britain as Europe's saviour. 'We Conservatives believe not in submerging Britain in some artificial United States of Europe, but in keeping our distinctive character as a nation state, ever present to protect our interests and guard our freedoms. Europe has more than once had need of such a Britain.' Rather than being an aberrant or pragmatic piece of pro-Europeanism on Thatcher's part, then, her use of Churchill here formed a bridge between the lukewarm 'Yes' campaigner of 1975 and the strident anti-Federalist of the 1988 Bruges speech.[81]

Attack from the Right-Flank

Thatcher's successor, John Major, did not make much use of Churchill in his rhetoric. On the other side of the Atlantic, President George H. W. Bush made plenty of references to Churchill in his speeches, but did so in a relatively casual and apparently non-calculating fashion. Bush was the last president to serve in the Second World War; Bill Clinton, the man who defeated him, had no striking interest in Churchill. It might have seemed that, with the advent of the post-war generation into political leadership, interest in Churchill was dying away.[82] Yet to a considerable extent, in nineties Britain, that interest was perpetuated by authors working at the interface between scholarly and popular writing. A number of books which presented themselves as conscious challenges to the standard Churchill myth had the effect of reinforcing the national fascination with him.

Interestingly, though, the critiques which gained most purchase came from the right rather than the left. These attacks were not a complete novelty. In 1987, the Holocaust denier David Irving published a work on Churchill that was a sustained attempt at character assassination.[83] Up until the very eve of his final disgrace in 2000, when he lost his libel action against the historian Deborah Lipstadt, Irving retained some credence in mainstream circles as someone who 'might well have emerged as one of the leading historians of the Third Reich' were it not for his extremist political views.[84] However, Irving was unable to find a publisher for this book in Britain, where its few reviewers largely or wholly dismissed it.[85] Unlike Irving, John Charmley was neither a fraud, an anti-Semite, nor a Nazi sympathizer. He was a serious scholar but also something of a provocateur. 'He calls people "old thing"' and swears "By Jove!" and nobody would imagine that he was brought up in a Birkenhead council flat, the eldest son of a docker and a bingo hall bar manageress', noted a *Times* profile.[86] A lecturer at the University of East Anglia, he was not yet forty when, in 1993, he achieved a *succès de scandale* with his political biography of Churchill. Charmley, who saw himself as a myth-buster, finished his account in 1945 because this point, he argued, marked the 'end of glory'. By this he meant that Churchill, whose obsession with Nazi Germany had led him to neglect the threat of the Soviet Union, had ended up sacrificing the interests of the British Empire and enforcing Britain's dependence on the United States.[87]

 Charmley's book gained huge attention, partly on account of a positive review by former Tory Defence Minister Alan Clark, a man who had difficulty persuading people he meant it when he explained, quite seriously, that he was Nazi.[88] Not surprisingly, Clark was also an admirer of Irving's work. In his article Clark argued that Britain should have made peace with Germany in the spring of 1941 (not, it should be noted, in 1940).[89] That was not a claim that Charmley made in the book, but he was prepared to defend it, and in the summer of 1995 he teamed up with Clark to debate it with two Conservative historians—the established and respected Robert Blake and the up-and-coming Andrew Roberts.[90] When the audience voted, Blake and Roberts won—although not before a heckler had been thrown out for shouting that those who opposed a negotiated peace were 'traitors'.[91] In a review essay the following year, the

historians Robin Prior and Trevor Wilson puzzled over 'historical revi-
sionism in its Clark-Charmley-Irving form'. It might have been expected,
they thought, that his Second World War 'finest hour' would have led
him to enjoy the regard of Conservatives forever. 'Why, in the 1990s,'
they asked, 'has this consensus regarding that central event of his career
vanished, so that what had once been his major unarguable achievement
has become the principal ground for condemnation?'[92]

In fact, as the victory of Blake and Roberts suggested, the consensus
around 1940 remained in robust health. Roberts himself, however,
now challenged the established Churchill legend from another direction. On 9 April 1994, the cover of The Spectator boasted a colourful
cartoon that depicted Winston Churchill sticking up two fingers to a
boatload of Caribbean migrants—'the Windrush generation', as we
would now call them. Inside was an article by Roberts (who had
previously made a name for himself as a biographer of Lord Halifax)
which labelled Churchill as an ideological racist. 'For all his public
pronouncements on "The Brotherhood of Man" he was an unrepent-
ant white—not to say Anglo-Saxon—supremacist', he wrote.
Moreover, 'for Churchill, negroes were "niggers" or "blackamoors",
Arabs were "worthless", Chinese were "chinks" or "pigtails", and other
black races were "baboons" or "Hottentots".'[93]

Churchill had been accused of 'malignant racism' before, but Roberts'
claims provoked a storm of criticism.[94] The historian Niall Ferguson
wrote that 'my friend Andrew Roberts has joined the growing ranks of
Churchill-bashers.'[95] Bill Deedes, who had served as a junior minister in
Churchill's final government, lamented in the Daily Telegraph that
'We live in times when greatness draws critics and genius attracts
iconoclasts—and iconoclasm sells books.'[96] Roberts' essay was soon
republished in extended form in his book Eminent Churchillians, together
with others that, for example, criticized the appeasement of the trades
unions by Churchill's peacetime government.[97] Lady Williams, a former
personal secretary to Churchill, lamented that Roberts' 'scurrilous allega-
tions' were symptomatic of a form of history that involved 'shooting
down great historic figures, especially Churchill'.[98]

Roberts, however, denied being a revisionist, and was at pains to insist
that he was not a 'detractor' of Churchill either. To draw attention to

Churchill's views was not to denigrate him, he argued. 'Nowhere did I criticise Churchill for his racist assumptions', he reassured *Telegraph* readers.[99] (This distinguished him from Clive Ponting, the former civil servant who had leaked details of the sinking of the General Belgrano during the Falklands War, who published a left-wing assault on Churchill's 'almost mythological' status shortly after the Roberts controversy broke.)[100] Rather, Roberts' purpose had been to show why in the 1950s, in spite of the prime minister's own hostility to non-white immigration, his government had failed to restrict it, partly due to his age, ill health, and lack of focus on domestic policy. There was, however, a contemporary dimension too. Even though Churchill's own views about Europe were not part of the argument at this time, the journalist Matthew d'Ancona correctly perceived that 'The Churchill debate is in large part an argument about the decline of British power and the origins of the European Union.'[101]

In order to understand d'Ancona's point it is necessary to remember that he was writing as the Conservative Party feuded with itself in the wake of the UK's ratification of the Maastricht Treaty. Roberts was firmly on the side of the Maastricht rebels; he even wrote a novel set in a tyrannical European super-state in the year 2045.[102] Alan Clark and his fellow Eurosceptics Michael Portillo and Norman Lamont were amongst the host of 'right-wing power brokers' present at the launch of *Eminent Churchillians*. 'The book the Tory grandees gathered to celebrate is unashamed Thatcherite history', noted Nick Cohen in the *Independent*. 'It is the old Conservative Party which is the subject of Mr Roberts's ire. Churchill is still the hero of the war years, but his 1951 government is condemned for being wet—too nice to the unions and too ready to allow black immigration.' Roberts was distressed above all by the collapse of British power, which Churchill's peacetime government had done little to avert. 'When I look at our country I see so much glorious past behind us and so little to look forward to', he told Cohen.[103] Thus, even though the 'Tory Nationalist' Roberts rejected the Clark/Charmley claim that the Empire could have been saved by doing a deal with Hitler, behind the acid commentary and ostensible cynicism of *Eminent Churchillians* there lay a deep nostalgia for times gone by.[104]

Puffing on an Invisible Cigar

In 1995, the National Heritage Memorial Fund added to the Major government's troubles through its decision to spend £12.5 million purchasing Churchill's papers for the nation, using money raised by the newly established National Lottery.[105] This was the culmination of a decades-long saga, wrapped up with the history of the Churchill Archives Centre at Cambridge (that opened in 1973) and the vexed question of who owned which documents.[106] The decision was not taken by ministers, but they took much of the heat. Gyles Brandreth, Parliamentary Private Secretary to the Secretary of State for National Heritage, noted that 'what we naïvely thought of as a timely triumph is turning out to be a colossal balls-up [. . .] in the run-up to the VE day anniversary, we thought "saving them for the nation" would have been greeted with loud hurrahs.'[107] Instead there was outrage that Churchill's 'privileged family were set for a multi-million pound "windfall"' at the expense of 'ordinary Lottery punters'.[108] 'This is our blackest hour', claimed *The Sun*.[109] Boris Johnson, at this time a columnist for the *Daily Telegraph*, suggested that buyers of lottery tickets might conclude that 'seldom in the field of human avarice was so much spent by so many on so little.'[110] John Charmley wrote that 'the whole business degrades the name of Churchill in a way that a regiment of revisionist historians could not, and would not, have done.'[111]

An opinion poll by the Harris Research Centre detected widespread anger.

> Of those asked, 52 per cent believed the family should have given the papers to the country for nothing. A further 35 per cent said that although the Churchill family had the right to sell the papers, the sum paid was far too much. Only 8 per cent agreed with the statement: 'His family has every right to sell the papers and this was a reasonable use of lottery money.'[112]

However, when the papers were briefly put on display in Cambridge later in the year, the public response was very warm. 'Almost everybody expressed interest in the subject material, and there was very little criticism of the use of national lottery money in saving the collection.'[113] The brand may not have been as heavily tarnished as Charmley suggested; the perceived money-grubbing of Churchill's descendants and 'the slight whiff of an Establishment stitch-up' did not necessarily diminish his own status in the eyes of the public.[114] Yet it did give a weapon to the resurgent Labour Party during the final stages of the 1997 general election campaign. Tony Blair criticized the use of Lottery funds for 'elite' enterprises such as the Royal Opera House and the acquisition of the Churchill Papers. 'That can't be right', Blair said. 'It is the people's lottery. It should address the people's priorities.'[115]

At the same time, though, Blair was beating the patriotic drum. In his early phase as Leader of the Opposition he had been happy to admit that his views coincided with those of Churchill in his Edwardian New Liberal phase, but he did not now attempt to harness the memory of the wartime Churchill explicitly.[116] (By contrast, Paddy Ashdown, leader of the Liberal Democrats, argued that 'Just as Winston Churchill had stood out for rearmament in the Thirties, so Britain needed now to re-educate to survive.')[117] Blair wanted to counter a surge in anti-European sentiment that seemed set to benefit the Tories.[118] Therefore, in one of its election broadcasts, New Labour deployed a three-year-old bulldog named Fitz. At first, it appeared torpid and weary, its spirit sapped by eighteen years of Tory misrule. Scenes of Blair speaking to camera ('I am a British patriot and I want the best out of Europe for Britain') were intercut with shots of the dog rising to its feet, progressively invigorated by a series of New Labour slogans. At last, it broke free from its leash and padded off towards the breaking dawn – or, perhaps, the sunlit uplands.[119]

A bulldog had recently been used in a cinema advert for James Goldsmith's Referendum Party, giving it 'inevitable anti-European associations'.[120] 'Fitz is there to tell floating voters that a vote for Labour is risk-free', observed Michael Ignatieff. 'It is a national party, alive to the happy associations of the bulldog with other fleshy incarnations of the national character such as Winston Churchill or Ernest Bevin, but also with the virtues of hearth and home.'[121] Before his only foreign policy speech of the campaign, Blair planned to say that he was 'proud of the

British Empire' but was dissuaded from doing so at the last minute—the sentiment was considered toxic.[122] Blair's 'Bulldogism', though, not only helped the party gain media coverage, it was sufficiently ambiguous to appeal across party lines and across the pro- and anti-European divide, speaking to the desire for strong national leadership.[123] Fitz evoked the spirit of Churchill whilst avoiding the potential pitfalls (for a Labour politician) of associating himself too closely with the memory of a Conservative.

As prime minister, when justifying British military intervention to prevent 'racial genocide' in Kosovo, Blair deployed the memory of the Labour movement heroes 'Clem Attlee and Ernie Bevin' rather than that of Churchill.[124] Yet that was in front of a Labour audience, where he had to be mindful of the party's penchant for nostalgia.[125] When he met with President Clinton he was happy to invoke Churchill, Roosevelt, and the Second World War in time-worn fashion.[126] There is no doubt that his emotion when he did so was genuine. In May 2000, anti-capitalist demonstrators vandalized both the statue of Churchill in Parliament Square (which was given a green turf Mohican as well as being sprayed with paint) and the Cenotaph. According to the diary of one of Blair's spin doctors, 'TB went a bit over the top saying "This sort of thing must never be allowed to happen again", and suggesting that such demonstrations should be kept out of London.'[127]

But equally certainly there was an instrumental dimension. During the presidency of George W. Bush, there was a continued willingness to exploit the resonances of Churchill. Christopher Meyer, the former UK ambassador to Washington, has noted that there was an existing store of goodwill towards the British from the Americans. He sensed this at various times, including 'when the memory of Winston Churchill was invoked, which was often, including in the White House'.[128] This explains why the British did their best to ensure that it was invoked as often as possible, by making Churchill a theme of diplomatic gifts, to which they gave considerable thought and worry.[129] This doubtless had the advantage of strengthening ties between the British and the Americans, although it opened Blair to domestic criticism that he was 'pandering to George Bush's Churchill complex'.[130] Thus, while Blair himself made relatively few overt references to Churchill, he certainly provided memory cues that encouraged Bush to do so.

The most famous Churchill object used in the diplomatic exchanges was actually lent rather than given. In July 2001, President Bush accepted the loan by the British government of a bust of Churchill by Jacob Epstein. At an Oval Office ceremony to mark the occasion, he observed:

> People said, why would you be interested in having the bust of an Englishman in your Oval Office. And the answer is because he was one of the great leaders in the 20th century. He was an enormous personality. He stood on principle. He was a man of great courage. He knew what he believed. And he really kind of went after it in a way that seemed like a Texan to me: he wasn't afraid of public opinion polls; he wasn't afraid of—he didn't need focus groups to tell him what was right. He charged ahead, and the world is better for it.[131]

This prefigured the use of Churchill's memory after the terrorist attacks of 11 September 2001, which went beyond a mere goodwill function. Bush now appeared to offer a conscious echo of Churchillian rhetoric in support of his own military objectives. 'We will not tire, we will not falter, and we will not fail', Bush told a joint session of Congress on 20 September.[132] Furthermore, when the rhetorical groundwork was being laid for the invasion of Iraq, Secretary of Defense Donald Rumsfeld drew a comparison between the then situation and the build-up to the Second World War:

> during that period, the voices of concern about what Adolf Hitler was doing were very few. There was not unanimity.... And as he—they occupied one country after another country after another country, it wasn't till each country was attacked that they stopped and said, 'Well, maybe Winston Churchill was right'. Maybe that lone voice expressing concern about what was taking place was the right voice.[133]

Rumsfeld did not state explicitly that it followed that Bush shared Churchill's gift of foresight, probably because he did not need to. Media commentators relayed the message that the president was seeking to appropriate Churchill's mantle, and thus flagged up the parallel, whether they agreed with it or not. They also worked to discover implicit Churchillian references in the statements of Bush and Blair themselves. For example, in September, one *Times* journalist wrote of how Blair had puffed 'on a large invisible cigar', during a Commons debate in which he argued that dictators would only respond to diplomacy when it was backed by the threat of force.[134] Churchill's reputation itself was also on the up, helped in part by Roy Jenkins' admiring biography. The book was published in October 2001 and 100,000 hardback copies were sold before Christmas.[135] His triumph in the Greatest Briton poll was further proof of his popularity; the label stuck.[136]

Once the invasion of Iraq was over, and as the occupation proved problematic, Bush administration rhetoric increasingly stressed not only Churchill's foresight but also his steadfastness. Now his 1946 'Iron Curtain' speech was used as a point of reference, and at the same time the comparison was widened from Iraq to the more generalized 'war on terror'. (The administration suggested that the Iraq War was part of this.) 'When World War II ended, Winston Churchill immediately understood that the victory was incomplete', Bush argued in February 2004:

> Today, we are engaged in a different struggle.... Yet in some ways, our current struggles or challenges are similar to those Churchill knew. The outcome of the war on terror depends on our ability to see danger and to answer it with strength and purpose. One by one, we are finding and dealing with the terrorists, drawing tight what Winston Churchill called a 'closing net of doom'.

Earlier in the same speech, he said that he saw 'the spirit of Churchill in Prime Minister Tony Blair'.[137] Interestingly, although even the president's closest supporters within the administration (unlike outside supporters) felt unable to state *explicitly* that Bush was like Churchill, it was apparently unproblematic for Bush to say that Blair was. Of course, the implicit corollary of the idea that Blair and Bush were, like Churchill, determined and unwavering, was that their opponents were vacillating and weak. Since 2004 was a US election year, the point was made with increasing directness, in order to undermine Senator John Kerry's bid to take back the White House for the Democrats. Vice President Dick Cheney used a speech in Fulton, Missouri, the site of the 'Iron Curtain' address, to ram this idea home.[138] 'There has arisen among America's elite a Churchill cult', observed the former Nixon aide and sometime Reform Party candidate Pat Buchanan a few years later. 'Its acolytes hold that Churchill was not only a peerless war leader but a statesman of unparalleled vision whose life and legend should be a model for every statesman.'[139]

Boom or Bust?

Buchanan's own arguments, which blamed Churchill for the decline of British power and indeed for most of the evils of the twentieth century and beyond, did little to damage the established core image based on his bravery and refusal to compromise. However, other critical interpretations did gain some purchase. As the situation in Iraq failed to improve, commentators increasingly drew lessons from his handling of the Mesopotamian issue as colonial secretary in the 1920s: 'Even Churchill Couldn't Figure Out Iraq', Joe Klein reminded the readers of *Time* magazine.[140] In 2005, South African President Thabo Mbeki spoke in Khartoum. Tactfully avoiding mention of the Sudanese government's human rights abuses in the Darfur region, he 'singled out Churchill as a progenitor of vicious prejudice who justified British atrocities by depicting the continent's inhabitants as inferior races who needed to be subdued'.[141] But at this time, within Britain, it was increasingly being suggested that the Empire should be actively celebrated.[142] Public discussion of Churchill's colonialist mindset may have discredited him in the eyes of some, but it cannot be assumed that this was the case across the board.

Consider, for example, the case of the Epstein bust. When Barack Obama took office as president in 2009, he returned it to the British embassy. An identical bust, which had been in the White House since the 1960s, remained on display close to the Oval Office.[143] Yet another bust, this one by Oscar Nemon, was installed in the Capitol as a pointed rebuke to Obama by the Republican Congress.[144] In a notorious *Sun* article, written at the end of his term as Mayor of London, Boris Johnson speculated about why Obama had had the bust removed, in the context of trying to explain what he regarded as the president's illogical opposition to Brexit. Being careful to put the words in the mouths of unidentified others, Johnson wrote: 'Some said it was a symbol of the part-Kenyan President's ancestral dislike of the British Empire—of which Churchill had been such a fervent defender.'[145] In this analysis, the problem was not Churchill's imperialism, but rather that Obama's prejudice against it made him irrationally anti-British.

Johnson's article was published two months before the 2016 EU referendum. Although one should not overstate the role played by Churchill's memory during the campaign itself, there was a significant pre-history of both pro- and anti-EU forces invoking his name. In 1995, Michael Heseltine, then president of the Board of Trade, published a newspaper article headlined 'Britain must march behind Churchill into Europe.'[146] The next year, the *Independent* published a piece reporting that 'A leading Conservative has come out in favour of the single European currency. He argues that Britain's future is "inseparably mingled" with that of Europe and suggests there should be coins with national images on one side and European images on the other.'[147] On the inside page it was revealed that the person concerned was Churchill. Eurosceptics fought back. In her book *Statecraft*, Margaret Thatcher, citing various Churchill statements that Andrew Roberts had helped her track down, argued that 'Even in his most visionary moods, Churchill does not seem to have envisaged Britain's ever being part of the United States of Europe, however much he thought that she should encourage and contribute to it.'[148] In 2013 the president of the European Commission, José Manuel Barroso, speaking in Zürich, described Churchill as a 'a committed and far-sighted British-European' and urged EU leaders to be inspired by him.[149] Although Prime Minister David Cameron was not mentioned, he was understood in Britain to be the target audience.[150] Boris Johnson responded to Barroso in his book *The Churchill Factor* (2014), published before he had firmly committed himself to the Leave cause. On the one hand, he made the familiar argument that Churchill had never actually intended Britain to be a member of the United States of Europe that he advocated. On the other, he suggested that it made no sense to argue about what line Churchill would have taken with regard to modern European dilemmas: 'The oracle is dumb.'[151] Churchill's pro-Europeanism, then, was something to be explained away or neutralized, as EU leaders increasingly sought to make play with it. To some extent, these leaders adapted their arguments in turn.[152]

Thatcher and Roberts made their claims on the basis of fairly detailed textual analysis; and there was an element of *logos* even in Johnson's annoyingly bumptious book. Others, though, put *ēthos* and *pathos* front and centre. The UK Independence Party selected Churchill for use on their posters in the 2009 European election campaign without making any claims about his actual beliefs. During the same campaign, BNP leader Nick Griffin also tried to lay claim to Churchill – in contrast to previous far right generations who had regarded him as a warmonger -albeit without making specific comments about his European views. Posed in front of a picture of him, Griffin stated:

> If you look at what Churchill said and wrote about the issues affecting our times, mass immigration, dangers of radical Islam, you would see that Churchill, were he alive today, would be thrown out of the Conservative Party for things he said and his political home would be with the British National Party.[153]

(Wrong, countered one Communist writer: 'the BNP is now too politically correct for Winston Churchill.')[154] No such news story was complete without a Churchill relative, very often his grandson Nicholas Soames MP, issuing a denunciation, but this did not necessarily dent the effectiveness of the technique. UKIP chose Churchill 'because he is a symbol of British sovereignty' and the powerful use of his core image simply swept arguments about his opinions to one side.[155]

For a variety of reasons, 'reclaiming' Churchill as a pro-European was not the winning card that those who deployed it appeared to imagine.[156] It is true that the use of this idea repeatedly forced Eurosceptics to try to rebut it, but these refutations were factually based and were not obviously absurd. The Europhiles were vulnerable to the charge that they were reading the evidence selectively.[157] Attempts to present

Churchill as the father of the European Convention of Human Rights (and by extension to label Human Rights as intrinsically 'British' and even 'impeccably Conservative') were less easily contested, although, of course, there was no institutional connection between the ECHR and the EU.[158] Fundamentally, all such efforts rested on the ability to connect the image of a 'virtuous', pro-European, and cosmopolitan Churchill to his core, bulldog image. Trying to harness Churchill's patriotic associations to a (supposedly) cosmopolitan or progressive project—tapping into nationalist sentiment in order to reject chauvinist nationalism—risked cognitive dissonance. These appeals probably worked most effectively when delivered by Pro-European Tories such as Heseltine (who had the rhetorical advantage of having lived through the Second World War).[159] By contrast, from the mouths of EU figures such as Barroso and Guy Verhofstadt they could appear—especially when presented through a hostile or sensationalist media lens—grating and discordant.[160]

It is striking, then, that during the referendum campaign itself, David Cameron chose to use Churchill's memory in a rather different way. This was during his appearance in a special BBC *Question Time* programme, in response to an audience member who described him (Cameron) as a twenty-first-century Neville Chamberlain. In an apparently spontaneous reaction, the prime minister did not attempt to argue that Churchill was himself a vigorous proponent of European integration.[161] Instead he deployed a response built on *ēthos* and *pathos*, which in combination with an element of *logos* amounted to a powerful appeal:

> At my office I sit two yards away from cabinet room where Winston Churchill decided in May to fight on against Hitler. The best and greatest decision perhaps anyone has made in our country. He didn't want to be alone. He wanted to be fighting with the French, the Poles and the others. But he didn't quit. He didn't quit on democracy, he didn't quit on freedom.

> We want to fight for those things today. You can't win if you're not in the room.[162]

Cameron thus implied a confrontational relationship with the present-day EU (a theme he had courted in the past) whilst also summoning up the spirit of cooperation with wartime European allies.[163] Crucially, he was working with the grain of Churchill's core image, not against it.

Returning the story to the present day, it is clear that that core image remained resilient, even in the face of attacks such as that of John McDonnell. Andrew Roberts, by this point, had completed his transition from *enfant terrible* to 'distinguished Churchill biographer'.[164] As such, in his new Life, he skated over the troubling issues he had raised a quarter-century before, such as his subject's attitude to immigration in the 1950s. Yet, at the same time, he argued that Churchill made the correct strategic choice in 1940 not in spite of being a white supremacist but because he was one. 'Churchill's lifelong belief in the superiority of the British people over all others ultimately served the cause of democracy well, convincing him of the correctness of fighting on against the Germans when many of those around him wanted to sue for peace.' Roberts made plain his belief that Churchill's racism sometimes had drawbacks (as when it led him to underestimate the fighting skills of the Japanese). But at the broadest level it was instrumentally valuable. This was because it strengthened the prime minister's will and made him, at the crucial moment, invulnerable to doubt. Roberts quoted Hitler asking sarcastically (in 1937) if the Almighty had handed Churchill the key to Democracy. 'The answer was yes', was Roberts' unambiguous reply.[165] It was not surprising, then, that Jacob Rees-Mogg MP hailed the book when asked on *Question Time* to comment on McDonnell's 'villain' remark. He claimed that 'the Second World War would not have been fought by us without Churchill, everyone else in the British Establishment was ready to seek peace terms.'[166] Given that Rees-Mogg wanted to present himself as anti-elitist, despite being a public school–educated Tory MP and the son of a *Times* editor, casting the aristocratic Churchill as an anti-Establishment figure was a useful move.

Meanwhile, the duplicate Epstein bust was back in the Oval Office, which was now occupied by Donald Trump. Normal service, it seemed, had been resumed. CIA Director Mike Pompeo's referenced Churchill (and Thatcher) when attempting to dissuade Theresa May's government from giving Chinese company Huawei access to British 5G networks—this was not dissimilar to LBJ's efforts to browbeat the British into supporting him in Vietnam.[167] When Donald Trump paid a state visit to the UK, the Queen presented him with a first edition of Churchill's *The Second World War*—Heath had given the identical gift to Nixon in 1970.[168] As rival Tories vied to replace Theresa May as prime minister, Churchill remained the measuring rod by which Conservatives were assessed—even progressives could use his superior stature as a reprimand to his midget successors.[169]

The Changing Face of British Nostalgia

Yet some things had changed over the previous decades. The Churchill being remembered was, in subtle ways, different from the icon in former days. He had been much criticized in his own lifetime, but never, in public, for his role in the Bengal famine of 1943. Archival releases and the publication of key diaries alone did not change this, but after the publication of Madhusree Mukerjee's highly critical study the issue became a significant point of reference even for those who wished to exculpate Churchill.[170] Furthermore, the Churchillian core image had undergone adjustment. President Trump was inspired to visit the Cabinet War Rooms by watching the feature film *Darkest Hour* (though its director, Joe Wright, intended it as a rebuke to him).[171] Yet the events that it portrays—Churchill's battle in May 1940 to ensure that there was no exploration of peace terms—only became public knowledge in the 1970s.[172] Churchill has ended up being most actively celebrated for an episode that he took pains to deny had ever happened.[173]

Nevertheless, it is striking that a politician who has been dead for over fifty years remains so caught up in current debates. These now involve not merely the long shadow of the Second World War but the re-excavation of events that took place before 1914. On *Question Time*, Rees-Mogg moved smoothly from the events of May 1940 to the claim that British Boer War concentration camps were designed to protect the internees ('where else were people going to live?'). Encouragingly, perhaps, there was a surprising degree of consensus amongst his fellow panellists that the hero/villain approach to Churchill was too simplistic.[174] At the same time, it appears likely that it will continue to bedevil public discussion of him for as long as the proponents of his rival and co-dependent myths remain trapped in their recriminatory cycles of praise and blame. That is to say, criticisms of Churchill provoke defensive reactions, reproductions, and re-evocations of his core image. Further attacks are launched in response, as are attempts to manipulate the core image for different ends. But while these repeated patterns are always similar, they are never quite identical. The arguments to and fro might be compared to the unfolding symmetry of a fractal—both remarkably regular and incapable of precise prediction in advance. They change in ways that, in the moment, defy observation by the naked eye. In this way, nostalgia, anti-nostalgia, and the mutual resentments that their interactions cause, are continuously renewed and adapted. Only when people realize that their problems are not really about Churchill will it be possible to discuss Churchill without rancour; but at that moment, perhaps, Churchill will no longer need to be discussed.

3

Persistence and Change in Churchill's Mythic Memory

The focus of this chapter is on the Churchill of popular myth—the divine Churchill and the damned Churchill, and those Churchills in between. Central to the question of mythic Churchill are the forms of his remembrance. Memory of the historical past is expressed in diverse ways, generated through different 'sites of memory', which includes 'film, television and radio, photography and the visual arts, journalism and propaganda, architecture, museums, music and literature'.[1] According to one of the leading figures in the field, Marita Sturken, such memory 'both defines a culture and is the means by which its divisions and conflicting agendas are revealed', indicating 'collective desires, needs and self-definitions' about the past which in its very forms simultaneously illuminates the present. As events become ever more distant, past and present are reconfigured. Sturken went so far as to describe the Vietnam War—the instance with which she was concerned—as 'no longer a definite event so much as it is a collective and mobile script in which we continue to scrawl, erase, rewrite our conflicting and changing views of ourselves'.[2] The same can be said of Winston Churchill, a figure who remains active in bringing the past into the present.

The big and small screen have played a decisive role in the making of mythic Churchill. This is not only due to the size of the TV and cinema audience, but also to the powerful ways in which the moving image impacts on social consciousness. Richard Attenborough, who directed the 1972 film *Young Winston*, spoke of how 'very daunting' he felt his role to have been, referring to its 'massive responsibility' because 'People who have no knowledge of Churchill's early life, now their knowledge is in that movie: it isn't from biography or major articles...it is from that movie.'³ Film and TV are uniquely persuasive, even as they play fast and loose with the historical record. Academic research indicates that audiences already primed with the facts are still likely to believe the most blatantly erroneous screen renderings of real historical events.⁴ This does not mean audiences are the passive victims of brainwashing: all fictions are open to contrasting interpretations, and people bring their own experience to bear when making sense of them.⁵ But if an individual screen drama does not usually overturn an audience's fundamental beliefs, it can at least reinforce prior opinions if these are in sympathy with the story.⁶

At the conclusion of the BBC's coverage of Churchill's funeral, the venerable broadcaster Richard Dimbleby, who had with great solemnity described the event for millions of viewers, read out a poem by teacher and amateur poet Avril Anderson, which ended: 'So Churchill sleeps; *yet surely wakes*, Old Warrior, where the morning breaks On sunlit uplands—but the heart aches'.⁷ The previous chapters have established how Churchill remains awake in the imagination of many politicians and historians. No other British political figure commands such lively post-mortem attention. This the anthropologist Katherine Verdery evocatively calls 'dead-body politics'. It is both a British and an international phenomenon.⁸ These dead characters, and Churchill more than most, can become even more important in their nations' lives than when they were alive. Their stories smother other kinds of explanation, distorting perceptions of the relations between past and present. The make-believe *persona* dominates the horizon, defining the nation by embodying it and claiming to speak for it.

Some figures, Churchill included, do even more than that. There is a current of contemporary political theory which now regards the modern nation state as a 'site of sacred experience'.⁹ Central to this approach is the willingness of citizens to sacrifice themselves for the nation in times of conflict, believing in a meaning beyond their own existence. In the case of Churchill this collective meaning is most fully embodied by the idea of the nation.¹⁰ The state provides individuals with a sense of the transcendent by creating symbols which express the nation *as* an eternal phenomenon. In this, threshold experiences—civil war or, in Britain's case, the war for national survival—give shape to the desire for certainty.¹¹ Thanks to his purported role in May 1940, Churchill became such a symbol of certainty, an icon of the British nation. By his eightieth birthday it became a commonplace, as we can see from *The Times*, to go further and anoint him the 'greatest man of *all* time'.[12]

After his death Churchill cast a long and deep shadow across the nation. Many actively sought comfort and illumination in the darkness of a post-war Britain thought to be in decline by embracing Churchill the war hero. Officiating at Churchill's state funeral in 1965, the Dean of St Paul's Martin Sullivan said, 'We shall think of him with thanksgiving that he was raised up in our days of desperate need to be a leader and inspirer of the nation, for his dauntless resolution and untiring vigilance and for his example of courage and endurance.' The Dean went on to hope, 'that the memory of his virtues and his achievements may remain as a part of our national heritage inspiring generations to come to emulate his magnanimity and patriotic devotion'. During the war, Sullivan had served as a Chaplain to the Forces, and he was—of course—remembering the figure who in the summer of 1940 determined Britain would fight on against Nazi Germany: it was the Churchill who in that bright, brief, moment in the nation's history mysteriously transmogrified the country's Darkest Hour into its Finest Hour. Churchill was at least partly responsible for this interpretation, writing that 'a white glow, over-powering, sublime...ran through our Island from end to end.'[13] His state funeral was then not the first act of remembrance, nor the last. But of those which followed not all would live up to the Dean's hopes: icons inevitably encourage iconoclasm.

From the outset Churchill was conscious of the power of representation. As a journalist and politician, he was moved by the power of rhetoric. As an amateur painter he knew how a picture might reflect—or distort—the truth. He wrote reams of prose: fiction, histories, speeches, autobiographical writings, the popularization of literary classics. Churchill also developed a keen interest in cinema. During the 1930s he was employed as a screenwriter by the movie mogul Alexander Korda. In 1941 his *confidant*, Brendan Bracken, even sold the film rights for *My Early Life* (1930) to Warner Brothers. When in 1959 Churchill's private secretary, Anthony Montague Browne, wrote to producer Jack Le Vien that 'Sir Winston has an objection, founded on practical arguments, against a film or play being made of his life', he was

therefore being somewhat disingenuous.[14] Part of Browne's job, however, was to protect Churchill's reputation by fending off those who
wished to exploit it. A wartime RAF pilot with a Distinguished Service
Order to his credit, after 1945 Browne joined the Foreign Office and
advised Churchill during his second term as prime minister, becoming
his public voice in the great man's retirement. But for some years Browne
and others close to Churchill had been negotiating with two Hollywood
studios about adapting *My Early Life* for the big screen, a process which
eventually concluded with the release of *Young Winston*. If Churchill had
objections to becoming a dramatized character he did not object to the
money it generated so long as his reputation was protected or even
enhanced. Yet Churchill needed others to project his version of the
past onto the screen. Therein lay the danger. After a protracted court-
ship, Le Vien convinced Churchill that his only object was to praise both
the man and his record, and that he was willing to pay handsomely for
the privilege of quoting from Churchill's six-volume *Memoirs of the
Second World War* (1948–53). Le Vien went on to produce the twenty-
six-part TV series, *Winston Churchill: The Valiant Years* (1960), the
documentaries *The Finest Hours* (1964) and *The Other World of
Winston Churchill* (1964), as well as the TV dramas *Walk with Destiny*
(in the US: *The Gathering Storm*) (1974) and *Churchill and the Generals*
(1979). These screen events played a key role in ensuring that in the
immediate post-war period—along with the publication of his own
accounts, the statues in his honour, the outpouring of histories which
commemorated his commanding role—'the Churchillian version of the
Second World War was hammered home', as David Reynolds put it.[15]

In 1972, such was the popular power of this 'Churchillian version', the
Daily Telegraph film critic wrote that, 'Churchill as a character can be
said to have a preservation order on him, as it were, placed there by
common admiration and affection.'[16] As Le Vien's activities proved, this
admiration was not confined to Britain; many of the films and TV
programmes could not have been made without American money and
the promise of an American audience. The dominating Churchill myth
was a transatlantic production.

Yet even while the myth was taking form, any number of particular
Churchills were recalled. As we saw in the previous chapters, in different

historical circumstances different Churchills were fashioned. But we also need to acknowledge Churchill's own mercurial character. More than most, Churchill was composed of contrary personalities; more than most, he was impossible to capture in a single image. When Graham Sutherland was commissioned to paint Churchill's eightieth birthday portrait, one of the prime minister's first comments was: 'How are you going to paint me? The bulldog or the cherub?'[17] The artist was determined to avoid these clichés: 'There are so many Churchills...I have to find the real one.' When Sutherland discovered what he believed to be the authentic Churchill, his sitter complained the artist made him look half-dead and half-witted (Figure 3.1).[18] The film-maker Bryan Forbes also struggled to 'find' Churchill. In the early 1960s he laboured to write a script about Churchill's early life. Writing to Anthony Montague Brown, in desperation, he explained:

Figure 3.1 Churchill reluctantly accepts Sutherland's 'half-dead and half-witted' 80th birthday portrait

As you can imagine I live and breathe and sleep with your employer at the moment—my study is crammed with books about him, and yet he still eludes me in some way. I am not suggesting that a meeting [with Churchill], however, brief, would be of great material assistance, but it would bring everything into sharp focus—just as, though one may admire and cherish a brilliant reproduction of a great painting, to stand before the actual work is an experience without parallel.[19]

'Finding' Churchill is a project assailed by ambiguities. This was dramatically exemplified when Richard Burton attacked Churchill in the *New York Times* just days before the broadcast of *Walk with Destiny*. This was the first ever television dramatization of Churchill's life, produced by Le Vien and the BBC to mark the centenary of his birth: it starred Burton (Figure 3.2). Dennis Potter described the programme as 'Churchill worship', the dramatic equivalent of a commemorative

Figure 3.2 Richard Burton as a 'great man' but a 'bad man'

plaque. Burton, who significantly had given voice to Churchill's words in previous celebrations, played Churchill, according to the *Daily Telegraph* critic, as 'a far-sighted, even noble saviour'.[20] Yet Burton, who came from the mining valleys of South Wales, was said to be possessed by a long-standing 'love-hate obsession' with the wartime prime minister.[21] This became apparent when he declared: 'I hate Churchill and all his kind.' For, while the actor considered him a 'great man', at the same time he looked upon him as a 'bad man'; motivated by the desire for bloody revenge, he was a 'vindictive toy soldier child'. To Burton's eyes he was no bulldog but a coward; his celebrated use of the English language the actor found bizarre and on occasion impossible to understand.[22]

Precedents and Parallels

Churchill is a unique historical figure; but there is nothing unique in how his memory has been sustained. Verdery's concept of 'dead-body politics' encapsulates how prominent figures have continued to enjoy significance through their funerals, entombments, and commemoration as statues. In this way, she claimed, their bodies emulated those of earlier religious figures believed to possess magical powers, arguing that by fixing their image in an eternal present, they were brought 'into the realm of the timeless or the sacred, like an icon'.[23] Verdery's main focus was Eastern Europe during the collapse of Communism. This great transformation was accompanied by the disinterment of former state heroes, the hauling down of their statues and the reburial and memorialization of those once victimized by Communism, and the consequent revival of their ideas and values.[24]

If reburials and the destruction of statues are associated with unstable authoritarian states or new regimes, 'dead-body politics' is also present in well-established democracies where politicians once buried generally stay underground, and when statues raised in their honour tend to remain standing. After his assassination in 1863, Abraham Lincoln's cadaver was taken by train on a circuitous journey from Washington to his final resting place in Springfield.[25] That was, however, just the start of his deification, and the creation of what has been described as a

Lincoln cult, culminating in the construction of the massively imposing Lincoln Memorial in 1922, officially described as 'an enduring symbol of unity, strength, and wisdom'.[26]

While Lincoln's body remained in Springfield he has, however, and with great care been virtually disinterred first on the stage and page but then by Hollywood. Myth-making about the dead president began even before his body was cold, so that to some he became 'an earthly incarnation of the Saviour of Mankind'.[27] Lincoln's screen dramatizations heightened this process, reanimating his corpse for the edification and entertainment of successive generations of Americans. Notably, from *The Iron Horse* (1924) by way of *Young Mr Lincoln* (1939) to *Cheyenne Autumn* (1964) director John Ford presented Lincoln, as national myth dictated, to be a serene bringer of unity and arbiter of justice. This was due to Ford's genuine regard for his subject, speaking as he did of Lincoln with, 'such an extraordinary sense of intimacy... [and] affection... that somehow it was no longer a director speaking of a great President, but a man talking about a friend'.[28] Steven Spielberg felt a similar emotional connection with the long-dead president, recalling of his visit to the Lincoln Memorial as a four-year-old, 'the comfort that I found looking at his face, there was a warmth and a safety, I felt really safe'.[29] Many years later he directed *Lincoln* (2012), which once more brought the president to life, presenting him as bending a flawed democracy to his compelling and righteous desire to free the slaves in a nation remade.

Lincoln has no exact British counterpart. But for a time after his death in 1881 the Conservative Prime Minister Benjamin Disraeli also continued to live on in various ways. This was largely thanks to his reputation for saving the Empire by securing control of the Suez Canal in 1875 thereby guaranteeing British ships a direct route to India. Disraeli was memorialized through the Primrose League, formed in his honour in 1883 the same year his statue was placed in Parliament Square. Dedicated to supporting the ascendency of British imperialism, and named after Disraeli's favourite flower, the League grew to claim a membership of two million by 1910.[30] And on the anniversary of his death, League members recalled Disraeli by processing to his statue where they laid down garlands of primroses.

Like Lincoln, Disraeli was periodically reanimated, first on stage and then on the big screen, most notably in Louis Napoleon Parker's 1910 play *Disraeli*, which dramatized his purchase of the Canal. Parker's play toured North America for many years to great acclaim and was three times adapted for the screen, including in 1929 by Warner Brothers, the star of which, George Arliss, won the Oscar for Best Actor. Warners' executives had their own reasons for remembering the British prime minister, and it had little to do with imperialism. Like them he was of Jewish origin, and they hoped American audiences would respond well to a film showing such a minority figure promoting the national interest. The film was also popular in Britain for more established reasons, to such an extent Arliss—dressed as Disraeli—filmed an appeal to voters to support the Conservatives in the 1935 general election.[31] American and British film-makers returned to Disraeli throughout the 1930s. But one of his last significant outings as a big screen protagonist came in *The Prime Minister* (1941) which, while made in a British studio, was financed and scripted in Hollywood. This was a wartime propaganda picture with Disraeli a surrogate for Churchill, the former's dealings with an expansionist German Chancellor Bismarck drawing obvious parallels with the latter's policy towards Adolf Hitler.[32] Film-makers used Disraeli as a stand-in for Churchill because Britain's cinema regulator prohibited the dramatization of living political figures. This restriction would, however, not long survive the end of the war, by which time Churchill had supplanted Disraeli as the screenwriters' favourite prime minister, having saved not just the Empire but the nation itself.

Celebrating the National Icon

In a moment of despair not long before his death, Churchill said, 'I wish I had died in 1945.'[33] In some ways he had, if by 'Churchill' is meant the divine national saviour, the icon of the 'Finest Hour'. His central role in world history had effectively disappeared as soon as the Soviet Union and the United States both entered the war in 1941. Even so, domestically Churchill was still regarded as a special figure: as the war drew to a close many Britons favoured the continuation of a coalition government in peacetime (albeit with Labour enjoying a greater voice) with Churchill as prime minister.[34] During the 1945 campaign, however, he destroyed his status as a figure of national unity by claiming any Labour government would employ some kind of Gestapo to push through its policies.[35] The Churchill who lived on after the war was then a walking ghost: on the occasion of his eightieth birthday in 1954 *The Times* even claimed he was the 'embodiment of living history'. In 1965, while paying tribute in the Commons, Prime Minister Harold Wilson observed that Churchill had become a 'legend...long before his death'.[36] Appropriately enough, when illustrated boys' weekly *The Eagle* published a year-long biographical series dedicated to Churchill's life during 1957–58, it ended with victory over Germany.

While Churchill claimed that the BBC was 'run by reds', the Corporation's role was initially and subsequently critical to enhancing his iconic status.[37] How the BBC saw its role was summed up by the Labour peer Lord Simon of Wythenshawe, who chaired its Board of Governors between 1947 and 1952. For Simon, during the Cold War the BBC had a duty to 'do what we can to maintain and strengthen democracy and the belief in democratic values'.[38] This meant representations of all contemporary political figures, but especially those of Churchill, were strongly discouraged if not actually prohibited, for fear of *lèse majesté*. But BBC censors could not be everywhere, and despite this injunction the popular surrealist radio comedy series *The Goon Show* got away with a few episodes which guyed Churchill. In October 1954 this included 'The Dreaded Batter Pudding Hurler of Bexhill-on-Sea' in which the then-prime minister is suspected of throwing a batter pudding at the Leader of the Opposition Clement Attlee. If that seemed harmless enough, in December that same year an episode made direct reference to a controversy provoked by Churchill claiming that in 1945 he had sent a telegram ordering Field Marshal Montgomery to stack surrendered German arms so they could be easily reissued to rearm the former enemy in case of a Soviet attack on the West. Montgomery denied receiving the order and the telegram could not be located, forcing Churchill to withdraw the claim. But it still led some Labour MPs to refuse to sign his Eightieth Birthday Book in protest at what they saw as his war-mongering.[39] In the offending Goons episode, Churchill forlornly looked for a telegram and in response BBC managers explicitly banned the show from making any further reference to the prime minister.[40]

In contrast, the BBC was keen to celebrate the real Churchill. Despite the controversy provoked by Churchill's missing telegram rumbling on, to mark his eightieth birthday both Houses of Parliament held a ceremony in Westminster Hall to present him with a commissioned portrait by the artist Graham Sutherland. It was widely expected that Churchill would use the occasion to announce his retirement as prime minister. With that in mind, in addition to broadcasting the event at Westminster Hall live, during the evening the BBC put together a television tribute with the prime minister's full cooperation; indeed, he appeared at its end to respond to participants, which included President Eisenhower.[41] If it had been dedicated to a politician other than Churchill, it could have well been judged as partisan. But the BBC's mostly middle-class viewers reportedly greeted it very positively, many of them finding it an emotional experience, with one seeing it as an entirely appropriate way 'of letting all the world share in the recognition of the most remarkable man of our time'.[42]

While the BBC was careful to avoid the idea that the programme was in any way an obituary that, in essence, is exactly what it was. Churchill's status was confirmed by those war films based on real events in which the prime minister enjoyed a spectral presence, like God in Hollywood Bible films. His voice might be heard, as in *The Man Who Never Was* (1956). In the movie Peter Sellers—the member of the Goons banned by the BBC from impersonating Churchill—gave a restrained rendition of the prime minister speaking unseen in the Commons. In *I Was Monty's Double* (1958) Churchill is credited with backing the audacious plan to fool the Germans into thinking the Allies were planning to invade the South of France in 1944 instead of Normandy. But all the audience sees is another character in the film smoking a cigar in the presence of a hidden and silent prime minister. At the beginning and end of *Operation Crossbow* (1965), an uncredited Patrick Wymark was allowed to embody the prime minister although he was mostly filmed from behind and always in dark shadows. Even though *The Battle of Britain* (1969) was released four years after his death it still dared do no more than depict a silent Churchill shot discretely, at a distance and in shade, notwithstanding the presence—as in *Operation Crossbow*—of his signature cigar. As a celebration of the RAF, the film however inevitably concluded with Churchill's written words, now enjoying the status of Holy Script, rehearsing how much so many owed to so few.

Churchill's funeral was the critical moment in the reinforcement of his reputation as the nation's preeminent wartime hero and was explicitly designed to reflect his status as a national icon.[43] It is therefore worth assessing how it was created and received. Arrangements for Churchill's last journey began in 1953 after he suffered a massive stroke and nearly died. The Queen readily granted him a state funeral, one on an unprecedented scale, befitting, as she put it, 'his position in history'. It was arranged, she informed the Commons in 1965, so the British people 'should have an opportunity of expressing their sorrow at the loss and their veneration of the memory of that outstanding man who in war and peace served his country unfailingly for more than fifty years and in the hours of our greatest danger was the inspiring leader who strengthened and supported us all'.[44]

It was estimated that 320,000 people filed past Churchill's body as it lay in state in Westminster Hall for three days, his coffin draped in the Union Jack and guarded by solemn soldiers. On the day of the funeral on 26th January 1965 the nation came to a halt as the spectacle was covered live on both television channels. Millions watched his body slowly transported by a gun carriage pulled by servicemen to St Paul's Cathedral, the streets lined with silently crying crowds where—in a break with precedent, monarchs being considered too elevated to attend their prime ministers' funerals—the Queen attended the service. The procession through the City of London, 'was beautiful', wrote the *Observer* correspondent, 'in the way that great works of art are beautiful.... [T]he City was stopped and was turned into a theatre and it was all performed as a drama that all men understand.'[45]

After the service Churchill's coffin was taken by the *Havengore* along the Thames, the cranes of London docks bowed in tribute, to Waterloo station and then by train to be buried in the modest graveyard of the family parish church in Bladon, Oxfordshire.

Churchill's grandson Nicholas Soames recalled of that final train journey, in every field we passed it seemed there were small groups of people waiting to say their goodbyes. I remember one field full of mounted members of the Pony Club with their hats off; a farmer standing with his head bowed; a Thames lock-keeper standing to attention at the salute, with his medals up; and on the flat roof of his house, an old man wearing his RAF uniform. At every station the platforms were thronged with people who had come to watch Winston Churchill's last journey home.

If the state funeral was minutely choreographed, and benefited from Churchill's own input, it evoked a genuine and popular emotional response, such that at the end of a very long day Soames remembers that as Churchill's widow retired to bed she said to her daughter, as one might the first night of a successful West End play: 'It wasn't a funeral, Mary—it was a triumph.' (Figure 3.3)[46]

As many as 100,000 people visited Churchill's final resting place during the week following his funeral. In 1998 a new tombstone had to be laid due to the erosion caused by the number of visitors. As a relative stated, when Churchill decided to be buried at Bladon, 'no one knew that it would become a shrine.'[47] Even so, Bladon's location, 65 miles from London, has meant his burial site has played a limited role in the dead-body politics of which Verdery has written. Instead, his statues, strategically placed at the heart of the capital, by fixing Churchill's image in an eternal present, have become the means of transporting him 'into the realm of the timeless or the sacred, like an icon'.[48]

Given their permanent and public display, statues sometimes proved a source of anxiety for those who wished Churchill's reputation to be preserved, which was of course their principal purpose. Those who authorized them wanted the *right* kind of Churchill to be represented. In 1958 the Woodford constituency Conservative party in Essex commissioned a statue to mark his thirty-three years as an MP representing the area. The commemoration committee, as one member put it, desired to see 'Sir Winston in the prime of his wartime triumph, the determined man whom the world knows' and commissioned David McFall who willingly sought to depict 'Churchill the Legend'. If the committee had

Caption: The funeral of Sir Winston Churchill
The procession approaching Trafalgar Square
London, 30 January 1965   Credit: TopFoto

Figure 3.3 'It wasn't a funeral, Mary—it was a triumph'

some concerns about early versions of the statue, when unveiled in Churchill's presence by Field Marshall Montgomery, it met its members' hopes, with one resident stating: 'He looks like a real bulldog.'[49]

Within a fortnight of Churchill funeral, the House of Commons agreed to set aside its stipulation that no member could be commemorated by statue in the Palace of Westminster until a decade had elapsed since their death. Oscar Nemon was selected as the artist largely because of his long-established links with the Churchill family. As with the McFall statue, Nemon depicted the Churchill of Legend and—as a consequence—was widely praised. When Lady Churchill unveiled it, according to the *Guardian* correspondent, 'there was an audible intake of breath' from those present. 'It was', he went on, 'for all the world as though Churchill had himself thrown off his coverings by taking a sudden step forward. There he stood once more...avid for new burdens.'[50] *The Times* in similar vein had it that, 'Churchill in bronze returns home'. The Speaker of the Commons hoped the statue would come to 'inspire through the years those who come to serve parliamentary democracy.'[51] Perhaps it did, but such were the statue's presumed magical qualities it also quickly became the favourite practice of Conservative MPs and sympathetic visitors to the Commons to stroke its left foot for luck, a practice that saw the foot almost worn away.[52]

During this wave of celebratory statue-building, another part of Churchill's sculpted anatomy played a vital role in Joe Orton's surrealist farce *What the Butler Saw*, completed just before the playwright's death in 1967 and first staged in 1969. Orton was an iconoclast who aimed to offend the respectable, the director of the Liverpool Playhouse production describing his last work as like 'when one's grandmother passes wind'.[53] The plot of *What the Butler Saw* involves the shattering of a Churchill statue due to a gas explosion. Orton has the wartime premier unmanned, and his detached flying penis kill a female bystander; as a character suggestively has it, the woman was 'violated by the hero of 1940'. As Orton's collaborator Kenneth Halliwell noted, this was symbolically significant, for Churchill the 'father-figure' had been 'castrated'.[54] When the statue is reconstructed his vital piece is, however, missing. As 'a matter of vital importance to the country' a police sergeant seeks to reunite Churchill with his member and at the play's climax succeeds, leading to lewd comparisons between it and his famed cigar. When the play was submitted to the Lord Chamberlain's Office, to be approved for production, the censor whose authority was soon to be abolished dictated that Churchill's phallus could not be displayed. But by the time it was produced theatre censorship had been liberalized and the ban no longer prevailed. Even so, the actor Sir Ralph Richardson's sensibilities were such he substituted a cigar for the phallus.[55] Critics might have found the play laboured, but, perhaps by now professionally immune to *lèse-majesté*, they did not feel the Churchill reference offensive: any outrage was reserved for its sexualized content.[56] Indeed, for some Orton's method had become predictable. As Irving Wardle wrote in *The Times*, it consisted of 'simply reversing normality and expecting to produce a laugh. Churchill is a national idol, so Churchill gets one in the teeth.'[57] Even when his sculpted phallus was revealed for the first time in the play's 1975 production, Wardle saw fit to not even mention the unveiling.[58] By then, however, the *Guardian* critic considered the play dated rather than shocking.[59] Churchill was safe from Orton's iconoclasm: it merely highlighted his iconic status.

Despite Orton's mockery, the demand for more statue-building continued to be expressed. While Nemon was still working on his Commons commission, in May 1968 the Conservative MP John Tilney in a question to Harold Wilson wondered if another statue 'of perhaps the greatest leader of this nation and the greatest Parliamentarian for centuries...be put up while those of us who remember and were inspired by his speeches are still alive?' Wilson's response to this suggestion showed that there were limits to Churchill worship, at least on the Labour side. The prime minister dissembled while the Welsh Labour MP Emrys Hughes—who, as we have seen, was a long-time critic of Churchill— sarcastically stated that another memorial was 'absolutely unnecessary because nobody can forget him.'[60] Undeterred, Tilney raised the matter a few months later, claiming, 'Those who remember his splendid speeches would like to see such a statue before we are all dead.' But Wilson, who was clear that such a statue would be financed, not by his cash-strapped government but by public subscription, was unwilling to support the move until evidence of broad support was established, something about which he expressed doubt.[61] The matter was also raised in the second chamber. While the Labour Leader of the Lords, Lord Shackleton, declared he was not unsympathetic to the initiative, he proceeded to list the Churchill statues at Woodford, in the Guildhall, and in Churchill College, Cambridge; the memorial stone in Westminster Abbey; the plaque commemorating the lying-in-state; and concluded by noting that Nemon's statue was shortly to be erected in the Members' Lobby of the House of Commons. Another Labour peer, Lord Blyton, a former miner first elected to the Commons in the party's 1945 landslide victory, pointedly added that, 'I think we should remember that he [Churchill] did not win the last war by himself. He had men like Clem Attlee and Ernie Bevin.'[62]

Despite this lack of cross-party enthusiasm, Tilney received the support of 150 MPs and of Churchill's widow. This forced Wilson to endorse the formation of a committee, which Tilney chaired, to raise the necessary £30,000, appoint a sculptor, and identify a site.[63] While the committee liked Ivor Roberts-Jones's submission, which took as its subject Churchill from the mid-1950s, they asked him to depict him as a 'younger man', specifically the one who inspired the country in 1940. This would be yet another iteration of 'Churchill the Legend'. Roberts-Jones's modified statue was unveiled by Lady Churchill on the north-east corner of Parliament Square in November 1973, with the full complement of state personnel in attendance, including the Queen, prime minister Edward Heath along with all his living predecessors, and a crowd of over 1,000 watching the ceremony in all. Despite some concern that early designs looked too much like Mussolini, Roberts-Jones's likeness was well received. Dwarfing the other statues in Parliament Square, the sculptor clothed his subject in a British Army officer's greatcoat and had his jaw, as *The Times* correspondent put it, 'jutting in bulldog resolution and defiance'. Tilney was certainly pleased, declaring Churchill's 'grit and greatness are here for all to see' (Figure 3.4).[64]

A Transatlantic Churchill

Compared to movies or television, statues were a relatively cheap way of memorializing Churchill, cultural objects whose creation involved no hope of financial return. Moreover, even if the sculptor was the ultimate arbiter, they were also subject to the approval of the commissioning

Figure 3.4 Roberts-Jones's 'bulldog' Churchill, Parliament Square

committee and of the Churchill family, whose members had definite ideas about what constituted an appropriate representation. But productions for the big and small screen involved those beyond this small charmed circle, often Americans: while they might also have seen Churchill in heroic terms, their approach was shaped by other, often market-based, concerns.

The first significant transatlantic memorialization of Churchill was a product of Jack Le Vien's courting of the wartime leader: the twenty-six-part documentary series *Winston Churchill: The Valiant Years*, a co-production between the American network ABC and the BBC, although the latter was very much the junior partner. This led to resentment. One British critic regretted the series had not been produced entirely by the BBC, commenting, 'They were, after all, our valiant years.' Another begrudged the American narrator, thinking a British voice preferable.[65] Such criticisms were not assuaged by a commentary designed for US audiences, which led at one point to Churchill being described as 'a maverick in the best American style'.[66]

The series was broadcast in Britain on Saturday evenings during 1961 and repeated as a tribute in 1965 after Churchill's death. Indeed, the series was so popular that the BBC took the unprecedented step of reshowing episodes before the end of its 1961 run.[67] Based on Churchill's *History of the Second World War*, its script was written by an Anglo-American team, among whom numbered playwrights, journalists, and historians. They were informed by their American producer Edgar Peterson that the series' 'cardinal principle' is that 'our leading man is WINSTON CHURCHILL, and that every creative and dramatic technique must be used to bring *him* to life'. If Churchill was the central protagonist, however, the writers were told to make use of any occasion in which Hitler's story paralleled his, given the extent to which they represented 'good and evil—the lead and the heavy, the cowboy and the Indian'. Peterson also informed the team they should 'think of the series as a "*DOCU-DRAMA*"'.[68] Unlike Peterson, BBC executives wanted to maintain a deep and wide trench between documentary and drama, that is, between 'sober' fact and 'emotionalizing' fiction. Peterson was soon replaced by someone more to the BBC's—and Churchill's—tastes, but the basic thrust of his approach survived in the scripts.[69] The emotional and dramatic impact of the series was further enhanced by Richard Rodgers' rousing Emmy Award-winning score and Richard Burton's voicing of Churchill's words. But *The Valiant Years* also included scenes from feature films masquerading as contemporary footage, while others were completely fabricated. The appearance of redoubtable comedic actor Rita Webb (and future Benny Hill stooge) as an East End housewife caused some to wonder about the series' authenticity, with Maurice Wiggin in the *Sunday Times* believing it indicated 'a degree of casualness in the presence of the sacred fact'.[70]

As history, *The Times* critic also found the series treatment 'on an entirely superficial level of a junior school history book'.[71] Peter Black in the *Daily Mail* similarly attacked the 'superficial, uncritical, over-simplified' narrative and even wondered if television should still be producing series about the war 'made on this primitive, unquestioning level.'[72] The Communist *Daily Worker*'s critic was alone in noting how

The Valiant Years overlooked Churchill's support for Franco and Mussolini and ignored pre-war efforts by the Soviet Union to oppose Hitler.[73] Yet, while the *Guardian* reviewer complained about its 'brassy American technique', he still considered it compulsive viewing.[74] Even Black admitted the series occasionally provoked 'the old tingling of the spine', while his *Mail* colleague Peter Lewis claimed to have been 'gripped' by the series because he felt he was watching the great events of the war, like the Dunkirk evacuation, 'as they actually happened'.[75] Such was its visceral impact, *The Valiant Years* could still be recalled by some of its younger viewers over fifty years later.[76] If, as Wiggin had it, 'it is all rather a razzmatazz, which vulgarises the Churchillian epic right heartily', *The Valiant Years* did so very effectively.[77]

The series was a huge success on both sides of the Atlantic, but concerns about its methods of production meant Anthony Montague Brown was determined to assert greater control over Le Vien's next project, *The Finest Hours*, a cinematic biography released in 1964. Despite widespread praise for Burton's rendering of his words, Churchill remained wary of allowing his voice to be impersonated in future productions.[78] In the end, Churchill's advisers relented, if only to limit any damage. Montague Browne conceded it was 'very important to have two voices—one for the narrative and the other for Churchill. If you have one only, the temptation to "ham it up" to indicate quotation would be irresistible.' He was, however, unhappy with the choice of Orson Welles as narrator, believing he 'is really too orotund and "juicy", and will ham it up unmercifully'.[79]

If he lost that battle, Montague Browne enjoyed greater success with the script. Le Vien employed dramatist Victor Wolfson, who won an Emmy for his contribution to *The Valiant Years*. Montague Browne was nonetheless advised to keep an eye on Wolfson 'fact-wise as he is very inclined to let drama take precedence over accuracy'.[80] Conscious of the need to protect Churchill's reputation, Montague Browne called for numerous changes in the various drafts of the script. He successfully had sections on the 1926 General Strike and the social unrest of the interwar period cut while references to the abdication crisis were significantly curtailed. Montague Browne however failed to have the narrative indicate that the disastrous Norway campaign was only a qualified failure—although it did avoid mentioning Churchill's involvement. He was also unable to get the movie to show that it was 'followers of the saintly Gandhi who encouraged the Japanese adventure in Asia'. On the other hand, the claim that the military vote was responsible for Labour's success in 1945 was excised. Perhaps because of its American provenance, *The Finest Hours* did, however, do as Montague Brown wished by criticizing the Nazi–Soviet pact and by drawing parallels between Churchill's warnings about interwar Nazism and post-war Communism.[81]

For the most part Montague Browne knocked on an open door, given that this was a film Le Vien's publicity declared was: 'the story of the greatest man of his age, perhaps of any age', someone able to, 'express the sentiments and resolves of the British nation... His spirit pervaded every aspect of national life', and his leadership 'inspired' the British to victory.[82] The final script emphasized Churchill's status as a 'warrior-statesman' rooted in English history, a man with a 'destiny' to save those it quotes Churchill himself describing as 'our loyal, brave people' from Nazism. It also overlooked or played down awkward episodes, even suggesting he was courageous in standing up to Edwardian suffragettes and blaming the 1915 Dardanelles disaster on delays and lack of resources for which Churchill was not responsible. The film also fails to note his changing party affiliations, while the reasons for his 1945 defeat are left unexplained.

If Le Vien's intention was to reiterate the central Churchill myth for cinema audiences, it certainly had the desired impact on one Harrow school girl who saw the documentary with the rest of her class. 'It was', she wrote, 'the most moving and most wonderful film I have ever seen and I shall never forget it, as long as I live.' While she had no memory of the war, she went on,

I have always been told, though, by my parents and many others, at how nobody could have led the nation as you did [and how you] willed them to strive for Victory and not let this country which you and which they, loved so dearly, especially at that time of trouble, be overrun by a despicable alien power. Until today, I heard all this but could not quite believe it, as I had no first hand knowledge of it. This morning was, however, for me and for many of my friends, enlightening. Your colossal courage and invincibility, your unfailing sense of calm, your sense of humour, but most of all your inspiring, masterful, encouraging speeches, awakened in us a new sense of patriotism and loyalty towards our country, and one of its greatest men. It made us realize how worthless our 'pop' idols and films stars are, compared to you, Sir Winston.[83]

Given the then-current popularity of the Beatles and their peers, it is unclear for how many of her generation this young woman spoke. The critics were, however, definitely divided over its merits. If in London's *Evening News* William Hall believed *The Finest Hours* conveyed an 'objective' perspective, Philip Oakes in the *Sunday Telegraph* complained of the 'inflated, bogus, and patronising idiom' in which the narration was written and a 'blinkered' view of the past.[84] Echoing Peter Black's comments about *The Valiant Years, The Times* critic thought it 'sycophantic' and argued that 'the time for this sort of unqualified eulogy is by now some little way back in history'.[85] Even so, Isabel Quigly, who rarely minced words, believed it spoke for those like her who had directly experienced the war, writing that 'to anyone who remembers Churchill's speeches ... as urgent talks for a particular, unknown, fearsome and exhilarating moment', *The Finest Hours*, 'can hardly fail to arouse some, at least, of the exhilaration.'[86] Thus it seems as if it was the subject rather than the film's treatment which touched reviewers. As Thomas Wiseman in the *Sunday Express* stated: 'Churchill is a part of all of our lives', so watching the film, however obvious it might have been, 'is like listening to a playback of part of one's past'.[87]

The Long Road to *Young Winston*

Churchill was first dramatized on the big screen in *Mission to Moscow* (1942) in which he is shown, during his wilderness years, warning the American ambassador to the Soviet Union of the Nazi threat. This Hollywood rendering of Joseph E. Davies' memoirs of his time in Moscow bent over backwards to look favourably on Stalin's regime, which was then bearing the brunt of the war against the Nazis.

Churchill had been too busy to see the movie, but his wife reported to him 'that somewhat trying film' was 'thought very vulgar' in Britain.[88] The Churchills remained wary of vulgarity when Hollywood came calling in 1956. Dore Schary, then Head of production at MGM, wrote to Churchill to argue that 'there was a magnificent and significant film to made from the story of the early life of one of the great men of this or any other era ... We feel that such a film could be exciting, romantic and inspirational to a wide audience throughout the world.' Schary was a serious man, a long-standing and active Democrat, and was sincere when promising it 'would be our earnest intention to make a picture which would genuinely further international understanding'. The mooted film would end with Churchill's first election to the Commons, as Schary claimed it would be 'tasteless and premature' to dramatize his later career—although it was clear he wanted the movie to emphasize how Churchill's early years 'foreshadowed the greatness which was later to make its indelible mark on the history of our times'.[89] He did not mention the movie, but the template for this film sounded very similar to John Ford's *Young Mr Lincoln*.

Churchill was interested in Schary's approach but had apparently forgotten that Brendan Bracken had already sold Warner Brothers the film rights to *My Early Life* during the war. This was understandable as Warners did not get far in developing their property. Soon after purchasing the rights the studio put a movie into development, but got little further than mooting portly actor Robert Morley as its star.[90] Warner's Managing Director Max Milder claimed that the war had inhibited work on a film, but with Japan on the verge of surrender in August 1945, and with a synopsis in hand, he said once the script had been written, the movie could be completed in twelve weeks. But Morley having now been cast aside, Warners had no star to play the lead. Warner's suggestion of Charles Laughton (an actor then well into his forties) as a young Churchill indicated that much work was still to do. The studio's hope that Churchill might be persuaded to play himself, now he was no longer prime minister, suggested its sense of reality also required some recalibration.[91]

After protracted wrangling, Warners sold on their rights to MGM, but by then Schary had been sacked as head of MGM. Despite that, the

studio remained interested in the project, albeit wary of a purely biographical film, having recently lost money on similar ventures. Churchill
and his representatives, while keen on the money a Hollywood film
would generate, also wanted to exert significant control over its production and negotiated a veto over the script, director, and who was to play
Churchill. The British thriller writer Eric Ambler and playwright Terence
Rattigan were initially mooted to write the film, but, by 1958, Nigel
Balchin was given responsibility for producing a draft. Balchin was a
renowned novelist and had scripted the critically respected war movies
The Man Who Never Was and *Malta Story*. He had also served as a
brigadier during the war. After meeting Churchill to discuss the project,
Balchin reported the former prime minister wanted the script to avoid
any changes to chronology and 'does not wish us to invent fictional
incidents, except perhaps on a very minor scale. In particular, to use his
own words, "this is a story without women".' Churchill was also keen for
the film to avoid any depiction of his childhood and wanted scenes
showing his relationship with his father to be as brief as possible, as 'it
is not our real story.' Balchin's suggestion of *Young Winston* as the film's
title did, however, please him.[92]

Marjorie Thorson, MGM's executive story editor, was alarmed by
Balchin's initial treatment, which faithfully adhered to Churchill's stipulations, informing the writer he had been 'unduly influenced by your
recent talks with the old man'. For Balchin's draft, Thorson believed, was
'a straight factual documentary account because of a very natural fear
you have of taking liberties with the truth'. But, she warned, 'Dramatic
liberties of some sort will have to be taken' or the film would not be
made. That meant producing something that would be a 'commercial
screen entertainment' which they should then persuade Churchill to
accept. To that end, Thorson suggested creating a composite character
to help link events. She also wanted to include Mrs Churchill in the story
and have the narrative suggest that meeting her changed Churchill's
opposition to female suffrage. Thorson was also keen to have at least
some suggestion of a romance towards the end of the film, as Balchin's
treatment lacked 'human interest', concluding that, 'if a good incident
cannot be unearthed, it should be invented.'[93] She confided to Churchill's
legal advisor Anthony Moir her dismay at Balchin's 'high narrative tone',

as well as his 'virtual failure to omit *anything* from the book', believing he was 'terrified' of offending Churchill.[94] Despite her entreatments, Balchin stuck to his Churchillian guns, leading MGM to pass the project on to Paramount.

At this point, responsibility for the script was assumed by C.S. Forester, author of the 'Horatio Hornblower' series of novels that celebrated British sea power during the Napoleonic era, much admired by Churchill. But after labouring for a long time he produced a treatment that Hugh French, Churchill's representative in Hollywood, considered 'kind of dull'. French told Montague Brown English writers were 'rather awed by your boss', thinking that for them 'it is like a devout Roman Catholic being asked to write the life story of the Pope.' With Paramount unpersuaded by Forester's work, despite Montague Brown thinking it 'dignified and truthful', the search began for what French termed a 'slightly more vigorous and less formal writer'—and an American.[95] The trail led first to Borden Chase but ended with Guy Trosper, experienced in writing biographical movies, albeit only ones about baseball, although one, *The Pride of St. Louis* (1952), had been nominated for an Academy Award. As Thorson had earlier advised Balchin, to give the story dramatic structure, Trosper created imaginary protagonists, such as a Sergeant Singh and the Duke of Shropshire, with whom Churchill struggled throughout the story. This, French admitted, 'leaves us bordering on the edge of fiction'.[96] If Paramount liked Trosper's work, Montague Brown considered his script, 'utterly useless. It is so full of impossibilities of taste, of fact and of dramatic construction that I can only regard it as a bad joke . . . . to read it makes me hover between nausea and hysterical laughter.' So little was based on *My Early Life* he wondered if Trosper had even read it.[97]

Once again Terence Rattigan was approached, but after a few months considering the project, he turned it down.[98] At this point the actor, writer, and director Bryan Forbes stepped up. He was regarded with special favour, for, as Montague Browne observed, Forbes was 'a rather unusual animal in the film world, holding agreeably right-wing views'.[99] Forbes said he wanted 'to tell the tale of the greatest Englishman of all time' and produce, true to Schary's original conception, an adventure story about the man in the making. Crucially, while arguing that 'the last thing we want to produce is a dry-as-dust would-be documentary on Churchill's life', and 'our primary aim is to entertain', he stated we cannot take 'dozens of ludicrous liberties'.[100] If that calmed Churchillian nerves after their experience with Trosper, they must have jangled when Forbes was quoted in the press saying Errol Flynn would have been an ideal Churchill due to their shared 'swashbuckling quality'.[101] However, they need not have worried. When Forbes met Churchill he was virtually struck dumb, being 'stupefied with nerves', and recalled what Churchill had meant to him as a young man: 'how his broadcasts in the darkest days of the war had imbued me with courage and resolve to join the Home Guard', and when he had looked upon him as 'something akin to a god'.[102] Given that level of hero-worship, it was perhaps no surprise Lady Churchill liked Forbes' final treatment, as did the family's other advisors. But Paramount did not.[103]

Having arrived at this impasse, Paramount were willing to relinquish their rights to Columbia and in particular to producer Carl Foreman. It was Foreman who came up with an approach that met both the approval of Hollywood and the Churchills: the relationship between Churchill and his father. As the son of Jewish immigrants, Foreman claimed, 'It suddenly occurred to me that this man from the great Marlborough family and I from a family which went over from Russia steerage had one thing in common: we didn't know our fathers.' At that point Foreman decided he could produce a story that satisfied all parties: while in possession of outward privilege, Churchill was a 'deprived youth', lacking parental affection.[104] This was, he wrote, 'a relationship at once unique and yet universal, very human, essentially sad, and one apparently never resolved in the lifetimes of the two men.' It was

a great story, of classical stature and almost biblical flavour, and for that reason a story that people of all classes will understand and be affected by. In fact, I think it is the only story, and that, without sentimentality or bathos, with dignity and restraint, it will raise what might otherwise be a simple adventure story for children, lacking weight or ballast, into an important film on all levels, and one not without considerable inspirational values.[105]

It was of course the very approach a more vigorous Churchill had dismissed when speaking with Balchin five years before.

Forbes was disappointed to have lost out to Foreman, arguing that 'The Churchill story should be made by an Englishman.'[106] Yet according to Richard Attenborough, Foreman's adoration for Churchill was undeniable, despite being forced to work in Britain, having been black-listed in Hollywood for Communist sympathies, not usually a recom-mendation in Churchill's eyes.[107] Attenborough, who directed the eventual film, was another unlikely Churchillian. For while 'Churchill holds a special place for me and my generation', he admitted that, 'I don't agree with many of his political views. But those of us in World War Two remember someone who said "Enough" to the Machiavellian barbarian sweeping across Europe. This man gave us our voice. He spoke for us and galvanised us into action.'[108]

Young Winston was, as Foreman put it, 'faithful to the truth, as Sir Winston saw it' and set at the time when Churchill was striving to find a place in the world, from his childhood to first becoming an MP.[109] Beginning and ending with VE Day, it is an 'origins' story, as had been Ford's *Young Mr Lincoln*; both outlined how their protagonists demon-strated the qualities necessary to guide their two nations through differ-ent crises. In Ford's 1939 film these were Lincoln's empathy for the people, from whom he had himself emerged, his cool command of their passions, and dedication to the principle of justice for all. Churchill's privileged background dictated Foreman take a very different tack: it was not principles but person upon which he focused. So *Young Winston* presents Churchill as having to live on his wits: despite an aristocratic background he was short of money and lacked the appropri-ate contacts. As the *Daily Telegraph* critic had it, the result was 'some-thing of a Cinderella story' (Figure 3.5).[110] The movie suggests Churchill's striving to enter Parliament was motivated by his desire to vindicate his father, a man he claims had strong convictions, although these are never made apparent. Churchill wants to serve his country in Parliament but also to advance himself. There is then some ambiguity in the film that overall supports Churchill's claim to have possessed a 'destiny'. David Lloyd George most notably tells Churchill 'You're a

Figure 3.5 Churchill's early years as a 'Cinderella story'

child of your class and you may never outgrow it…but you've got something.' The *Morning Star* critic, alone amongst reviewers to refer to Churchill sending troops to deal with a Welsh miners' strike, clearly did not believe Churchill transcended his class—but Foreman presumably expected most other members of the audience to accept he had.[111]

The film, like Churchill, took the Empire for granted and raised no critical questions about its propriety, simply using it is as a thrilling background for his adventures. Even so, a scene which saw British colonial troops set fire to a native village must have evoked in the minds of some the contemporary activities of American soldiers in Vietnam. Yet Churchill gives a speech in the Commons which effectively concludes the film, in which he takes up the baton left by his father who ended his brilliant career by resigning from the cabinet over increases in military expenditure. The speech as delivered in the movie was a truncated version of the one Churchill actually delivered in 1901.[112] Through careful editing, it gives the strong impression he was a man of peace, calling as he does for Britain to exert 'moral force' in the world rather than risking a bloody European war, one the audience knows is coming in 1914. By then, something the film does not mention, Churchill was one of the loudest members of the Liberal cabinet to demand that Britain declare war on Germany.

Baiting the Myth

Alexander Walker, a critic of a conservative bent, claimed of *Young Winston* that, 'No other national hero of recent memory has ever received such a thorough going-over.'[113] In contrast, the critic in Britain's leading left-wing weekly, the *New Statesman*, believed Foreman was a 'prisoner of the Churchill myth'.[114] If film reviewers disagreed about the kind of relationship Foreman's film had to the dominant Churchillian mythology, this was not true of all the dramas produced in the immediate aftermath of his death, some of which took an undeniably critical stance.

Just prior to Churchill's death, Dennis Potter, then establishing himself as one of the country's most radical and innovative television dramatists, submitted a draft treatment to the BBC that, albeit covertly, explored the very dynamics of Churchill's mythology. The set-up for what would become *Message for Posterity* involved a Conservative politician widely regarded as a 'great man' sitting for a portrait commissioned by Parliament to celebrate his long life. This obviously evoked Churchill's experience with Graham Sutherland. But those responsible for commissioning the play persuaded themselves it contained no further Churchillian echoes, perhaps because Potter's initial outline left out other parallels.[115] However, the final script made Potter's intent obvious, and as the transmission date loomed, in May 1967, Corporation executives were increasingly uneasy.[116]

For while the 'great man' is called Sir David Browning, there can be little doubt upon whom he was closely based. Potter reveals Browning sent in troops to end a miners' strike in South Wales, played a prominent role in the General Strike, opposed appeasement, and led his country in the war against Nazism. If no other figure shared those characteristics with Churchill, James Player, the modernist artist selected to paint his portrait, is nothing like Sutherland. He is instead a contemporary of Browning, from the Welsh proletariat and of socialist views and so a severe critic of a man he considers to be the enemy of his class. Player wants his portrait to be 'the final judgement of a much-abused people' that would decisively reveal Browning's true nature. Yet in labouring on his work, Player is turned mad and the portrait never sees the light of day. His reputation now protected from attack, at the end of the drama Browning declares with smug satisfaction: 'We always win in the end.' The old statesman suffers a heart attack during his final sitting but is given the kiss of life by his granddaughter. This was, so far as critics of the dominating Churchill mythology were concerned, amongst whom the socialist Potter undoubtedly numbered, a bleakly defeatist work. For, not only would the myth survive; it would be given new life by a younger generation.

In public Potter denied Browning was based on the wartime prime minister, but most critics saw the glaring parallels.[117] In the *Sunday Times* Maurice Wiggins complained that Potter's Churchillian figure was depicted 'rather vindictively, he left out the magnanimity and courage of the finest hour'.[118] The reaction was however curiously muted.

This might have been because, as Milton Schulman wrote: 'Straight-jacketed by convention and by the limitations of putting on the screen a really vicious portrait of Churchill, Potter obviously had to comprom-ise. He gave us a timorous bleep rather than a full-bloodied cry of outrage. He was trapped by his own inhibitions.'[119] Certainly, most viewers were unimpressed, the BBC audience panel giving it a low rating and reportedly seeing it as 'both tasteless and boringly uneventful'. Most appreciated Browning was modelled on Churchill, which was 'a far from comfortable consideration' for many. As with the professional critics, the play left many viewers with a general sense of unresolved unease.[120]

Message to Posterity was broadcast in the BBC's Wednesday Play slot, an established ghetto for plays the Corporation considered controversial. Few watched it: only 6 per cent of BBC panellists. In the same slot seven years later Churchill appeared in *Days of Hope*, a series of four films which traced the working-class experience from the First World War to the General Strike. Written by the Trotskyist Jim Allen and directed by Ken Loach, the series was criticized by Margaret Thatcher in her first Conservative conference speech as leader for representing an attack on 'our national self-respect'.[121] In the final episode, which dealt with the General Strike, Churchill appears briefly and has just one line—in which he expresses his contempt for the Trade Union Congress—but Allen has a number of characters refer to him as an extremist wanting to crush the strike. Once again, relatively few viewers saw the episode, preferring instead to watch *The Morecambe and Wise Show*.

Even so, when the popular period drama *Upstairs, Downstairs* dealt with the 1926 strike in an episode broadcast in November 1975, Churchill's bloodthirsty desire to defeat the miners was also put on show—and criticized by the moderate and consensual Conservative peer Richard Bellamy, the paternalistic head of the household.

Those writing for the stage, as opposed to television, were freer to write what they liked about Churchill. Few enough chose to use the platform to criticize the legend, however, with Rolf Hochhuth's experi-ence showing the limits of what it was possible to say.[122] Hochhuth was a young and iconoclastic German playwright whose *Soldiers*, which was mooted to be staged by the National Theatre in 1967, accused Churchill of being responsible for the death in 1943 of General Sikorski, leader of

Poland's exiled government, and condoning the mass bombing of German cities. It was selected by the Theatre's literary manager Kenneth Tynan, a keen public *provocateur* made infamous for saying 'Fuck' on television in 1965. He would subsequently create *Oh! Calcutta!*, an all-nude revue which dealt with sex in direct terms to invite accusations of obscenity. Tynan saw *Soldiers* as one more way of further goading the Establishment. The Theatre's artistic director, Sir Lawrence Olivier, agreed to stage the play. Olivier was no controversialist. He had voiced Churchill's words during ITV's coverage of his state funeral, but nonetheless believed Hochhuth expressed a legitimate point of view.[123] Olivier was, however, overruled by the Theatre's board, which accused *Soldiers* of grossly maligning Churchill. Certainly, there was no convincing evidence that Churchill had connived to kill Sikorsky, although the prime minister's support for mass bombing was there for all to see. One reason for the board's decision was that its chair happened to be Lord Chandos, a member of Sir Winston's wartime government. Yet even had the board agreed to stage *Soldiers*, the Lord Chamberlain's Office would have forbidden it. In response Tynan looked for a theatre prepared to stage the play in the commercial West End, but few owners wanted to be associated with an attack on Churchill. After a venue was finally found, the production was subject to bomb threats, accusations of Nazi sympathies, and found an audience hard to find, running for just four months.

Despite the outrage his play provoked, Hochhuth claimed to revere Churchill as the 'saviour of civilization', a heroic giant in the German tradition. But he also saw him as a tragic figure. For, he argued, Churchill was right to order the murder of Sikorksy and support mass bombing as the price for keeping the Soviet Union in the war. Hochhuth suggested the prime minister had no choice, even though he knew the consequences would be terrible. In this reading, Churchill was a pragmatist forced to do regrettable but necessary things.[124] But Hochhuth fell foul of opinion by mixing the historical Churchill, who was performed on the stage in uncannily realistic terms, with highly contentious, not to say false, claims about Sikorksy's death. Those few, like the critic Ronald Bryden, who could see the play as a purely theatrical enterprise and put aside considerations of fact or fiction, saw what it was that Hochhuth endeavoured to argue.[125]

Dennis Potter had avoided controversy by attacking a partially fic-tionalized Churchill. Perhaps in 1967 it was too soon to air a critique of the unadorned historical Churchill. Attitudes had certainly changed two decades later. In 1989 the BBC television drama *Bomber Harris* written by Don Shaw had Churchill privately support Harris's strategy of mass bombing and encourage him to attack Dresden. But after that raid killed up to 135,000 and was widely criticized as immoral, Churchill—in the programme—hypocritically sided with Harris's detractors. In some ways, *Bomber Harris* cast an even darker light on Churchill than did *Soldiers*, but it provoked little fuss.

To make his points, Hochhuth had used the device of a play-within-a play, something also employed by Howard Brenton in *The Churchill Play* (1974). Brenton was one of a number of young socialist playwrights who emerged from the far-left politics of the late 1960s to produce work for the subsidized theatre. He was associated with debunking conventional national wisdoms and being especially critical of the shortcomings of the 1945 settlement. Speaking in 1972, Brenton described the theatre as the place 'to bait our obsessions, ideas and public figures'.[126] In that spirit, *The Churchill Play* was commissioned by the Nottingham Playhouse, then at the heart of Britain's radical theatre, to mark the centenary of Sir Winston's birth.

The play is set in an internment camp in an authoritarian Britain of the near future. The inmates, mostly dissident journalists and trade unionists, stage a play about Churchill for visiting dignitaries. This has him come back from the dead during his lying-in-state to talk to the squaddies charged with guarding him (Figure 3.6). During these macabre exchanges Churchill is attacked for being an enemy of working people and in particular for sending in troops in 1910 to end a Welsh miners' strike, a standard left-wing rebuke. But most critical to the central Churchill myth is this exchange:

Private. But 'e won the war. 'E did that, 'e won a war.

Marine. People won the War. He just got pissed with Stalin.

When Churchill speaks of wartime heroism, the soldiers talk of their parents' suffering during German bombing: there was, according to

Figure 3.6 Churchill rises from the dead in *The Churchill Play*

Brenton, no unity in the war under Churchill's leadership. This of course raised significant questions about Churchill's relationship with the British people during the conflict, the centrepiece of the main Churchill myth. It was one which Angus Calder's *People's War* (1969) explored by looking at the conflict through the eyes of ordinary people. Calder's book was read by many radical dramatists of Brenton's generation and shaped how they looked on the conflict, especially so in the case of David Hare.[127] It is likely Brenton was influenced by it, especially as he and Hare together wrote *Brassneck*, a broad satire critical of the betrayal of popular wartime hopes, also staged at the Nottingham Playhouse the year before *The Churchill Play*.

Brenton's play was well received by critics when in opened it Nottingham and although not banned, like *Soldiers*, due to what one described as Brenton's 'explosive material' and 'audacious iconoclasm', it has rarely been performed elsewhere.[128] Certainly, while some of Brenton's work reached television screens—even *Brassneck*, in which Churchill did not appear—*The Churchill Play* never did.

The Great Man

Young Winston introduced audiences to an unfamiliar Churchill in order to show that the youth was destined to be the man who saved the nation: it was Whig History. Later biopics played safer with audience expectations and gave them the Churchill with whom they were more accustomed, to different degrees drawing from a conception of the Great Man. They generally retold the same story, one with strong religious resonances, of a prophet crying in the wilderness, his inexorable vindication and the fulfilment of his destiny by bringing Britons out of darkness and into their finest hour. These biopics came in three waves. First, within seven years of each other were *Walk with Destiny* (1974), *Churchill and the Generals* (1979), and the mini-series *Winston Churchill: The Wilderness Years* (1981). Then, after a gap of twenty years came *The Gathering Storm* (2002) and *Into the Storm* (2009), followed within a decade, finally, by the movies *Churchill* (2017) and *Darkest Hour* (2018). There was a good reason why these dramas mostly repeated the same glorious narrative: it was what audiences wanted. Richard Last, the *Daily Telegraph* critic, complained of being bored by *The Wilderness Years*. This spent eight hour-long episodes exploring Churchill's time out of power between 1929 and 1939, including in great detail his battles over Indian Home Rule. Once the Nazi threat appeared over the horizon and the series reached more familiar ground, it was only then that Last's interest returned.[129]

These dramas were all in some shape or form Anglo-American works, usually in terms of production, often involving the BBC in cooperation with a US production company, and always in regard to the intended market. A few, like *Darkest Hour*, were exclusively Hollywood products (Figure 3.7). This was not a new phenomenon, but, as with *The Valiant Years*, there was some initial concern about its implications amongst

Figure 3.7 An anachronistic Churchill for our own times

British critics and BBC managers.[130] By the time of the second wave these worries had disappeared, if only because the reality of producing such expensive dramas meant they simply could not be made without American investment or the promise of a US audience.

All were, of course, based on real history. Yet as the chronological distance increased between the events depicted and their onscreen representations, so writers became ever more willing to enhance their stories with invention. This temptation was, as we have seen, not new. In the earliest iterations the dramas did, however, stick closely to the facts, or at least to Churchill's version of them. His official biographer, Martin Gilbert, was even involved as a co-writer on *The Wilderness Years*. But however much they claimed to be based on the historical record—just like professional historians—these dramas nonetheless manipulated their narratives through omission, over- and under-emphasis of certain events, the way they characterized their protagonists, or in the casting.

Initially history acted like a straight-jacket on these works. Potter's jibe that *Walk with Destiny* was the dramatic equivalent of a commemorative plaque was echoed by many others. Joan Bakewell said the script wove familiar events and quotes together 'in a civilised but unsurprising order'.[131] Yet four decades later, *Darkest Hour* showed that in the battle between drama and history, the former had won hands down, most egregiously when the prime minister talks to Tube passengers. Director Joe Wright, in admitting the invention, claimed the scene—and others in the movie—was actually 'a fictionalization of an "emotional truth"' because he claimed Churchill was known to disappear and to have visited the people of London to 'seek their counsel, and have a little cry with them sometimes'.[132]

If *Darkest Hour* found new ways to restate the central Churchillian myth, the film also showed how far Churchill could, by the second decade of the twenty-first century, be represented as a flawed figure, a drinker, a shouter, a man of passion as much as reason. Burton's 1974 portrayal of Churchill was in contrast subdued, the passion held largely in check while his domestic enemies—notably Thorley Walter's rendering of Stanley Baldwin—were almost avuncular. In contrast, Gary Oldman's 2018 portrayal celebrated Churchill's oddness, making it a virtue. As Clemmie tells her husband in *Darkest Hour*: 'you are strong *because* you are imperfect.' God had assumed the shape of a gargoyle, but only to retain his divinity. In contrast, Churchill's opponents are presented as buttoned-up, cold, calculating, almost vampiric figures: if they are stereotypical 'politicians', *he* is a human being. This manner of representation had been gently anticipated in *The Wilderness Years*, which pitched a warm but imperfect Churchill against his two main protagonists, Sir Samuel Hoare and Neville Chamberlain who, to the eyes of one reviewer, were respectively 'odiously reptilian' and a 'contemptible toady'.[133]

Despite such differences these dramas mostly share the same unremitting focus, viewing their subject through the prism of the Great Man. These are works about a leader and his leadership: the fate of the many is in the hands of the one. National salvation comes through the decisions of an exceptional figure. The roots of this idea can be traced back to Plato, who in *The Republic* argued that as the people were captives of selfish passions, government needed to be the preserve of a supreme guardian elevated by Nature above them. Plato's vision remains at the heart of much thinking about the necessity for leaders. Through the years, many have reworked his metaphor of the 'ship of state', which envisaged the leader as a captain at the helm. For people from a seafaring city like Ancient Athens this was an obvious parallel to draw; but it is a fundamentally undemocratic metaphor.

Plato certainly influenced Thomas Carlyle's conceptualization of the Great Man, outlined in the 1840s, when he argued that, 'the history of what man has accomplished in this world, is at bottom the History of Great Men.'[134] Like Plato, Carlyle believed the people needed Great Men, their role being to '*command* over us, to furnish us with constant practical teaching, to tell us for the day and hour what we are to *do*'. Equality he saw as ridiculous because it contradicted a Nature based on the impermeable hierarchies of gender, class, and race.[135] And as more Britons gained the right to vote, Carlyle expressed himself with ever-greater vituperation. Democracy he predicted would promote only politicians willing to pander to the people's 'blockheadism'.[136] The unity and purpose necessary for national greatness could only be achieved through a Great Man, for 'the basis of all human culture' was 'commanding and obeying'. Carlyle's Great Man was a martial leader imposing a collective purpose on millions of individuals oblivious of their deepest need: his leadership completed an imperfect people, and through him they also became great.

Some of Carlyle's contemporaries questioned his sanity. But his reworking of Plato remained an important reference point for many. While unlikely those who produced the Churchill dramas had read, let alone endorsed, Carlyle, elements of his thinking permeate their renderings of the past, if only because they are infused by Churchill's own conception of his role as a leader. Churchill's only novel, the political romance *Savrola* (1900), shows how a fickle people required a firm leader able to rhetorically persuade them to see the world as did he. Nevertheless, in the novel, Churchill has his fictional heroic leader ask at one point: 'Do you think I am what I am, because I changed all those minds, or because I best express their views? Am I their master or their slave?'[137] When addressing Parliament on his eightieth birthday, Sir Winston seemed to believe that during the war he had acted as the people's slave, for, 'It was the nation and the race dwelling all around the globe that had the lion's heart. I had the luck to be called upon to give the roar.' Despite that, his biopics mostly suggest it was more a case of Churchill being the people's master.

The dramas in any event outline a High Political History, with the people, except as faithful Chartwell servants, largely left out. None of the dramas are able to explain why Britons were deaf to Churchill's crying in the wilderness, an awkward paradox given the audience knows that he was right to issue his warnings about the Nazi threat. *The Wilderness Years* comes closest to suggesting that popular support for appeasement was due to the desire for government to spend more money on social projects rather than on arms. It has Chamberlain declare that 'I want to make this country great once more', not by war and conquests, 'but by looking after all our people'. It was their 'happiness' to which Chamberlain was dedicated. In this account, if appeasement was due to a combination of naive idealism and greedy self-interest, then Churchill's opposition was based on putting the supreme national interest first: guns before butter. Carlyle would have approved.

While the British people are largely absent or flawed historical agents in these dramas, Churchill's agency is everywhere and often explicitly expressed in terms of the Great Man. In *Walk with Destiny*, following his isolation after the abdication of Edward VIII Clementine tells her husband: 'Perhaps what the people need today is not what they want, but you must rouse them: you alone can do it.' Soon after he becomes prime minister she again makes the vital point, albeit in the form of a rhetorical question: 'I wonder if there has ever been a time when our future depended on the courage of one man?' *Churchill and the Generals* has the Chief of the Imperial General Staff Alan Brooke assure Churchill: 'If there's one thing that will save us it's your voice.' The prime minister modestly demurs, as he did in 1954, and claims he is only saying what is already in people's hearts. Yet later he angrily states: 'only I can win this war...I have the steady power of England inside me. I am its strength, its teeth, its bite. I must survive or we will lose.' The drama makes its normative position clear, with Brooke at the end of the war quoting from a newspaper which states of Churchill: 'we owe him everything.'

In the two HBO dramas written by Hugh Whitemore, *The Gathering Storm* and *Into the Storm*, there is greater ambiguity. In the former, Clemmie tells her husband, 'You have the ability to make people carry on no matter what.' But in the latter, after verbally abusing his butler, she indignantly tells Winston, 'It's people like him that won the war.' And yet the latter drama has its cake and eats it, by ending with the recently deposed prime minister greeted as 'The Saviour of our Nation' when visiting a West End theatre. If *Into the Storm* quietly suggests the people themselves played a part in the war, that proposition is taken further in *Darkest Hour*. At one point Churchill declaims just before making a radio speech 'I am going to imbue them [the people] with a spirit of feeling they don't yet know they have.' But he fails in his task because he does not tell them the truth about the dire situation into which Britain has fallen. To rescue himself and the country, he consults the people in that infamously invented Tube carriage. The scene has been criticized for its anachronism. But it is there to make flesh his claim about being the 'lion's roar'. This is its 'emotional truth'. Now armed by the people's will, Churchill takes the fight to the Establishment, then plotting for his removal, and Britain enters its Finest Hour.

The great exception to these biopics is *Churchill*, partly because it is set as Britain prepares for D-Day. The Finest Hour is now in the past and the prime minister is suffering severe doubts about the invasion, fearing it will turn out a disaster. Faced with the need to prepare a radio address to be broadcast on the day of the invasion itself, and so before anybody knows its outcome, he runs away from the task. That is, until his young secretary reminds him that her *fiancé* is part of the invasion fleet and she—like millions of others—need reassurance and hope that their sacrifice will be worthwhile. Reminded of his duty to the nation, Churchill produces an inspirational speech.

Churchill was also distinct in the lengths to which the movie illustrated Churchill's occasional incapacity due to depression, the 'black dog' to which he had often referred. This was done not to attack the Churchill myth but, as its script writer stated, to 'take it in a different direction'.[138] Previous dramatists had mentioned, but briefly, or skated over entirely, Churchill's mental state—although his dependence on Clemmie for reassurance was indicated as early as *Walk with Destiny*. But *Churchill* was produced at a time when mental illness was becoming a more acceptable issue to discuss openly. It was not, however, something the keepers of the established Churchillian flame appreciated, and they attacked *Churchill* for making it so central to its understanding of the prime minister.[139] The movie also underlined the brevity of Churchill's Finest Hour. It presents him in June 1944 as almost irrelevant; indeed, he has become an obstacle to the success of D-Day and is reduced to the status of a backseat driver. It is the Supreme Commander, Dwight Eisenhower, who takes all the decisions. This draws Churchill into an existential crisis, such that he asks his wife: 'who will I be when it's all over?' 'You'll always be the man who led us through this', she replies.

Sir Winston's rapid fade into History had also been highlighted in *Churchill and the Generals*, which showed that once the Americans entered the war he quickly lost his strategic authority. This is also explored by *Into the Storm*, which shows Churchill waiting for the result of the 1945 election, having been told by Attlee that the people 'want a different sort of future' from the one he offers.

Despite such shifts in focus, these dramas therefore largely focus on the familiar Churchill, the Great Man, the wartime hero. They might increasingly depict him as a flawed person, if only to reinforce his greatness, but in contrast merely genuflect or completely ignore the more problematic aspects of his career. This is especially the case with Churchill's imperialism, and racism, which were increasingly difficult to defend in post-war Britain. If later versions, such as *The Gathering Storm*, show him opposing Indian Home Rule and attacking Gandhi, these fleeting moments are the equivalent of the clearing of the throat before the high drama of The Finest Hour can begin. If only because the series covered the whole of the 1930s, it was impossible for *The Wilderness Years* to avoid the Indian question: it actually dominates three episodes. The series deals with the issue in an ingenious way, so that Churchill's opposition to India being granted Dominion status is presented as just one of the many instances in which, as producer Richard Brooke has it, 'Churchill had to choose between his party and his conscience.'[140] Churchill is then shown to be an honest imperialist, despite its cost to his political career—in contrast to those who supported Dominion status, notably the duplicitous Sir Samuel Hoare, Secretary of State for India. When Prime Minister Baldwin creates a Select Committee, ostensibly to look at the evidence for the proposed policy, he is shown as packing it with supporters. Even so, Hoare feels he must see in advance evidence to be presented to the Committee from Lancashire's cotton manufacturers. This he expects to be damaging to the cause of Home Rule. Hoare has the evidence redrafted so that, when formally submitted, it helps his cause. In so doing Hoare broke parliamentary protocol. When made aware of this, Churchill forces an inquiry which, thanks to further manipulation, finds Hoare innocent of impropriety.

The series thereby sidesteps the basic reason for Churchill's opposition to Indian Home Rule—his racism and imperialism—in favour of casting him as a stalwart defender of parliamentary integrity: it even has him claim Hoare's actions were just one step away from Nazism. History was distorted, by omission and unwonted emphasis, to avoid showing Churchill in what by the 1980s many would have seen in an unfavourable light. Three decades later, *Darkest Hour* took this process of rehabilitation a stage further in the fictional Tube scene, when Churchill gratefully touches the arm of a black passenger who has helped him finish Lord Macaulay's poem *Horatius*.

The Reassertion of a Deeper Myth

Due to her respect for Churchill's iconic status, Queen Elizabeth twice broke with royal convention, first in 1954 by visiting Downing Street for a dinner to celebrate the prime minister's eightieth birthday, and then in 1965 by attending his St Paul's funeral service. During the twenty-first century, however, the traditional constitutional order has been restored, with Churchill's subordination to one of the truly hegemonic myths of British history: the caring monarch. If Churchill's wartime role was memorialized by statues and state pageantry, and in various screen documentaries and dramas, the monarch's position, as Tom Nairn had it, as Briton's 'enchanted glass', has been reinforced on an almost daily basis.[141] This is one reason why, during Britain's Brexit crisis, support for the monarchy was about the one thing that united an otherwise divided country.[142]

Since they were first able to depict Britain's head of state, screen dramas have reinforced belief in monarchy—especially in the case of Victoria and Elizabeth II—as the loving heart of a heartless political world, the only figures who put the people's interests first. Initially Victoria, just like Churchill, was a spectral presence, referred to but not seen, except as a shining light, as in *Disraeli* (1929). Once the prohibition on depicting her on the screen was lifted thanks to Edward VIII, Herbert Wilcox produced *Victoria the Great* (1937) and, owing to its popularity, *Sixty Glorious Years* (1938), in which one critic noted, the Queen's prime ministers, 'succeed one another like patient dogs'.[143] These films set the template for later movies and outlined the role expected of a monarch's first minister: to enact their desire to look after the people. *Victoria the Great* even has it that Robert Peel only abolished the Corn Laws because, after reading of the suffering of the poor in *Oliver Twist*, the Queen demanded the price of bread be reduced.

Churchill had a deeply sentimental view of the monarchy: if anybody was captive to its mythology, he was.[144] But Sir Winston's relationship with the institution has presented dramatists with problems. His support for Edward VIII during the abdication crisis did not go down well with his younger brother, who was forced to succeed him. Moreover, on

becoming George VI, the new King supported appeasement, even stand-
ing with Prime Minister Neville Chamberlain on the balcony of
Buckingham Palace to acknowledge the crowd gathered to celebrate
the 1938 Munich agreement. The King was also a personal friend of
Lord Halifax, Chamberlain's Foreign Secretary; in May 1940 he wanted
Halifax, not Churchill to succeed Chamberlain.

Recent dramas focusing on the abdication crisis have tended to sym-
pathize with Edward's position, reflecting times when divorce had lost its
stigma and the pursuit of private happiness over public duty can be seen
in a more positive light. The major ITV series *Edward and Mrs Simpson*
(1978) generally took Edward's side as a modernizing monarch, concerned for the poor but confronted by a stuffy Establishment. It presented Churchill as, like many in the audience, sensitive to the King's
personal dilemma. He is cast as a pragmatic friend who merely wants
Edward granted more 'time and patience' so the issue might be resolved
without abdication. This is in contrast to a braying Commons, whom
Churchill accuses of wanting to break the King. But he is also shown to
be a responsible statesman: if Baldwin's government resigns, should the
King marry Mrs Simpson, Churchill would support it. This is essentially
the position of the later TV movie *Wallis and Edward* (2005), which has
Churchill state that Edward had the potential to be a 'modern king' and
compares his empathy for a suffering people with a hypocritical and
hidebound Baldwin who wants to be rid of his awkward monarch.

There has, however, in recent years been an increasing dramatic
interest in George VI. As it focused on the lives of the monarch and
his wife, the ITV drama *Bertie and Elizabeth* (2001) criticized Edward's
motives while obscuring brother George's support for appeasement and
mistrust of Churchill. Instead the drama highlighted the wartime monarch's strong sense of public service and his willingness to embrace self-
sacrifice. As he angrily informs his elder brother, who here is presented
as selfishly putting himself before duty, the monarchy is 'an office whose
existence is at the very heart of what English democracy and English
liberty means'. This highly romanticized drama also shows the King and
Queen visiting Blitzed East Enders to, as the latter puts it, 'keep 'em
smiling'. To emphasize their shared vulnerability to German attack it
also has the royal couple melodramatically scurrying to a shelter as

bombs blow out Buckingham Palace's windows, showering them with broken glass. Despite much of the drama being about the war, Churchill's contribution is almost entirely overlooked.

The King's Speech (2010) went a stage further in the reconstitution of history in favour of the monarchy by radically rearranging the roles and attitudes of George and Churchill. Most egregiously, it is the monarch whose voice is presented as vital to Britain's wartime survival rather than, as in the central Churchillian myth, his prime minister's radio rhetoric. Hence it is not just for personal reasons that George needs to overcome his debilitating stammer, which is the focus of the movie, because, as is stated at its end: 'Through his broadcasts George VI became a symbol of national resistance.' The relationship between the two men was also recast to make them appear close *confidantes* before the outbreak of war. Churchill is cast as a critic of Edward and a friend of George, even suggesting he take his father's name as king rather than Albert because it sounded too Germanic. George's own support for appeasement is in addition craftily finessed by simply avoiding any reference to his support for Chamberlain while emphasizing his elder brother's sympathy for Nazism. Instead George agrees with Baldwin's parting words on his resignation as prime minister that 'Churchill was right all along' about Hitler.

Those dramas in which Churchill is the principal protagonist have also played fast and loose with the reality of Churchill's relationship with King George. *Walking with Destiny* has George in possession of no qualms when appointing Churchill prime minister, and even has him commenting that Churchill has always been 'a good friend of my family'. Later iterations, such as *Into the Storm* and *The Darkest Hour* do, however, allow the King to express initial doubts about Churchill's suitability to lead the country. If in that sense accurate, the latter film has a truly novel take on Churchill's decision to fight on against Nazism. For having himself been converted to the cause of fighting on, despite his friend Halifax's continued opposition, the King visits his prime minister, who is suffering from doubt. In Churchill's decision-making, at this critical juncture, it is the King's advice that is presented as supreme, for he tells Churchill: 'go to the people, let them instruct you.'

The subordination of Churchill to the mythology of the caring monarch has recently been further reinforced and chronologically developed in the Netflix series *The Crown* (2016–). Peter Morgan's *The Queen* (2006) showed Elizabeth II at bay after the death of Princess Diana in 1997 and has her assailed by a hysterical public, attacked by an unfriendly media, and surrounded by political forces ambiguous about her survival. Elizabeth's only crime, according to Morgan's script, was that she took her inherited public duties seriously. Morgan's 2013 play *The Audience* built on that portrait and in a series of vignettes in which Elizabeth meets her successive prime ministers, she emerges a wise and witty figure whose happy life has been turned upside down by an unwanted job as monarch, a task she nonetheless executes with admirable skill. Indeed, such was Morgan's treatment of his subject, *The Audience* was described by Jonathan Freedland as 'a two-hour exercise in propaganda for Elizabeth Windsor'.[145]

The Crown expands on that propaganda, with many of the scenes in which Churchill appears in the play sometimes repeated word for word. Churchill is omnipresent during the first season, but with his wartime role as 'the Father of Nation', as Anthony Eden puts it, well behind him. Morgan does not question the central myth, but he rather undermines it by presenting Churchill as an old man, hunched and reliant on his stick, desperate to cling onto power and delusional about his continued importance. This was the figure sculptors in the 1950s and 1960s had been warned against depicting, in favour of 'Churchill the Legend'. Sir Winston's shameless milking of the limelight when he attends Elizabeth and Philip's wedding, in one of the opening scenes of the first episode, frames this other, rather camp, Churchill.

In the series, Churchill is depicted as an elderly member of a crumbling Establishment that stands in the way of a young and modernizing Royal couple. He is, for the most part, an impediment which they have to overcome. His physical slowness is a subject of Philip's jokes while Elizabeth is advised by her mother to 'smile politely while he drones on'. If words are still his weapon—his eulogy for George VI helps shape the expectation of a 'New Elizabethan Age'—Churchill is nonetheless one of the forces of conservatism intent on preventing its emergence. As prime minister he heads an ineffective government stuck in stasis due to his own frailties. This is brought to the fore in the episode 'Act of God' in which he is presented as directly culpable for a toxic fog that descends upon the capital. Instead of taking preventative action, having been warned of the dangers, he insists on burning coal to give the impression of a booming economy. This creates a medical emergency in which one overstretched doctor is shown pointedly saying the prime minister has created a crisis worse than in the war. Churchill, however, manages to extricate himself from public blame for the crisis by a cynical manipulation of the press and his facility with words. This episode comes close to being a dark reflection on Churchill's iconic wartime role: if he showed leadership then, he fails to show it now, and at the cost of many Londoners' deaths, including that of a hero-worshipping young secretary enamoured by the heroism of the precocious author of *My Early Life*.[146]

Churchill is, however, a second-order character in *The Crown*, which stresses the importance of the dutiful Elizabeth, who wants to do the right constitutional thing. Her serious sense of Divine Calling, duty to the constitution and country, is contrasted to the childlike, sometimes comic, desire for personal power exhibited by the politicians, Churchill included. Indeed, he delays her Coronation to help him cling to power. The Queen is the only serious person in the room, as demonstrated in the episode 'Scientia Potentia' which has Churchill endeavour to prevent Elizabeth learning about his two strokes, fearing her awareness of his temporarily incapacity will lead to his permanent loss of power. When she discovers Churchill's deception she gives those members of the cabinet who participated in it, including the prime minister, a dressing down to remind them of their responsibilities, just as a mother would do to her child.

In the end, however, *The Crown* provides audiences with a touching depiction of a frail man past his best but clutching to power, as to life, the subject of the episode 'Assassins'. This deals with Churchill's hostility to Graham Sutherland's eightieth-birthday portrait and apart from his ageing pains reveals a hitherto overlooked emotional hinterland: Churchill's continued sadness for the death of his young daughter Marigold in 1921.

Adapted from Jonathan Smith's 2015 novel *The Churchill Secret KBO*, *Churchill's Secret* (2016) evoked *The Crown*'s depiction. Presenting an old man's struggle to hold on to power, this drama does at least suggest that his ambition for one last victory, the achievement of some kind of peace with the Soviet Union, is genuine. But the emphasis overall is on the personal rather than the political. Churchill's fractious family has often been represented, but the price they all paid for their father's 'greatness' in particular is brought home, as is—uniquely—his wife's neglect of her children in his favour.

The centrepiece of the drama, however, is Millie Appleyard, who alone is an invented character, a young nurse drafted in to care for the ailing Premier. Millie was presumably created to provide readers and the television audience with a sympathetic character and through whose eyes they can grasp the narrative. She also creates a bridge between the audience and Churchill. For Millie is the daughter of a socialist Yorkshire miner and no fan of the prime minister. Despite that, they nonetheless establish a rapport, identifying common ground through a shared love for English literature. While mention is made of Churchill sending in troops to end a Welsh miners' strike, it is brushed aside in favour of this more profound bond.

Millie is a nurse, proud of her work in the National Health Service, but is on the verge of leaving for Australia where she is to marry a *fiancé* who expects her to abandon her career in favour of motherhood. She is therefore faced with the prospect of subordinating her dreams for his, in the same way Clemmie did for Winston. While listening to Churchill's speech to his party's annual conference, which demonstrates his recovery from the stroke and capacity to keep hold of power despite his wife's wish for his retirement, Millie decides to stay in Britain and continue her nursing career. If the drama has a feminist theme, and not one from which Churchill emerges with much credit, it also ends on a triumphant note for a man battling the ravages of time. 'Growing old is not for cowards', he tells Millie at one point. Churchill's battle against physical incapacity echoes the play *Sunrise at Campobello* (1958), made into a movie in 1960, which showed Franklin Roosevelt overcoming polio and thereby demonstrating the strength of character that made him a great wartime president. It also concludes with a speech, this time Roosevelt's address to the 1928 Democratic convention. The play was written by

Dore Schary who, as we have seen, as head of MGM in 1955 wanted to produce a Churchill biopic.

A Confusion of Churchills

Churchill's assimilation within the myth of the caring monarch suggests that—perhaps—he is coming to the end of his long innings as Britain's supreme national icon. However, despite this and the proliferation of various other kinds of Churchill that have appeared in recent years, the central myth still retains much of its power. For the more sceptical contemporary readings of Churchill have not replaced those which reiterate the traditionally dominant mythology: they instead interweave with each other. The picture is more opaque than once it was, but Churchill the hero whose destiny led him to the save the nation is still clearly observable.

The political theorist Harald Wydra suggests citizens need 'a web of symbols and meanings' by which they can identify markers of certainty, and when that certainty disappears they look for new symbols to give a new order to events.[147] Churchill became a symbol of certainty thanks to Britain's 1940 crisis, his role in the resolution of which has been described as constituting 'modern Britain's founding myth'.[148] To Richard Attenborough, director of *Young Winston*, who also served in the wartime RAF, Churchill was 'the lion who looked after us all'. Without him, Attenborough believed, Britons would not have had the courage to continue fighting Hitler.[149] To those growing up in the shadow of the Second World War, Churchill assumed a similar paternal shape. As one member of that generation wrote:

> I remember some years back seeing a documentary on Churchill's life which ended with his funeral (which I can still remember vaguely as a child) and feeling inconsolable grief for a few minutes. There was something very big about Churchill and very small about the island he was trying to protect which I think resonates with the child within us and the father we have . . . lost.[150]

The cultural memorializations discussed in this chapter promulgated Churchill's status as national saviour to these and later generations of Britons. As noted earlier, Katharine Verdery suggested that in becoming statues, dead leaders were brought 'into the realm of the timeless or the sacred, like an icon'.[151] But if statues freeze time, the world around them still moves on, and while the British do not tend to tear down effigies of the great and the good, they do sometimes repurpose them. During London's May Day protests of 2000, a strip of grass was famously placed on the head of Churchill's statue in Parliament Square to give the impression he sported a Mohican haircut (Figure 3.8). Those responsible evaded the police, but James Matthews, the twenty-five-year-old former soldier who sprayed the mouth of the statue with red paint so it looked as if blood was dripping from it, did not. Matthews gave a full explanation for his actions, stating that

Churchill was an exponent of capitalism and of imperialism and anti-semitism. A Tory reactionary vehemently opposed to the emancipation of women and to independence in India. The media machine made this paunchy little man much larger than life—a colossal, towering figure of great stature and bearing with trademark cigar, bowler hat and V-sign. The reality was an often irrational, sometimes vainglorious leader whose impetuosity, egotism and bigotry on occasion cost many lives unnecessarily and caused much suffering that was needless and unjustified.[152]

By daubing Churchill's statue, Matthews hoped to turn the dominant Churchillian myth on its head. Ten years later in what the *Daily Mail* described as an attack on 'respect and common decency', young protestors at a demonstration against a significant increase in university tuition fees showed what they thought about that myth by urinating on the statue's plinth.[153] In 2012, in a more sober and focused way, so as to highlight the need to tackle problems associated with mental illness, campaigners placed a straightjacket on the statue, in recognition of Churchill's increasingly well-known bouts of depression.[154]

If contemporaries can give Churchill's solid bronze statue different meanings, his dramatizations were even more open to reworking. On the

Figure 3.8 Roberts-Jones's Churchill defaced, May Day 2000

big and small screen, Churchill now pops up anywhere and everywhere, in diverse iterations. A 2006 ITV adaptation of Agatha Christie's Miss Marple story, *The Sittaford Mystery*, set the tale in 1952 and had a benign prime minister give sound advice to a glamourous Conservative MP who the revised plot insisted wished to succeed him at Number 10. In a 2015 episode of the BBC situation comedy *Up the Women*, about an ineffective group of Edwardian suffragists, Churchill appeared as a bombastic, hard-line opponent who, when accused of having no respect for women, takes it as a compliment. The inaugural episode of the BBC drama series *Peaky Blinders* (2013–) set in 1919, saw Churchill unleash the forces of violent state oppression to restore order to working-class Birmingham, ordering that, 'if there are bodies to be buried, dig holes and dig them deep.'

Dramatists are, it seems, now freer than ever to imagine any Churchill they wish. Perhaps the last time censorship was exercised occurred in the 1982 Frankie Howerd BBC sitcom *Then Churchill Said to Me*. In this Howerd played a version of the crafty, lazy, and cowardly put-upon slave he had made famous in earlier historical comedies set in the Ancient World. For the purposes of this series he was Private Potts, the prime minister's batman in his underground Westminster war rooms. Each of its six episodes began with an excerpt from a Churchill speech and Howerd in the prime minister's chair greeting the audience with a V sign. Howerd then proceeded to mock the speech, often unconsciously echoing Richard Burton's earlier angry claim that sometimes his words made no sense. If referred to many times, Churchill nonetheless never appears, apart from his discarded cigar butts which Potts sells to American service personnel. *Then Churchill Said to Me* was low *lèse-majesté* comedy, mostly comprising laboured double entendres such as the repeated claim that the most important room in the complex is marked 'W.C.'. If this was an anti-heroic view of the war, the Churchill legend was never challenged, in the series theme tune it was even celebrated. But, as luck would have it, *Then Churchill Said to Me* was set to be broadcast just as the Falklands War blew up. With the BBC under attack from Prime Minister Margaret Thatcher for what she saw as its unpatriotic news coverage of the conflict and fearing the series would give offence at this sensitive time, it was shelved, not to appear on the BBC until 2000.[155]

From once being afraid to present him except as a spectral presence, film and TV producers are now responsible for a contemporary confusion of Churchills. A diverse Britain now has a diversity of Churchills. There are still those like Jim Sweeny, who in 1965 pulled the gun carriage upon which rested Churchill's coffin from Westminster to St Paul's, who recall the occasion fifty later with tears in their eyes.[156] And there are others like Arthur Matthews who look upon the funeral as comically anachronistic. Together with Matt Berry, Matthews wrote the cult Channel 4 sitcom *Toast*. A 2013 episode reveals that the bizarre Stephen Toast and his equally eccentric friend Ed Howzer-Black watch a recording of Churchill's state funeral every year. As Matthews relates, 'it just seemed a good fit for two old-school actors who believe that things were better in the old days to watch an event which conjured up memories of Empire and victory over Germany in World War 2.'[157]

Within this chaos of meaning, Churchill's dark side still remains largely unexplored. We await a screen writer and production company brave enough to ignore audience preferences and take on his attitude to India, and not pull their punches.[158] In contrast, the wartime iconic figure remains visible within the dramatic swirl, albeit in forms that would have foxed the Dean of St Paul's. When Doctor Who is greeted by the wartime prime minister at the height of the London Blitz in the 2010 episode *Victory of the Daleks* they do so as old friends. For fans of the series had created a detailed backstory for the pair, which involved the Doctor appearing at various times in Churchill's life.[159] In the episode, Churchill's greatness is confirmed, despite having inadvertently given the evil Daleks a foothold on Earth. Thus, Amy, the Doctor's young companion tells him: 'you're a beacon of hope' (Figure 3.9). And while the prime minister fails to persuade the Doctor to help him beat the Nazis after he has seen off the Daleks, the Time Lord declares: 'The world doesn't need me. The world has Winston Churchill.'

The film *Jackboots on Whitehall* ostensibly parodies hyper-patriotic movies about the war by imagining a Nazi invasion of Britain during which it satirizes one of Churchill's speeches by having him state, 'Never in the field of human conflict was so much buggered up by so few for so many.' But the movie still has the prime minister, albeit as an animated puppet, defiantly wield a Tommy Gun on the steps of 10 Downing Street

Figure 3.9 Churchill as the 'beacon of hope' in *Doctor Who*

and lead his ragbag army to victory over the invader (Figure 3.10). As ever, Churchill is part of a wider international cultural process, in which patriotic icons have become embroiled in various anachronistic narratives, the relationship between past and present, the invented and the imagined having been thrown into apparent chaos.[160]

In more straightforward ways the pivotal importance of 1940 and Churchill's critical role within it continues to be reiterated, if recalibrated, most obviously in *Darkest Hour*. In 2004 and across three hours the BBC docudrama *Dunkirk* faithfully reconstructed events based on eyewitness accounts. While its focus was on the desperate events in France, it nonetheless showed Churchill rejecting attempts to abandon the fight and make peace with Germany. During one especially defiant Churchill speech, played by Simon Russell Beale, the 'drama stopped and reality took over', according to the military historian John

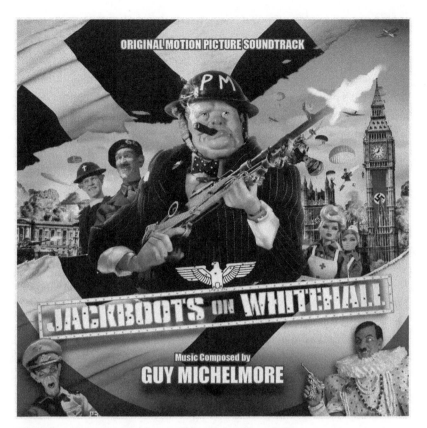

Figure 3.10 A parodic—but still heroic?—Churchill

Keegan, who reviewed the production.[161] A year later, to mark the 40th anniversary of Churchill's death, BBC Radio 4 broadcast Robin Glendinning's drama-documentary *Playing for Time: Three Days in May 1940*. This showed how the prime minister's faith in the British people's fortitude strengthened his resolve to reject Lord Halifax's proposal that Britain, with the outcome of the Dunkirk evacuation still uncertain, seek peace with Germany. Six years later Ben Brown's stage play *Three Days in May* covered the exact same moment, although he presented Churchill as momentarily wobbling over whether to sue for peace. Both works, however, innovatively suggest that behind the famous declamatory rhetoric lay a Churchill who was a skilful manipulator of men.[162] Glendinning and Brown also give Labour ministers Clement

Attlee and Arthur Greenwood—who barely feature in *Darkest Hour* and earlier dramas that cover this ground—more importance than hitherto in supporting Churchill. Despite that, however, for them Churchill remains the crucial and singular figure in determining that Britain should fight on. Brown's play even ends by quoting Stalin, who said of that period: 'he could think of no other instance in history when the future of the world depended on the courage of one man.'

Churchill continues to play a part in Britain's political culture. If his corpse lies quietly in St Michael's parish cemetery in Bladon, Oxfordshire, he is figuratively reanimated at regular intervals and for increasingly miscellaneous purposes. The myth of the Great Man who saved Britain as the country stood Alone during its Finest Hour retains its hold over the popular imagination, but time has allowed it to be finessed, challenged, and even mocked. In Britain they do not disinter their leaders or pull down their statues, but Churchill's body is something to which they—with more than a little help from some Americans friends—return again and again upon which to write stories about who they were and who they are and who they might become.

Epilogue

On 24 July 2019, Boris Johnson at last fulfilled his long-standing ambition to become prime minister. Having accepted the Queen's commission to form a government, he stood at a lectern in Downing Street and argued that it was time 'to recover our natural and historic role as an enterprising, outward-looking and truly global Britain, generous in temper and engaged with the world'.[1] The speech did not include any Churchill quotations, although the next day in the House of Commons he spoke of 'bend[ing] our sinews to the task', an obvious sub-Churchillian trope.[2] Perhaps overt references were unnecessary. After all, during his campaign to become Conservative Party leader, Johnson had been unafraid to echo Churchill, as when, speaking to activists in London, he commented that 'the hour is darkest before the dawn.' The reference was to the movie *Darkest Hour*, which dramatized Churchill's decision to fight on against Germany in 1940. This was an evocation of the Churchillian past rather than a literal reference. But such are the workings of mythic thought.[3]

This, of course, built on an established pattern. During the 2016 referendum campaign Johnson claimed to see parallels between the choice that confronted Britain in 1940 and the decision then facing voters.[4] Later, as he battled to grasp the keys to Number 10, Johnson continued to plough this fertile soil. Ninety-five per cent of Conservative Party members looked upon Churchill with favour, making him the most popular of their former leaders.[5] Remarkably, this meant they regarded Churchill more positively than did the British public during the Second World War itself.[6] True, only 4 per cent of Britons considered Johnson himself to be 'Churchillian', but the figure was surely higher among the mostly elderly, well-off Tory members who had the final pick of leader.[7]

Certainly, some influential media figures took the comparison seriously. Andrew Roberts believed he saw in Johnson the 'ability to inspire hope in others' which showed he had 'learnt some lessons from the great man'. In anticipating his election as party leader Roberts argued Johnson also needed to 'to show remarkable boldness' the moment he crossed the threshold of Number 10, just as Churchill had in May 1940. So far as Roberts was concerned, this meant proroguing Parliament in order to get through a No Deal, if that was required to ensure Britain left the EU as scheduled, on 31 October 2019. This would, he argued, be Johnson's 'Churchill moment'.[8] Others took a different view. Max Hastings, Johnson's former boss at the *Daily Telegraph*, was like Roberts a Churchill biographer and a Conservative, but believed Britain should remain in the EU. Hastings thought Johnson closer to the inept comic character Alan Partridge than to Churchill. Drawing a very different lesson from the same comparison used by Roberts, Hastings argued Churchill—unlike Johnson—was a 'profoundly serious human being' who far 'from perceiving anything glorious about standing alone in 1940 [...] knew that all difficult issues must be addressed with allies and partners'.[9]

Yet the most significant Churchillian moment of the leadership campaign involved the revelation of an episode that had taken place the year before. Alison Klayman, a film-maker who was about to release a documentary on the alt-right white nationalist and former Trump adviser Steve Bannon, unveiled footage of her subject captured on 16 July 2018. On the face of it, the big revelation was that, in spite of Johnson's previous suggestion that such claims were 'a lefty delusion', he and Bannon had been in close touch. Bannon explained that the two men had 'gone back and forth over text [message]' as Johnson drafted his resignation statement as Foreign Secretary. Behind this, though, was a shared affinity, captured in Bannon's rambling comments: 'Boris is a journalist, before he was Mayor of London, before he was Foreign Secretary, wrote a great book on Churchill, that's one of the things I did tell him over the weekend, that his great love of Churchill, his great study of Churchill, he wrote a really fantastic book for a modern audience on Churchill.'[10]

These remarks were more significant than they first appear. Bannon likes to refer to a Chinese word *'laobaixing'* meaning 'old 100 names', which refers to the common people, to which he claims to belong. 'The "old 100 names" is basically the working class of China, which is always getting screwed over by every emperor. It's the backbone of society', Bannon told another interviewer.

I say 'old hundred names' is nothing but the 'deplorables', and that's what we see everywhere, the same working-class people, that same working class that had Churchill's back to take the Nazis on, and I think there was a lot of the same elements that were there then were also apparent in Brexit.[11]

For Bannon, the working-class is racialized as white. What he sees in Churchill, then, and also in Johnson, are figures committed to a global, white, Anglo-Saxon Commonwealth. International white patriotism is to him more important than more parochial national patriotisms. Here we see, in Bannon's mind, the realization of the race-empire envisaged by Anglo-world Victorian thinkers. As Duncan Bell has explained:

It was common to refer to the race itself as an actor—as doing, thinking, feeling. But Angloworld discourse often went further, implying that the 'nervous system' and 'brain' [formed by communications technology] allowed a form of distributed intelligence, deliberation, and decision-making. Communications infrastructure was envisaged as a constitutive element of the Anglo-Saxon or English-speaking peoples.[12]

This deep well of racist cosmopolitanism was what Churchill drew upon when in 1943—following a passage about the merits of Basic English as a future international language—he said that 'The empires of the future are the empires of the mind.'[13] Some might think that linking Churchill, Johnson, Bannon, and the weaponization of social media for white nationalist purposes is a stretch. Yet for Bannon, at least, the connections are clear—and while 'the reality-based community' sits and wonders whether they really hold up, Boris Johnson has entered Number 10 and, as we finish this book—is planning a No Deal Brexit on behalf, as he no doubt sees it, of Global Britain's 'old 100 names'. The 'Darkest Hour' may be yet to come. Or perhaps by the time our book's been published, it will already have arrived.

Endnotes

Introduction

1. Richard Toye, 'Churchill (in)flexible', in Étienne François and Thomas Serrier (eds), *Europa: Notre Histoire* (Paris: Les Arènes, 2017), 523–6.
2. Above all, Claude Lévi-Strauss, *Totemism* (London: Penguin, 1969), with its scintillating introduction by Roger Poole.
3. Roland Barthes, *Mythologies* (London: Vintage, 1993), 131–2.
4. Barthes, *Mythologies*, 154, 183, and 168, emphasis added.
5. Christopher Hill, 'The Norman Yoke', in John Saville (ed.), *Democracy and the Labour Movement. Essays in Honour of Dona Torr* (London: Lawrence & Wishart, 1954).
6. For theorizations of this approach, the most fruitful starting point remains Peter Stallybrass and Allon White, *The Politics and Poetics of Transgression* (Ithaca: Cornell UP, 1986).
7. @Conservatives, 6.11 a.m., 24 Jan. 2019 Tweet; @traquir, 12.57 p.m., 25 Jan. 2019 Tweet.
8. 'Churchill: "More blood on his hands than Hitler"', *The Citizen* (Gloucester), 12 Oct. 1951, quotes a local Labour councillor to this effect. (Copy in Conservative Party Archive, CRD 2/47/6, Bodleian Library, Oxford.) Raphael Lemkin coined the term 'genocide' in 1944. Thirty years later, the actor Richard Burton accused Churchill of advocating it, with particular reference to comments that he allegedly made about wiping out the Japanese. ('To Play Churchill Is to Hate Him', *New York Times*, 24 Nov. 1974).
9. *Daily Mirror* (25 Oct. 1951).
10. 'Churchill: The Nation's Farewell', BBC1 (28 Jan. 2015).
11. Interview with Jeremy Paxman, 'The One Show', BBC1 (23 Jan. 2015). The media controversy began before the programme was broadcast.
12. Randolph Churchill, 'Sir Winston Churchill Would Make Mincemeat of Paxman' (21 Jan. 2015), https://www.telegraph.co.uk/history/11357871/Sir-Winston-Churchill-would-make-mincemeat-of-Paxman.html (accessed 16 June 2019).
13. https://www.independent.co.uk/arts-entertainment/music/news/geri-halliwell-horner-interview-spice-girls-reunion-winston-churchill-original-a8794446.html
14. Boris Johnson, 'The Rest of The World believes in Britain. It's Time That We Did Too', *Daily Telegraph* (16 July 2018).

15. https://www.dailymail.co.uk/news/article-2680183/Is-EU-just-German-racket-Europe-Nearly-25-years-ago-Tory-minister-told-DOMINIC-LAWSON-lost-job-firestorm-followed-right-along.html

16. https://www.telegraph.co.uk/news/2016/05/14/boris-johnson-interview-we-can-be-the-heroes-of-europe-by-voting/

17. https://gerardbattenmep.co.uk/2016/05/16/boris-hitler-and-the-european-union/

18. https://twitter.com/nigel_farage/status/889971797386514434?lang=en

19. https://www.express.co.uk/news/uk/1125162/Brexit-News-Ann-Widdecombe-news-update-latest-party

20. https://twitter.com/Nigel_Farage/status/980175102456279041

21. https://www.express.co.uk/news/uk/1147508/Nigel-Farage-brexit-party-big-vision-rally-birmingham-air-raid-sirens-world-war-2

22. https://www.nytimes.com/2009/09/19/world/europe/19iht-letter.html

23. Nicolas Foulkes, 'Times Must Be Hard. They Are Running Those Old Ads Again', *Independent on Sunday* (17 May 2009).

24. https://www.telegraph.co.uk/news/politics/4935429/BNP-uses-Polish-Spitfire-in-anti-immigration-poster.html

25. J.H. Plumb, 'Churchill as Historian', in A.J.P. Taylor (ed.), *Churchill. Four Faces and the Man* (Harmondsworth: Penguin, 1973), 123.

Chapter 1

1. Winston S. Churchill, 'The Scaffolding of Rhetoric' (unpublished; Nov. 1897), https://winstonchurchill.org/wp-content/uploads/2016/06/THE_SCAFFOLDING_OF_RHETORIC.pdf

2. J.B. Priestley, *Out of the People* (London: Collins, 1941), 110.

3. Boris Johnson, 'Cancel the Guilt Trip', *Spectator* (2 Feb. 2002), when postcolonial rule in Africa was exercising him.

4. Elizabeth Bowen, *In The Heat of the Day* (London: Vintage, 1998; first pub., 1948), 92.

5. Robert Rhodes James explains why: *Churchill: A Study in Failure* (Harmondsworth: Penguin, 1973).

6. Winston Churchill, 'Their Finest Hour' (4 June 1940), in Robert Rhodes James (ed.), *His Complete Speeches, 1897–1963. Vol. VI. 1935–1942* (New York: Chelsea House, 1983), 6231–8.

7. For the telephone, Andrew Roberts, *Churchill. Walking With Destiny* (London: Allen Lane, 2018), 11.

8. According to *Newsweek* (11 Feb. 2018), president Trump was so moved by the film he expressed the wish to visit Churchill's Cabinet War Rooms in Whitehall. On his first official visit to London this never happened, but he did dine at Blenheim Palace, Churchill's birthplace. A year later, on his state visit, the tour took place.

9. For Alexander Boris de Pfeffel Johnson: there occurs a revealing photo of two overgrown Eton boys—Johnson and Charles Moore, onetime editor of the *Telegraph*—at the East Sussex and Romney Marsh Hunt, clad in the appropriate gear. They *look* as if they know the whole thing to be an end-of-the-pier, Archie Rice masquerade: Andrew Gimson, *Boris. The Rise of Boris Johnson* (London: Simon & Schuster, 2006). Gimson shares Johnson's affiliations to private schooling, Oxford, and the *Spectator*; their shared history is evident throughout. For an evocative correlate: Boris Johnson, 'Politics', in Rachel Johnson (ed.), *The Oxford Myth* (London: Weidenfeld & Nicolson, 1988). And Sonia Purnell, *Just Boris: A Tale of Blond Ambition—A Biography of Boris Johnson* (London: Aurum Press, 2012).

10. Heathcote Williams demonstrates a relentless *ad hominem* hostility toward Johnson in his *Brexit Boris. From Mayor to Nightmare* (London: Public Reading Rooms, 2016). This, though, substantially does nothing to damage his historical case.

11. Jennifer Rankin and Jim Waterson, 'How Boris Johnson's Brussels-Bashing Stories Shaped British Politics', *Observer* (14 July 2019).

12. Boris Johnson, *Desert Island Discs* (BBC Radio 4, 30 Oct., 2005).

13. But not to universal conservative acclaim. Simon Heffer, for one, declared Johnson's interpretation 'a travesty': 'The Churchill Myth', *New Statesman* (9 Jan. 2015). Heffer had been part of the *Spectator* crew while Johnson had been editor, though he was hostile to Johnson's bid to become Mayor of London in 2008. Heffer is never reticent in pursuing his own species of undiluted, high-proof conservatism, as he displays in his biographies of Thomas Carlyle and Enoch Powell; or in a different domain of the cultural world, in his loving recuperation of his own boyhood dreamworld, mediated through his movie memories, which provides a heady spectacle of a man radically out of time: 'Fifties British War Films. Days of Glory' (BBC4, 1 Jan. 2013). For Heffer the genre marked the aesthetic pinnacle of British cinema. The connection between the war movies and mythic Churchill is close.

14. Some of Johnson's books defy readers making headway beyond the earliest pages: Harry Mount (ed.), *The Wit and Wisdom of Boris Johnson* (London: Bloomsbury, 2013). Mount was a crony of Johnson's at the *Telegraph*. In response Jonathan Coe noted that Johnson 'has become his own satirist: safe, above all, in the knowledge that the best way to make sure the satire aimed at you is gentle and unchallenging is to create it yourself', 'Sinking Giggling Into the Sea', *London Review of Books* (18 July 2013). In this Johnson was following in the footsteps of Churchill: there are countless collections parading his 'wit and wisdom': for example, Richard M. Langworth, *Churchill's Wit. The Definitive Collection* (London: Ebury, 2009). Lordy, Lord.

15. Boris Johnson, *The Churchill Factor. How One Man Made History* (London: Hodder & Stoughton, 2015), 10. In this he was repeating the sentiments of Mrs Thatcher, who'd earlier claimed: 'Winston Churchill illustrates dramatically that

whatever theory one espouses, a place has to be found for personality, for leadership, for individual drive and determination, for history has shown many times that the fortunes of nations can be transformed, for good or ill, by the character and deeds of individuals', 'Sir Winston Churchill, Fifty Years On' (9 May 1990), cited by John Ramsden, 'How Winston Churchill Became "The Greatest Living Englishman"', *Contemporary British History*, 12/3 (1998), 22.

16. Johnson, *The Churchill Factor*, 34.

17. Richard Evans, '"One Man Who Made History" by Another Who Seems Just to Make It Up: Boris on Churchill', *New Statesman* (13 Nov. 2014); Steven Fielding, 'Boris Johnson Makes a Bid to Appropriate the "Churchill Brand"', *The Conversation* (27 Oct. 2014), https://theconversation.com/boris-johnson-makes-a-bid-to-appropriate-the-churchill-brand-33377

18. We follow Martin Gilbert, *Winston S. Churchill. Vol. VI. Finest Hour. 1939–1941* (London: Heinemann, 1983), 411–22. Churchill's morning began with his statement to the Commons on Belgium's surrender, which had occurred the previous evening with full effect from dawn on the 28th: Churchill, 'The Fall of Belgium' (28 May 1940) in *Complete Speeches. VI*, 6223–4.

19. Paul Addison, *The Road to 1945. British Politics and the Second World War* (London: Quartet, 1977), ch. 4, 'New Deal at Dunkirk'; and more recently, John Bew, *Citizen Clem. A Biography of Clement Attlee* (London: Riverun, 2016). This reading, while not overturned, is questioned by David Edgerton, *The Rise and Fall of the British Nation. A Twentieth-Century History* (London: Allen Lane, 2018).

20. For the younger Tories who moved into Churchill's slipstream, Lynne Olson, *Troublesome Young Men. The Churchill Conspiracy of 1940* (London: Bloomsbury, 2008). More details are available in Alistair Horne, *Macmillan, 1894–1956* (London: Macmillan, 1988); and Robert Rhodes James, *Bob Boothby. A Portrait* (London: Hodder & Stoughton, 1991).

21. Nicholas Shakespeare is good on Halifax the private man during these tempestuous days, and on his relationship with Lady Alexandra 'Baba' Metcalfe, Lord Curzon's daughter and wife of Major Edward 'Fruity' Metcalfe. They'd first met in Simla in 1926, when Halifax was viceroy, as her own father had been. This resituates the 1940 antagonism between Churchill and Halifax, bringing into play also the dynamics of the splits within the traditional colonial hierarchy; important in this regard were the divisions between the two of them over the Government of India Act of 1935, when Churchill positioned himself as the reactionary, and Halifax as the (relatively) less blood-curdling proponent of empire. *Six Minutes in May. How Churchill Unexpectedly Became Prime Minister* (London: Vintage, 2018).

22. Gilbert, *Finest Hour*, 422.

23. John Lukacs, whom we come to in a moment, is of the opinion that Churchill had already arranged this second meeting of the cabinet: *Five Days in London. May 1940* (New Haven: Yale UP, 1999), 183. He goes on to explain

that 'some'—unnamed historians—have called this a 'coup', although he doesn't believe it was such, 184.

24. Hugh Dalton, *The Fateful Years. Memoirs, 1939-1945* (London: Frederick Muller, 1957), 336. Ben Pimlott, *Hugh Dalton. A Life* (London: Macmillan, 1986) doesn't feel compelled to refer to the story, nor does he include it in his edition of Hugh Dalton, *Political Diary. 1918-40; 1945-60* (London: Cape, 1986).

25. Roy Jenkins, *Churchill* (London: Pan, 2002; first pub., 2001), 608. For Roberts, 'This was no mere bravado', *Churchill*, 547.

26. Winston S. Churchill, *The Second World War. Vol II. Their Finest Hour* (London: Cassell, 1949), 88.

27. Johnson, *The Churchill Factor*, 18.

28. This deep suspicion and antagonism run through Julian Jackson's riveting story, *A Certain Idea of France. The Life of Charles de Gaulle* (London: Allen Lane, 2018).

29. Bill Schwarz, 'Conservatism and Caesarism, 1903-1922', in Mary Langan and Bill Schwarz (eds), *Crises in the British State, 1880 to 1930* (London: Hutchinson, 1985); and Schwarz, 'Ancestral Citizens. Reflections on British Conservatism', *New Formations*, 28 (1996).

30. George Dangerfield, *The Strange Death of Liberal England* (London: Paladin, 1970; first pub., 1935), 31. Who could be identified as a 'man of destiny' of course was an open matter. Neville Chamberlain was sure he should be counted among their number: Shakespeare, *Six Minutes in May*, 12. For the continuing history: Jo Fox, 'Winston Churchill and the "Men of Destiny": Leadership and the Role of the Prime Minister in Wartime Feature Films', in Richard Toye and Julie Gottlieb (eds), *Making Reputations. Power, Persuasion and the Individual in Modern British Politics* (London: I.B. Tauris, 2005).

31. Harold Nicolson, a self-styled aesthete and aficionado of the operations of the state, imagines this counterfactual scenario in his novel, *Public Faces* (Harmondsworth: Penguin, 1945; first pub., 1932): 'The wedge driven into the Third National Coalition by the Anglo-Egyptian crisis of December 1935, the subsequent "Union Jack" election and the return to power of the Churchill-Mosley combination in March 1936', 5.

32. Cited in Johnson, *The Churchill Factor*, 185.

33. Antonio Gramsci, *Selections from the Prison Notebooks* (London: Lawrence & Wishart, 1973), 220.

34. Churchill, 'Scaffolding of Rhetoric'. For Johnson's discussion of Churchill's thinking on this matter, *The Churchill Factor*, 88. The theme recurs in Winston S. Churchill, *Lord Randolph Churchill* (2 vols) (London: Macmillan, 1906); and in his only published fiction, *Savrola* (Bath: Cedric Chivers, 1973; first pub., 1900). For reflections on the relations between mass democracy and political rhetoric, Richard Toye, *Rhetoric. A Very Short Introduction* (Oxford: Oxford UP, 2013); Bill Schwarz, 'The Language of Constitutionalism. Baldwinite Conservatism', in *Formations of Nation and People* (London: Routledge & Kegan

Paul, 1984); and Schwarz, 'Politics and Rhetoric in the Age of Mass Culture', *History Workshop Journal*, 46 (1998).

35. Cited in Johnson, *The Churchill Factor*, 91–3; originally in a letter to his mother, 1897, and quoted from Norman Rose, *Churchill: An Unruly Life* (London: I.B. Tauris, 2009), 45. The complete quote from Rose here is reproduced here.

36. Churchill, 'Their Finest Hour' (18 June 1940). He delivered the speech first in the House of Commons, where it was well received. He was persuaded to relay it again that evening on the BBC. He was tired and he was faced with a microphone instead of a live audience. It was commonly perceived to have been a flop: Richard Toye, *The Roar of the Lion. The Untold Story of Churchill's World War II Speeches* (Oxford: Oxford UP, 2015), 57–9. A few days later, and repeated in his war memoirs nine years after, Churchill was claiming 'Rhetoric was no guarantee for survival'. On 26 June he cabled the British ambassador in Washington, Lord Lothian, saying: 'I don't think words count for much now.' His views on the power of rhetoric were as mobile as his views on anything else, dependent in part on the success or failure of his last speech. Both cited in John Lukacs, *Blood, Toil, Tears and Sweat. The Dire Warning* (New York: Basic Books, 2008), 115 and 116.

37. Johnson, *The Churchill Factor*, 93.

38. For a prescient reflection on Johnson's future career, predicting that his political prestige would be *enhanced* by his TV buffoonery, Mark Lawson, 'Cometh the Hour...', *Guardian* (29 Oct. 2003).

39. Johnson employs the phrase, although it has a longer genealogy. Its provenance is not clear. It's possible that the term originated with the journalist Beverley Nichols. Or maybe it was first coined by the celebrated US journalist, Ed Murrow, who was stationed in London during the Blitz and whose broadcasts home caught the popular imagination, both in the US and the UK. Andrew Roberts, *'The Holy Fox'. A Biography of Lord Halifax*, presents these events from Halifax's point of view, 220–7. Yet notwithstanding Roberts' sympathy for Halifax, his reading of the situation converges with Johnson's. For Roberts, Halifax is equated with reason, Churchill with theatrics. His final verdict is to conclude that 'Halifax had attempted to bring logic and reason to a problem long since devoid of either', 226. The idea of 'theatrics' in relation to Churchill comes from Alexander Cadogan, permanent undersecretary for foreign affairs and a supporter of the strategies of Chamberlain and Halifax: *Diaries of Sir Alexander Cadogan, O.M., 1938–1945*, ed., David Dilks (London: Putnam, 1972), 292, from the entry for 29 May 1940. On the 26th he'd complained that Churchill was 'too rambling and romantic and sentimental and temperamental', and on the 27th that he, Cadogan, was bored with Churchill's 'rhodomontades', 290 and 291.

40. Gerry Hassan, 'Why Churchill Still Matters. The Power of the Past and the Postponement of the Future', *Soundings*, 70 (2018). There's a further dimension to these memories of 1940 in their dystopian mirror image, in the vortex of imagining how things would have turned out had the Allies been defeated.

Fintan O'Toole, *Heroic Failure. Brexit and the Politics of Pain* (London: Head of Zeus, 2018), a magisterially profane interpretation from Ireland, ch. 2: 'SS-GB: Life in Occupied England'. Older—pre-Brexit—is Malcolm Smith, *Britain and 1940: History, Myth and Popular Memory* (London: Routledge, 2000).

41. John Charmley, *Lord Lloyd and the Decline of the British Empire* (London: Weidenfeld & Nicolson, 1987).

42. John Charmley, *Churchill. The End of Glory. A Political Biography* (London: Hodder & Stoughton, 1993), in which he argued for the long-term merits—that is, for Charmley, the salvation of Empire—in arriving at an accommodation with Germany. See too, David Carlton, 'Churchill in 1940: Myth and Reality', *World Affairs*, 156/2 (1993). The exact terms of the divide at this point between Churchill and Halifax remains unresolved in the historiography.

43. Charmley, *Churchill*, 3 and 649. This coincided with Clive Ponting, *Churchill* (London: Sinclair Stevenson, 1994) who, from some way distant from Charmley on the political spectrum, promised to deliver 'a less soothing view', p. xii. Published somewhat later was Gordon Corrigan, *Blood, Sweat and Arrogance: the Myths of Churchill's War* (London: Weidenfeld & Nicolson, 2006). The author was an experienced soldier who argued that although Britain possessed the most technologically argument in the world, its training for policing the Empire disqualified it for fighting a major land war. The navy and the air force prevented Britain from losing the war, while the army didn't win it. Churchill's military experience was 'almost nil', 24.

44. Lord Moran, *Winston Churchill. The Struggle for Survival, 1940–1965* (London: Sphere, 1968), 310.

45. Andrew Gamble offers an outstanding analysis: *Between Europe and America. The Future of British Politics* (Houndmills: Palgrave Macmillan, 2003).

46. Paul Addison, 'The Political Beliefs of Winston Churchill', *Transactions of the Royal Historical Society*, vol. 30 (1980); his *Churchill on the Home Front, 1900–1955* (London: Pimlico, 1993); and Bill Schwarz, 'The Tide of History. The Reconstruction of Conservatism, 1945–1951', in Nick Tiratsoo (ed.), *The Attlee Years* (London: Pinter, 1991).

47. Charmley, *Churchill*, 647.

48. In this regard Churchill becomes a *lieu de mémoire*. For a discussion of Pierre Nora's use of the concept, Bill Schwarz, 'Memory, Modernity, Temporality', in Susannah Radstone and Bill Schwarz (eds), *Memory: Histories, Theories, Debates* (New York: Fordham UP, 2010).

49. When the new UK polymer banknotes were introduced in September 2016, the image of Elizabeth Fry, the prison reformer, was removed from the five-pound note and replaced by Churchill. The governor of the Bank of England, the Canadian Mark Carney, had unveiled the new note the previous June at Blenheim Palace, Churchill's birthplace. He took the opportunity to reflect on history: 'The new fiver will commemorate the achievements of the only prime minister to win the Nobel Prize for literature and one of the greatest statesmen of

all time—Sir Winston Churchill. As he himself said, "a nation that forgets its past has no future". Our banknotes are repositories of the United Kingdom's collective memory and, like Churchill, our new polymer notes will stand the test of time', *Guardian* (9 Sept. 2016). A handful of grammarians was disturbed that Churchill's words reproduced on the notes—'I have nothing to offer but blood, toil, tears and sweat'—appeared without quotation marks, *Telegraph* (28 April 2017). Sean O'Grady, 'Winston Churchill: Legend or Myth, Why Do We Want Him on the New Fiver?', *Independent* (15 Sept. 2016).

50. Anthony Barnett is good on this: *The Lure of Greatness. England's Brexit and America's Trump* (London: Unbound, 2017).

51. Farage can be heard and seen on https://www.independent.co.uk/news/uk/politics/eu-referendum-nigel-farage-4am-victory-speech-the-text-in-full-a7099156.html

52. Johnson, *The Churchill Factor*, 224.

53. In this light readers may wish to consult Johnson's 'comic' novel about an Islamic terror attack on Westminster: *Seventy-Two Virgins* (London: HarperCollins, 2005; first pub., 2004). Fintan O'Toole offers a bravura reading: 'The Ham of Fate', *New York Review of Books* (15 Aug. 2019).

54. Winston S. Churchill, *My Early Life* (London: Thornton Butterworth, 1930), 73.

55. Paul Addison, 'Churchill's Three Careers', in David Cannadine and Roland Quinault (eds), *Winston Churchill in the Twenty-First Century* (Cambridge: Cambridge UP, 2004), 9.

56. Obituaries appeared on 6 May 2019 in the *New York Times* and the *Washington Post*.

57. John Lukacs, 'Churchill's Funeral', in his *Churchill. Visionary. Statesman. Historian* (New Haven: Yale UP, 2002), 163.

58. John Lukacs, *The Duel. Hitler vs Churchill: 10 May–31 July 1940* (London: Bodley Head, 1990); the US edition, published one year later, took a different title: *The Duel. 10 May–31 July 1940: The Eighty Day Struggle between Churchill and Hitler* (New York: Ticknor & Fields, 1991).

59. Lukacs, 'Preface', *Churchill*, p. xi.

60. Lukacs, 'Churchill's Funeral', 172.

61. Richard Crossman, *The Crossman Diaries: Selections from the Diaries of a Cabinet Minister* (London: Hamish Hamilton and Jonathan Cape, 1979), 66; entry for 30 Jan. 1965.

62. Lukacs, 'Churchill's Funeral', 164–7 and 172.

63. Lukacs, 'Churchill's Funeral', 184.

64. Lukacs, 'Churchill's Funeral', 172.

65. Lukacs, 'Churchill's Funeral', 192.

66. Lukacs, 'Churchill's Funeral', 175.

67. Examples are legion. A random illustration will have to do. 'Halifax was a very British type, in the sense that he knew how to adjust his mind to circumstance, rather than attempt to adjust circumstances to his ideas. This does not mean that he was a hypocrite or opportunist—except in the habitual Anglo-Saxon way which is not really Machiavellian, since the innate practice of that kind of English hypocrisy often serves purposes that are higher than those of individual prestige or profit', Lukacs, *The Duel. Hitler vs Churchill*, 97.

68. Lukacs's flurry of Churchill monographs coincided with two volumes which strained to work through the wall of myth-making: Geoffrey Best, *Churchill. A Study in Greatness* (London: Penguin, 2002; first pub., 2001), who endeavours to bring the 'super-real' Churchill of May 1940 down to the historical-real, p. ix; and, particularly, Paul Addison, *Churchill. The Unexpected Hero* (Oxford: Oxford UP, 2005).

69. Isaiah Berlin, 'Mr Churchill', *The Atlantic* (Sept. 1949), republished as *Mr Churchill in 1940* (London: John Murray, n.d., 1949?/1950?). However, the mythic and the historical were inseparable from the start. In this Winston S. Churchill's six volumes of *The Second World War* (London: Cassell, 1948–54) were of the first importance. The most sustained subsequent analysis, with a revealing title, is David Reynolds, *In Command of History. Churchill Writing and Fighting the Second World War* (New York: Basic Books, 2005), although earlier and wider in scope is John Ramsden, *'That Will Depend on Who Writes History'. Winston Churchill as His Own Historian* (London: Department of History, Queen Mary and Westfield College, 1997); Ramsden, 'How Winston Churchill Became "The Greatest Living Englishman"'; and his later, comprehensive, *Man of the Century. Winston Churchill and His Legend Since 1945* (London: HarperCollins, 2002), which has the virtue of attending to the global ramifications of legendary Churchill. On Trump's state visit to Britain his gift from the queen was a first edition of Churchill's *The Second World War*: *Telegraph* (3 June 2019).

70. Ramsden, *Man of the Century*; Martin Gilbert, *Churchill and America* (London: Simon & Schuster, 2005); Christopher Hitchens, *Blood, Class and Empire. The Enduring Anglo-American Relationship* (London: Atlantic Books, 2006; first pub., 1990), 'Preface', and chs. 7–9; and Neal Ascherson, 'Atlantic Fogies Flatter America', *Observer* (19 Jan. 1986). We're grateful to Ascherson for searching out and sending us a copy of his article.

71. Perry Anderson, 'Components of the National Culture', *New Left Review*, I/50 (1968). This is a *tour de force*. Berlin himself features in Anderson's roster of Central and Eastern European intellectuals who found themselves on British shores in the period before the Second World War. It's remarkable, though, that in the fifty-four pages of the article their shared Jewish heritage is not once mentioned.

72. For the politics of the management of the Churchill archives, which has done much to organize how he has been recalled, Warren Dockter and Richard Toye, 'Who Commanded History? Sir John Colville, Churchillian Networks, and the "Castlerosse Affair"', *Journal of Contemporary History*, 54/2 (2019).

73. For the larger context, providing effectively an authorized reading, Martin Gilbert, *Churchill and the Jews* (London: Simon & Schuster, 2008).

74. Cited in Arie M. Dubnov, *Isaiah Berlin. The Journey of a Jewish Liberal* (London: Palgrave, 2012), 156. This provides an incisive account of Berlin's mental world, full of thought.

75. Cited in Dubnov, *Isaiah Berlin*, 186.

76. Berlin, *Mr Churchill*, 33.

77. Berlin, *Mr Churchill*, 10, 12–3, and 19.

78. Dubnov, *Isaiah Berlin*, 188. Before the essay was published Berlin sent it to Deakin to look over, because 'I would not dream of wishing anything to appear which would in any way upset or annoy or even slightly irritate the Old Man', cited in Dubnov, *Isaiah Berlin*, 189.

79. In this instance Churchill of 1940 was conscripted as the (negative) foil to Tony Blair, on account of the latter's 'formalized and progressive destruction of the Cabinet system', David Owen, *Cabinet's Finest Hour. The Hidden Agenda of May 1940* (London: Haus, 2016), 259.

80. https://twitter.com/tradegovuk/status/1040903048892018688. This was the same Liam Fox who declared on 20 July 2017 that a new British trade deal with the EU would be 'one of the easiest in human history', cited in George Eaton, 'The Ship of State Goes Down', *New Statesman* (26 Oct. 2018).

81. Matthew Weaver, 'Theresa May Will Not Be Flying to Brussels in Spitfire, BBC Clarifies', *Guardian* (31 Jan. 2019).

82. Falling just outside our chronological scope, but important thematically, was the 2017 film titled simply, *Churchill*. This reconstructs Churchill's tribulations on the eve of the Normandy landings, showing him tormented by memories of Gallipoli. The role it gives Jan Christian Smuts is distinctive: he's dragooned (along with Eisenhower) to join with 'Clemmie's' ministrations to her husband, in a bid to temper Churchill's outlandishly rash strategic ideas. This provides an unusually domestic Smuts.

83. We follow here Richard Toye's response in the *Times Literary Supplement* (31 Oct. 2018).

84. The term itself originates with Niall Ferguson: Toye, *Times Literary Supplement*.

85. Roberts, *Churchill*, 982.

86. Roberts, *Churchill*, 977; for the historical record, Richard Toye, *Churchill's Empire. The World That Made Him and The World He Made* (London: Macmillan, 2010).

87. Roberts, *Churchill*, 39.

88. In popular fiction the irrepressible Michael Dobbs—Tory tyro; adviser to Mrs Thatcher; creator of *House of Cards*—has fashioned a panoramic Churchill, from Munich to Yalta: *Winston's War* (London: HarperCollins, 2002); *Never Surrender. A Novel of Winston Churchill* (London: HarperCollins, 2003); *Churchill's Hour* (London: HarperCollins, 2004), in which for some reason the liaison between Pamela Churchill, Churchill's daughter-in-law, and Averell Harriman, then serving as Roosevelt's special envoy to Europe, comprises much of the action; and closing with *Churchill's Triumph* (London: Headline, 2005). This last volume is much preoccupied with the matter of Churchill's legacy. In this Dobbs centrally locates the Yalta Conference and the fate of Poland, which complicate the judgement signalled in the book's title, 'triumph'. His argument only moves into the open as the quartet closes: 'As much as any single man, Winston Churchill preserved the liberties of the people of Britain. He was the man who guided them—dragged them, at times—through their finest hour. Yet the freedom of the peoples of Europe, finally secured only many years after his death [by which we take him to mean the destruction of the Soviet bloc], was still a greater triumph—perhaps his greatest triumph of all', 462.

89. Saurabh Dube, 'Myth, Symbols and Community: Satnampanth of Chhattisgarh', in Partha Chatterjee and Gyanendra Pandy (eds), *Subaltern Studies. Writings on South Asian History and Society. Vol. VII* (Delhi: Oxford UP, 1993), 133.

90. A further indication of how such sensibilities enter the professional historiography, in unexpected contexts: Bill Schwarz, 'An Unsentimental Education. John Darwin's Empire', *Journal of Commonwealth and Imperial History*, 43/1 (2015).

91. Paul Gilroy, *After Empire: Melancholia or Convivial Culture?* (London: Routledge, 2004).

92. Brexit supplies endless examples of the syndrome. Late in April 2017 the first meeting of the British negotiators with their future adversary, Michel Barnier, at a Downing Street dinner is characteristic. It indicates a blithe ignorance of the situation they were in. All was going to be speedily resolved. And Britain, in the vocabulary of the time, was to have its cake and eat it: Denis MacShane, *Brexit, No Exit. Why (In the End) Britain Won't Leave Europe* (London: I.B. Tauris, 2017), pp. xviii–xix.

93. Andrew Pulver, 'Winston Churchill of *Darkest Hour*. A Rebuke to Trump, Says Film's Director', *Guardian* (28 Sept. 2017).

94. A subordinate element in mythic Churchill comprises mythic Clementine, Churchill's wife. For a persuasive account of the subjective costs for the family of living, day by day, cheek by jowl, with the myth—with 'The Greatest Living Englishman'—Sonia Purnell, *First Lady. The Life and Wars of Clementine Churchill* (London: Aurum Press, 2016; first pub., 2015). More can be gleaned from Mary Soames, *Clementine Churchill. By Her Daughter* (Harmondsworth: Penguin, 1981; first pub., 1979); Mary Soames (ed.), *Speaking for Themselves:*

The Personal Letters of Winston and Clementine Churchill (London: Black Swan, 1999); and Helen Jones, '"Let Us Go Forward Together". Clementine Churchill and the Role of Personality in Wartime Britain', in Toye and Gottlieb, *Making Reputations*.

95. Toye, *Roar of the Lion*.

96. Johnson, *The Churchill Factor*; Nigel Farage, *Flying Free* (London: Biteback, 2010), and *The Purple Revolution. The Year That Changed Everything* (London: Biteback, 2015); Arron Banks, *The Bad Boys of Brexit. Tales of Mischief, Mayhem and Guerrilla Warfare in the EU Referendum Campaign* (London: Biteback, 2016) performs its own commitments to a masculinist *jacquerie* which seeks to turn back the history of the past half century. More is revealed in Owen Bennett, *Following Farage. On the Trail of the People's Army* (London: Biteback, 2015). Those with an iron disposition might in addition contemplate sampling Jacob Rees-Mogg, *The Victorians: Twelve Titans Who Forged Britain* (London: W.H. Allen, 2019).

97. Significant is Robert Gildea, *Empires of the Mind. The Colonial Past and the Politics of the Present* (Cambridge: Cambridge UP, 2019), which follows the argument condensed in his subhead: 'Brexit: The Revenge of Colonial Nostalgia', 231; and the anticipations of two prominent historians, Linda Colley, 'Brexiteers are Nostalgics in Search of a Lost Empire', *Financial Times* (22 April 2016); and Pankaj Mishra, 'Brexiteers Are Pining for Empire', *Bloomberg* (29 April 2016): https://www.bloomberg.com/view/articles/2016-04-29/brexit-supporters-are-pining-for-the-days-of-empire. Danny Dorling and Sally Tomlinson, *Rule Britannia. Brexit and the End of Empire* (London: Biteback, 2019) is interesting on the Brexit components of the story, although notwithstanding the title it displays barely any curiosity about what the end of empire either entailed in the past, or entails in the present.

98. J.B. Priestley, *Postscripts* (London: Heinemann, 1940), 39.

99. Steven Fielding, Peter Thompson, and Nick Tiratsoo, *England Arise! The Labour Party and Popular Politics in 1940s Britain* (Manchester: Manchester UP, 1995), which brings to light the discrepancies between the lived experience of the people and its (radical, leftish, mythic) representations.

100. Bill Schwarz, 'Forgetfulness. England's Discontinuous Histories', in Astrid Rasch and Stuart Ward (eds), *Embers of Empire in Brexit Britain* (London: Bloomsbury, 2019).

101. Ramsden, 'How Winston Churchill Became "The Greatest Living Englishman"', 2.

102. A parallel shift can be tracked in the popular press: A.C.H. Smith, with Elizabeth Imirizi and Trevor Blackwell, Paper Voices. *The Popular Press and Social Change, 1935–1965* (London: Chatto & Windus, 1975).

103. Priestley, *Postscripts*, 70; John Baxendale, '"I Had Seen a Lot of Englands". J.B. Priestley, Englishness and the People', *History Workshop Journal*, 51 (2007); and Vincent Brome, *J.B. Priestley* (London: Hamilton, 1988).

104. Priestley, *Postscripts*, 27.

105. Priestley, *Postscripts*, 3.

106. Priestley, *Postscripts*, 23.

107. Priestley, *Postscripts*, 63.

108. Priestley, *Out of the People*, 33.

109. Cato, *Guilty Men* (London: Gollancz, 1940). This was first published in July 1940. We have been using here the eighth impression. This too is dated July 1940. There has occurred a singular attempt to revive the *Guilty Men* intervention of 1940 as a broadside against the 'guilty' perpetrators of Brexit: 'Cato the Younger', *Guilty Men* (London: Biteback, 2017).

110. Charles Madge and Tom Harrison, *Britain by Mass Observation* (Harmondsworth: Penguin, 1939), 9.

111. *The Penguin Hansard. Vol. I. From Chamberlain to Churchill* (Harmondsworth: Penguin, 1940). For its demise, ordered from above, *House of Commons Debates* (6 Aug. 1940), vol. 364, cc. 37–837.

112. To follow a theme: as late as 1958 Ealing Studios released its feature film, *Dunkirk*, the first of a long succession of Dunkirk epics. Churchill barely figured: right at the start there's a fleeting moment when, bizarrely, he walks as if by happenstance across the path of a newsreel camera; and later a single mention, where a conscript expresses the hope that he might represent a new start.

    On the back of the success of *Dunkirk* the movie, the BBC's docudrama *Dunkirk* of 2004, in three episodes, was rushed out as a DVD in 2017. Intriguingly, it marks a throwback to earlier conceptions of May 1940, in which the people take centre stage. It zooms in on the catastrophe of Dunkirk: on the disintegration of the army, as an army, and on the various spirals of subjective disintegration experienced by those fleeing the terrors. It's brutal. The usual cinematic Churchill is evident, but the image is largely off-stage and doesn't stand as the principal conduit through which history is realized. The courage it depicts is of the popular, everyday, pragmatic variety, largely agnostic about any elevated patriotism and free from the flights of high rhetoric which Churchill made his own. From this vantage, the notion that the social actors are *making history* doesn't appear to be a prime mover in the minds of those who found themselves making courageous and desperate sacrifices. For a classic statement in this vein, in literary form, Alexander Baron's fine novel, *From the City, From the Plough* (London: Black Spring Press, 2010; first pub., 1948).

113. We need also to acknowledge how the role of the people in the drama of 1940 was translated, after the fact, into a formal historiography. Angus Calder's *The People's War* (1969) and Paul Addison's *The Road to 1945* (1975) worked to give war radicalism historical form. The political properties of this populism have been much debated, and its relations to the Labour victory of 1945 remain a matter of dispute. But that an identifiable radical sensibility existed, across the classes, and that it shaped the mental climate from which 1945 emerged, were

explanations which underwrote the Calder and Addison generation of historians. See too, for a different trajectory, Angus Calder, *The Myth of the Blitz* (London: Jonathan Cape, 1991).

114. Addison, *Churchill*, 169–70 and 250.

115. Priestley, *Out of the People*, 11.

116. For thinking of populism in these terms we draw from Ernesto Laclau, *Politics and Ideology in Marxist Theory: Capitalism, Fascism, Populism* (London: New Left Books, 1977); his *On Populist Reason* (London: Verso, 2018); and Chantal Mouffe, *For a Left Populism* (London: Verso, 2018). And for the ideological configuration which underwrote this manifestation of mythic Churchill, Kit Kowol, 'The Conservative Movement and Dreams of Britain's Post-War Future', *Historical Journal*, 62/2 (2019).

117. Max Hastings, *Finest Years. Churchill as Warlord, 1940–45* (London: Harper, 2010), pp. xvii–xviii.

118. Stuart Hall, 'The Social Eye of *Picture Post*', *Working Papers in Cultural Studies*, 2 (1972); Schwarz, 'The Tide of History', 154–5.

119. As an example, Anne Scott-James, 'Why Women Don't Have Babies. An Enquiry', *Picture Post* (13 Nov. 1943), an eloquent attack on state pronatalism from the perspective of a feminist inflected conception of democratic welfare.

120. As editor-in-chief of the *Telegraph* from 1986 to 1995 it would have been his formal decision to employ Johnson after he'd been fired by *The Times*. It's not clear, however, the degree to which this was his decision or that of the proprietor Conrad Black. Despite Hastings' and Black's shared reverence for Churchill, their political and professional temperaments were radically different: Gimson, *Boris*, 154–5.

121. Max Hastings' verdict on Boris Johnson, for example, is unqualified. He 'supposes himself to be Winston Churchill, while in reality being closer to Alan Partridge': 'I was Boris Johnson's Boss: He Is Utterly Unfit to Be Prime Minister', *Guardian* (24 June 2019). This had long been Hasting's estimation of Johnson, going back to the time when he had first won Michael Heseltine's old seat of Henley in 2001. Or in similar vein: Sonia Purnell, 'Boris Johnson's Biographer: I Know Too Well the Fire and Fury Lurking Behind That Smile', *The Times* (23 June 2019).

122. For an early anticipation see E.P. Thompson's fulminations against the *Daily Express* journalist, and practitioner of the dark arts in political life, Chapman Pincher in 'A State of Blackmail' in his *Writing by Candlelight* (London: Merlin, 1980): 'It is difficult to explain how memories affect one in middle life. For months, the past stretches behind one, as an inert record of events. Then, without forewarning, the past seems suddenly to open itself up inside one— with a more palpable emotional force than the vague present—in the gesture of a long-dead friend, or in the recall of some "spot of time" imbued with

incommunicable significance. One is astonished to find oneself, while working in the garden or pottering about the kitchen, with tears on one's cheeks', 132.

123. The premier analysis remains Anthony Barnett, 'Iron Britannia', *New Left Review I*, 134 (1982). He adopted the term 'Churchillism'—'born in May 1940', he explained—as a key element in his enquiry. We were unsure about the efficacy of his approach as the organizing concept, Churchillism, has in our view too much explanatory work to do. 'Churchill*ism* was essentially the political flesh of national life: its skin, muscle tonality and arthritis at the same time', 33 and 43. Even so, Barnett's 'Churchillism' and our 'mythic Churchill' evidently are not a million miles apart.

124. J.H. Plumb, 'Churchill as Historian', in A.J.P. Taylor (ed.), *Churchill. Four Faces and the Man* (Harmondsworth: Penguin, 1973), 123. Sir Arthur Bryant was a popular historian of vigorously backward attachments.

125. We're not exercised by the liberties the film takes with the historical record. It is after all a *movie*. Attention to historical detail is not the issue; the unwilled bending of history so that it conforms to the stipulations of the Churchill myth is of greater consequence.

126. Bill Schwarz, '*Philosophes* of the Conservative Nation: Burke, Macaulay and Disraeli', *Journal of Historical Sociology*, 12/3 (1999), 202. Duff Cooper believed Macaulay 'the greatest rhetorician in the language', *Old Men Forget* (London: Rupert Hart-Davis, 1954), 15.

127. Cited in Roberts, *Churchill*, 20.

128. Schwarz, '*Philosophes* of the Conservative Nation'. Of Scottish descent, Macaulay was an esteemed Whig politician, an extraordinarily influential colonial administrator in India in the 1830s, essayist, and poet. In November 1848—the shock of the June Days in Paris still reverberating in the collective mind of the nation's governors—the first instalment of his *History of England* had been published to widespread popular acclaim: Catherine Hall, *Macaulay and Son: Architects of Imperial Britain* (London: Yale UP, 2012). It sought 'to make the past present' and as it did so advanced with unsurpassed rhetorical skill the case for England's exceptionalism: Thomas Macaulay, 'Hallam's Constitutional History', *Edinburgh Review*, 48 (1828), 97. Initially, Tories were far from enamoured by Macaulay's partisanship for the Whigs. But when through the course of the later nineteenth century the divisions between Whig and Tory attenuated, Conservative affiliations to Macaulay deepened. His direct influence on Conservatism—arising from his popular verses as much as from the histories—can be discerned in an unbroken lineage which stretches from Arthur Balfour in the early 1900s to Alec Douglas-Home in the 1960s. Piqued by Macaulay's inclination to be insufficiently deferential to his ancestor, the Duke of Marlborough, Churchill laboured to set the record straight in four programmatic volumes: Winston S. Churchill, *Marlborough: His Life and Times*

(4 vols), (London: Harrap, 1933). But just as part of Johnson wants to be Churchill, so one part of Churchill dreamt of being a historian of England as revered as Macaulay. Ever keen to have the last word, when the war came to its end Churchill set about reviving his four-volume manuscript, *A History of the English-Speaking Peoples* (London: Cassell, 1956–58). There's little to recommend it. It is twentieth-century Macaulay produced on classically Fordist principles, teams of hands organized in twelve-hour shifts, held in place by a despotic-philanthropic line manager. Defying reason, for this Churchill received the Nobel Prize for literature. On Macaulay and Churchill: Berlin, *Mr Churchill in 1940*.

129. In 2009 the film *Into the Storm* had already staked a claim on the Churchill–Macaulay relation, by referring twice to 'Captain of the gate', including in the opening sequence. Some sixty years ago Bill Schwarz remembers his primary school teacher—in a deadly final gasp of an exhausted history—reading the poem and enjoining the class to draw a picture of Horatius, still in his armour, diving into the Tiber. What was the pedagogic impulse behind the exercise? And why, more worryingly, should he remember it?

130. Much the same can said about the climactic scene in the 2010 film *The King's Speech* when the nation is projected as becoming unified under the spell of George VI's words on 3 September 1939, a modern form of the power of the king's touch. As he approaches the microphone, Churchill, providentially present whenever history is about to happen, is there to offer tender encouragement to his monarch.

131. This moment can be followed in more detail in the accompanying chapters, and in: Mattha Busby, 'Winston Churchill Was a Villain, Says John McDonell', *Guardian* (13 Feb. 2019); Daniel Finkelstein, 'Churchill Was a Racist But Still a Great Man', *The Times* (13 Feb. 2019); Ben Sixsmith, 'The War on Churchill', *Spectator* (14 Feb. 2019); Simon Jenkins, 'The Churchill Row Is Part of a Glib Approach That Gave Us Brexit', *Guardian* (14 Feb. 2019); and Andrew Roberts, 'We Have Been Warned', *Mail on Sunday* (17 Feb. 2019).

132. Stuart Hall, 'Popular-Democratic *vs* Authoritarian Populism: Two Ways of "Taking Democracy Seriously"', in Alan Hunt (ed.), *Marxism and Democracy* (London: Lawrence & Wishart, 1980).

133. O'Toole, *Heroic Failure* turns the historic tables. 'Vassalage' supplies one of its many comic turns.

134. Simon Kuper, 'The Oxford Files', *Financial Times Weekend* (22–3 June 2019). Kuper adds, 'the night after Brexit happened, I sensed I was rooted in 1980s Oxford'. This needs to be read alongside James Wood on the Eton component of this same political generation, where he describes one element of Brexit as 'a madness casually instituted, secretly engineered and noisily bolstered by a cabal of old Etonians born between 1962 and 1975, the year we joined the Common

Market', 'Diary', *London Review of Books* (4 July 2019). For Oxford see too the older *When Boris Met Dave* (ITV, 7 Oct. 2009). This attests to the historical reality of Brexit as an unlikely coalition between a fraction of the traditional ruling elite and a newly immiserated section of the working population possessed by a deep feeling that, in the new (Blairite) Britain, they no longer mattered.

135. Bill Schwarz, 'Wild Power. The Aftershocks of Decolonization and Black Power', in Daniel Geary, Camilla Schofield, and Jenni Sutton (eds), *The Global History of White Nationalism. From Apartheid to Donald Trump* (Manchester: Manchester UP, 2020).

136. Geoffrey Wheatcroft, *The Strange Death of Tory England* (London: Penguin, 2005), 235.

137. Schwarz, 'Forgetfulness. England's Discontinuous Histories'.

138. Gilroy, *After Empire*; Camilla Schofield, *Enoch Powell and the Making of Postcolonial Britain* (Cambridge: Cambridge UP, 2015).

139. O'Toole, *Heroic Failure*, 34–5.

140. Adrian Addison, *Mail Men: The Story of the* Daily Mail. *The Paper That Divided and Conquered Britain* (London: Oneworld, 2016), 262–3.

141. 'Who Will Speak for England?', *Daily Mail* (4 Feb. 2016).

142. Churchill, 'Scaffolding of Rhetoric'.

143. Roberts, *Eminent Churchillians* (London: Phoenix, 1995; first pub., 1994), 139, 147, and 210.

144. Johnson, *Churchill*, 34–5. Roberts equates Churchill oratory with Pericles and Abraham Lincoln, *Churchill*, 550; Johnson repeats the estimation, adding 'with a small but irrefutable dash of Les Dawson', 87.

145. Roberts, *Churchill*, 980.

146. Tom Nairn, *The Break-Up of Britain: Crisis and Neo-Nationalism* (London: Verso, 1981), 288.

Chapter 2

1. 'Winston Churchill "villain" over Tonypandy riots, says John McDonnell', 14 Feb. 2019, https://www.bbc.co.uk/news/uk-politics-47233605 (accessed 3 May 2019).

2. ITV news interview with John McDonnell, https://twitter.com/itvnews/status/1096007893491560453, posted 14 Feb. 2019, 3.26 a.m. (accessed 3 May 2019); Paul Addison, *Churchill on the Home Front 1900–1955* (London: Jonathan Cape, 1992), 142–5.

3. 'MSP Ross Greer brands Churchill "mass murderer"', 28 Jan. 2019, https://www.bbc.co.uk/news/uk-scotland-scotland-politics-47028246 (accessed 3 May 2019).

4. 'John McDonnell brands Sir Winston Churchill a "villain"', 13 Feb. 2019, https://www.telegraph.co.uk/politics/2019/02/13/john-mcdonnell-brands-winston-churchill-villain/ (accessed 7 May 2019).

5. Richard Toye, *The Roar of the Lion: The Untold Story of Churchill's World War II Speeches* (Oxford: Oxford University Press, 2013).

6. 'Winston Churchill "villain" over Tonypandy riots, says John McDonnell'.

7. H.G. Nicholas, *The British General Election of 1950* (London: Macmillan, 1951), 94.

8. HC Debs Vol 959, 30 Nov. 1978, col. 696.

9. 'Mr. Attlee on Family Gathering', *The Times*, 1 Dec. 1954.

10. 'Great Britons: Churchill', BBC2 (30 Jan. 2015), originally broadcast 2002.

11. Kate Watson-Smyth, 'Shakespeare voted greatest Briton', *Independent*, 2 Jan. 1999, https://www.independent.co.uk/news/shakespeare-voted-greatest-briton-1044484.html (accessed 7 May 2019).

12. Gary Alan Fine, 'Reputational entrepreneurs and the memory of incompetence: Melting supporters, partisan warriors, and images of President Harding', *The American Journal of Sociology*, 101/5 (1996), 1159–93. Quotations at 1160, 1162, 1163. It is important to acknowledge that reputational entrepreneurs do not always act out of self-interest. For example, Kay Halle, the American journalist who campaigned for Churchill to receive honorary US citizenship, appears to have acted on the basis of altruism.

13. Mark Pottle (ed.), *Daring to Hope: The Diaries and Letters of Violet Bonham Carter 1946–1969* (London: Weidenfeld & Nicolson, 2000), 140.

14. Benjamin Hufbauer, Presidential Temples: How Memorials and Libraries Shape Public Memory (Lawrence, KS: University Press of Kansas, 2006); Anthony Clark, *The Last Campaign: How Presidents Rewrite History, Run for Posterity & Enshrine Their Legacies* (North Charleston, SC: CreateSpace Independent Publishing Platform, 2015).

15. Warren Dockter and Richard Toye, 'Who Commanded History? Sir John Colville, Churchillian Networks, and the "Castlerosse Affair"', *Journal of Contemporary History*, 54 (2019), 401–19.

16. For example, Toye's *Roar of the Lion* reported contemporary criticism of Churchill's wartime speeches but was wrongly perceived as endorsing it. Merely proposing a rethink of what made the speeches successful was perceived as heresy (judging from social media reaction, letters and emails to the author, etc.). By contrast, Dockter and Toye's Channel 4 documentary 'Churchill's Secret Affair' (first broadcast 3 March 2018) brought a much more muted response, speculatively because the notion that Churchill had an affair with a socialite was less disturbing of his legend than the idea that his speeches often failed to have the effects conventionally attributed to them.

17. Accepting the Democratic nomination on 15 July 1960, John F. Kennedy remarked: 'A tired nation, said David Lloyd George, is a Tory nation—and the United States today cannot afford to be either tired or Tory.' He also used the quotation in at least two other speeches that year.

18. 'Ll. G.: statesman who played to win', *Daily Telegraph*, 25 March 1970.

19. David Dutton, *Neville Chamberlain* (London: Hodder Arnold, 2001); Philip Williamson, 'Stanley Baldwin's reputation: Politics and history, 1937–1967', *Historical Journal*, 47 (2004), 127–68.

20. Daniel Immerwahr, *How to Hide an Empire: A Short History of the Greater United States* (London: The Bodley Head, 2019); Peo Hansen and Stefan Jonsson, *Eurafrica: The Untold History of European Integration and Colonialism* (London: Bloomsbury Academic, 2014).

21. David Edgerton, *The Rise and Fall of the British Nation: A Twentieth-century History* (London: Allen Lane, 2018), 26. For the evolution of Churchill's bulldog image, see Jonathan Black, *Winston Churchill in British Art, 1900 to the Present Day: The Titan With Many Faces* (London: Bloomsbury Academic, 2017).

22. Chris McGovern, 'Massacred—the truth about the British Empire', 16 Apr. 2019, https://www.conservativewoman.co.uk/massacred-the-truth-about-the-british-empire/ (accessed 7 June 2019).

23. According to Dutch Prime Minister Mark Rutte, interviewed on Radio 4's Today programme on 20 June 2019, 'your campaign is done in poetry and governing is in prose, as I think Churchill said once.' The true author of the sentiment was New York Governor Mario Cuomo.

24. See Marco Duranti, *The Conservative Human Rights Revolution: European Identity, Transnational Politics, and the Origins of the European Convention* (New Yprk: Oxford University Press, 2017).

25. John Ramsden, *Man of the Century: Winston Churchill and his Legend since 1945* (London: HarperCollins, 2002); David Reynolds, *In Command of History: Churchill Fighting and Writing the Second World War* (London: Allen Lane, 2004). ˙

26. Winston Churchill to Clement Attlee, 29 May 1946, quoted in Ramsden, *Man of the Century*, 167.

27. 'Churchilliana', *Indian News Chronicle*, 27 Sept. 1951. Aneurin Bevan had previously made a similar claim about Churchill: 'He sub-edits history, and if there is any disagreeable fact, overboard it goes.' Parliamentary Debates, House of Commons, Fifth Series, Vol. 468, 29 Sept. 1949, col. 310.

28. Matthias Zeller, 'Rechenfehler in Europas Gleichgewicht', *Die Deutsche Zukunft*, 14 Apr. 1955, copy in Churchill Papers, CHUR 2/482A/15.

29. Emrys Hughes, *Winston Churchill in War and Peace* (Glasgow: Unity Publishing Company, 1950); Emrys Hughes, *Churchill: Ein Mann in seinem Widerspruch* (Tübingen: Schlichtenmayer, 1959); Emrys Hughes, *Winston Churchill: British Bulldog: His Career in War and Peace* (New York: Exposition Press, 1955).

30. David Stafford, *Roosevelt and Churchill: Men of Secrets* (London: Abacus, 2000), 300.

31. Eduard Mark, '"Today has been a historical one": Harry S. Truman's diary of the Potsdam Conference', *Diplomatic History* 4 (1980), 317–26, at 320.

32. R.H. Ferrell, *The Eisenhower Diaries* (New York: Norton, 1981), 222–4.

33. James Reston, 'Churchill and Truman Survey a Changed World', *New York Times*, 6 Jan. 1952.

34. John Young, Winston's Churchill's Last Campaign: Britain and the Cold War, 1951–5 (Oxford: Clarendon Press, 1996); Klaus Larres, *Churchill's Cold War: The Politics of Personal Diplomacy* (New Haven, CT: Yale University Press, 2002).

35. US London Embassy to Secretary of State, 18 June 1954, reproduced in the Declassified Documents Reference System database, Gale Group, Farmington Hills, MI.

36. Evelyn Shuckburgh, *Descent to Suez: Diaries 1951–56* (London: Weidenfeld and Nicolson, 1986), 75.

37. W.S. Lucas, Divided We Stand: Britain, the US and the Suez Crisis (London: Hodder and Stoughton, 1991), 160.

38. Dwight Eisenhower to Winston Churchill, 27 Nov. 1956, reproduced in the Declassified Documents Reference System database.

39. G. C. Peden, 'Suez and Britain's Decline as a World Power', *Historical Journal*, 55 (2012), 1073–96.

40. Geoffrey Skinner, 'The Development of Military Nuclear Strategy and Anglo-American Relations, 1939–1958', University of Exeter PhD thesis, 2019.

41. Martin Gilbert, *Winston S. Churchill Vol. VIII: 'Never Despair', 1945–1965* (London: Heinemann, 1988), 1225.

42. Michael P. Riccards, 'Waging The Last War: Winston Churchill and the Presidential Imagination', *Presidential Studies Quarterly* 16 (1986), 213–23, at 219.

43. J. D. Fair, 'The intellectual JFK: Lessons in statesmanship from British history', *Diplomatic History* 30 (2006), 119–42, at 139–40.

44. Ramsden, *Man of the Century*, 23, 28.

45. 'Mr. Wilson gives pledge of determined action', *The Times*, 30 July 1966.

46. Nicholas Garland, 'The artist and his model', *Daily Telegraph*, 1 Aug. 1966 (NG0072), and Michael Cummings, 'Why not? If President Johnson can think I'm a Churchill, you can think I won the World Cup', *Daily Express*, 1 Aug. 1966 (09476), archive.cartoons.ac.uk (accessed 13 May 2019).

47. Louis Heren, 'Anglo-US relationship comes under strain', *The Times*, 23 Feb. 1968, emphasis added.

48. Simon C. Smith, 'Anglo-American relations and the end of empire in the Far East and the Persian Gulf, 1948–1971', in Tore T. Petersen (ed.), *Challenging Retrenchment: The United States, Great Britain and the Middle East 1950–1980* (Trondheim: Tapir Academic Press, 2010), 9–40, quotation at 36.

49. Ramsden, *Man of the Century*, 574.

50. Stuart Ward, *The Untied Kingdom: A Global History of the End of Britain*, forthcoming with Cambridge University Press, Chapter 2.

51. 'Canadians and Mr. Churchill', *Manchester Guardian*, 16 Jan. 1952.

52. 'General Election 1964: The Manifesto of the Conservative and Unionist Party, Fifth Draft', 27 July 1964, R.A. Butler Papers, RAB 106/9, Trinity College, Cambridge.

53. Conservative Party manifesto, 1959, in F.W.S. Craig (ed.), *British General Election Manifestos 1918-1966* (Chichester: Political Reference Publications, 1970), 188–96.

54. 'Tories Make Bomb Election Issue', *The Times*, 23 July 1964. The original draft script featured an extract from Churchill's *World Crisis* and an 'Excerpt from Churchill recording about Britain having once again to face enemies alone', but it is unclear if these elements were included in the final version. 'Outline for Defence programme', n.d. but 31 Apr. 1964? Butler Papers, RAB H52/1, Trinity College, Cambridge. For a later use of Churchill in a Tory broadcast, see Fred Emery, 'New Tory TV film depicts Labour as dividing nation', *The Times*, 18 May 1978.

55. However, at this time voters seemed more interested in domestic issues than the 'problems for which the Conservative Party is thought best, such as the Power and Prestige of Britain, the Commonwealth and giving aid to Underdeveloped countries': 'Voters and the 1964 General Election Volume 1: Report: prepared for the Thomson Organisation Limited by Simon Broadbent', March 1964, Conservative Party Archive, CCO 10/11/2/1, Bodleian Library, Oxford.

56. Fine, 'Reputational entrepreneurs', 163–4.

57. Richard Nixon, 'Remarks at the airport on arrival in London', 24 Feb. 1969, *Public Papers of the Presidents of the United States: Richard Nixon, 1969* (Washington D.C.: General Services Administration, National Archives and Records Service, 1969), 139–41.

58. 'Remarks of welcome to Prime Minister Harold Wilson of Great Britain', 27 Jan. 1970, and 'Toasts of the President and Prime Minister Heath of Great Britain', 17 Dec. 1970, *Public Papers of the Presidents of the United States: Richard Nixon, 1970* (Washington D.C.: General Services Administration, National Archives and Records Service, 1970), 27, 1148–51.

59. Edward Heath, *The Course of My Life: My Autobiography* (London: Hodder & Stoughton, 1998), 146, 472.

60. Alan McGregor, 'Mr. Heath endorses a European summit', *The Times*, 18 Sept. 1971; Walter Terry, 'The new Europe—by Heath', *Daily Mail*, 18 Sept. 1971.

61. 'Churchill's Europe', *Daily Telegraph*, 18 Sept. 1971. The TV programme in question was an episode of the Thames Television series 'The Day Before Yesterday' entitled 'Set the People Free', broadcast on 16 September.

62. Winston S. Churchill to the editor of the *Daily Telegraph*, published 3 June 1975.

63. The photo is reproduced on the cover of Robert Saunders, *Yes to Europe! The 1975 Referendum and Seventies Britain* (Cambridge: Cambridge University Press, 2018).

64. On image events, see Davi Johnson, 'Martin Luther King Jr.'s 1963 Birmingham Campaign as Image Event', *Rhetoric and Public Affairs* 10 (2007), 1–25. On pseudo-events, see Daniel J. Boorstin, *The Image: A Guide to Pseudo-Events in America* (New York and Boston: Harper Colophon Books, 1964).

65. Speech by John Colville, undated but *c*.1968, Colville Papers, CLVL 2/46, CAC.

66. For a useful recent discussion of this term, and its limitations, see Rachel K. Bright and Andrew R. Dilley, 'After the British World', *Historical Journal* 60 (2017), 547–68.

67. Lord Moran, Winston Churchill: The Struggle for Survival, 1940–1965 (London: Constable, 1966).

68. Anthony Storr, 'The man', in A.J.P. Taylor et al., *Churchill: Four Faces and the Man* (London: Allen Lane, 1969), 205–46, at 245.

69. 'Toasts of the President and Prime Minister Margaret Thatcher of the United Kingdom at the Dinner Honoring the President', 27 Feb. 1981. Available online at: https://www.reaganlibrary.gov/research/speeches/22781c (accessed 1 March 2006).

70. Margaret Thatcher, speech at the Winston Churchill Foundation Award dinner, 29 Sept. 1983, https://www.margaretthatcher.org/document/105450 (accessed 16 May 1019).

71. Richard Aldous, *Reagan and Thatcher: The Difficult Relationship* (London: Hutchinson, 2012).

72. Interview of Margaret Thatcher by Geoffrey Smith, 8 Jan. 1990, https://www.margaretthatcher.org/document/109324 (accessed 16 May 2019). Emphasis in original.

73. POSTER 1984–01, 1984–02, 1984–03, 1984–04, 1984–05, 1984–06, 1984–07, Bodleian Library, https://www.bodleian.ox.ac.uk/cpa/collections/posters-collection (accessed 17 May 2019).

74. Jorgen Rasmussen, '"What Kind of Vision is That?" British Public Attitudes towards the European Community during the Thatcher Era', *British Journal of Political Science* 27 (1997), 111–118.

75. Paul Johnson, 'Still the best man in the Cabinet . . .', *Daily Mail*, 1 May 1982.

76. Ezequiel Mercau, *The Falklands War: An Imperial History* (Cambridge: Cambridge University Press, 2019).

77. Conservative Party Election Broadcast, 12 June 1984, https://www.margaretthatcher.org/document/105706 (accessed 17 May 2019).

78. Thatcher herself advanced the Commonwealth argument in 1975: TV interview for ITN (3 June 1975), https://www.margaretthatcher.org/document/102700 (accessed 17 May 2019). On her view of the Commonwealth in the 1980s, see John Campbell, *Margaret Thatcher Volume Two: The Iron Lady* (London: Vintage, 2008), 318–34.

79. Conservative Party Election Broadcast, 12 June 1984. Emphases added.

80. Peter Clarke, *Mr Churchill's Profession: Statesman, Orator, Writer* (London: Bloomsbury, 2012); Patrick Wright, *Iron Curtain: From Stage to Cold War* (Oxford: Oxford University Press, 2007).

81. Conservative Party Election Broadcast, 12 June 1984. Thatcher had also rejected the notion of 'a kind of United States of Europe' in 1975: interview on *Newsday*, BBC2 (3 June 1975), https://www.youtube.com/watch?v=zT3rx4RqhOU (accessed 17 May 2019).

82. Ramsden, *Man of the Century*, 578–9.

83. David Irving's *Churchill's War Volume One: The Struggle for Power* (Bullsbrook, Western Australia: Veritas, 1987).

84. Andrew Roberts, 'David Irving, truth and the Holocaust', *Sunday Telegraph*, 16 Jan. 2000. After Irving lost his legal case, Roberts, who had certainly not been wholly uncritical of him, became more openly contemptuous. See his ironically titled article 'Irving's Greatest Triumph', *Sunday Telegraph*, 16 Apr. 2000 and the letters by the two men in the same paper on 23 Jan. 2000.

85. 'Lowest ebb for finest hour', *Daily Telegraph*, 3 Nov. 1987; Piers Brendon, 'Dog's Dinner', *Observer*, 31 Jan. 1988; Norman Gash, 'Conclusions on a colossus', *Times Literary Supplement*, 27 May 1988; Peregrine Worsthorne, 'Paperbacks in Brief', *Sunday Telegraph*, 21 Jan. 1990.

86. Valerie Grove, 'The man who rewrote history', *The Times*, 8 Jan. 1993.

87. John Charmley, *Churchill: The End of Glory: A Political Biography* (London: Hodder & Stoughton, 1993), 649.

88. Ion Trewin (ed.) *Alan Clark: Diaries: Into Politics* (London: Weidenfeld & Nicolson, 2000), 103, 280 (entries for 27 Aug. 1977 and for 8 Dec. 1981).

89. Alan Clark, 'A reputation ripe for revision', *The Times*, 2 Jan. 1993.

90. Kathryn Knight, 'Churchillians defeat heretics', *The Times*, 12 July 1995.

91. Ion Trewin, *Alan Clark: The Biography* (London: Weidenfeld & Nicolson, 2009), 348.

92. Robin Prior and Trevor Wilson, 'Reassessments of Winston Churchill', *International History Review*, 18 (1996), 113–26.

93. Andrew Roberts, 'Winston Replied That He Didn't Like Blackamoors', *Spectator*, 9 Apr. 1994.

94. Christopher Thorne, *Allies of a Kind: The United States, Britain, and the War Against Japan, 1941–1945* (London: Hamish Hamilton, 1978), 725.

95. Niall Ferguson, 'They're just not playing the game', *Daily Telegraph*, 9 Apr. 1994.

96. W.F. Deedes, 'This Man Was No Racist', *Daily Telegraph*, 9 Apr. 1994.

97. Andrew Roberts, *Eminent Churchillians* (London: Weidenfeld & Nicolson, London, 1994).

98. Lady Williams to William Manchester, 8 July 1994, William Manchester Papers, B109 F9, Wesleyan University.

99. Andrew Roberts to the editor of the *Daily Telegraph*, published 11 Apr. 1994.

100. Clive Ponting, *Churchill* (London: Sinclair-Stevenson, 1994). The quotation is on the dust jacket.

101. Matthew d'Ancona, 'History men battle over Britain's future', *The Times*, 9 May 1994.

102. Andrew Roberts, *The Aachen Memorandum* (London: Weidenfeld and Nicolson, 1995).

103. Nick Cohen, 'Re-righting history', *Independent*, 31 July 1994. Note also Nigel Lawson's later claim that 'Churchill might have made Thatcher unnecessary' had he pursued the free market approach of the never-implemented Operation ROBOT in 1952: 'Robot and the fork in the road', *Times Literary Supplement*, 21 Jan. 2005.

104. Andrew Roberts, 'Churchill's Reputation: The State of the Debate', *Finest Hour* 131 (Summer 2006).

105. Anthony Seldon, *Major: A Political Life* (London: Phoenix, 1998), 549–50.

106. See PRO 57/ 955, PRO 57/956, PRO 57/957, TS 27/1584, and LCO 67/51, The National Archives, Kew, London.

107. Gyles Brandreth, *Breaking the Code: Westminster Diaries May 1990-May 1997* (London: Phoenix, 2000), 329–30 (entry for 26 Apr. 1995).

108. Carol Midgley, 'Never has so much been paid by so many to so few', *Daily Mirror*, 27 Apr. 1995.

109. Quoted in the NPR programme 'All Things Considered', 27 Apr. 1995, 4.30 p.m. ET, transcript available via Nexis UK.

110. Boris Johnson, 'How to fritter £400 million', *Daily Telegraph*, 27 Apr. 1995.

111. John Charmley, 'Churchill's Paper profit', *Guardian*, 28 Apr. 1995.

112. 'Public dismay at Churchill papers sale', *Independent*, 2 May 1995.

113. Allen Packwood to Perdita Hunt, 6 Dec. 1995. National Heritage Lottery Fund Freedom of Information release to Richard Toye, November 2014. The exhibition ran over four afternoons and was targeted at a local rather than a national audience; over a thousand people attended.

114. The phrase was Jon Snow's in his interview with Heritage Secretary Stephen Dorrell on 26 Apr. 1995. https://www.gettyimages.co.uk/detail/video/winston-churchill-speeches-bought-by-national-lottery-news-footage/1014267116? adppopup=true (accessed 3 June 2019).

115. Rebecca Smithers, 'Blair gives pledge of "people's lottery"', *Guardian*, 14 Apr. 1997.

116. Terry Coleman, 'The New Churchill...or the new Bambi?', *Mail on Sunday*, 2 Oct. 1994.

117. Patrick Wintour, '"I'm the better Brit" says Blair', *Guardian*, 20 Apr. 1997.

118. Donald Macintryre, *Mandelson and the Making of New Labour* (London: HarperCollins, 2000), 377–9.

119. Labour Party Election Broadcast 15 April 1997, https://www.youtube.com/watch?v=i0uouyO-whY (accessed 6 June 2019).

120. Rebecca Smithers, 'You've seen the chickens, bears and rhino. Now meet Labour's bulldog', *Guardian*, 15 Apr. 1997.

121. Michael Ignatieff, 'A pedigree chum for Tony Blair', *Observer*, 20 Apr. 1997.

122. John Kampfner, *Blair's Wars* (London: Free Press, 2004), 4. See also Inderjeet Parmar, '"I'm Proud of the British Empire": Why Tony Blair Backs George W. Bush', *Political Quarterly* 76 (2005), 218–31.

123. Macintryre, *Mandelson*, 379; David Butler and Dennis Kavanagh, *The British General Election of 1997* (Houndmills, Basingstoke: Macmillan, 1997), 183.

124. 'Blair's Speech: Highlights', 28 Sept. 1999, https://www.theguardian.com/politics/1999/sep/28/labourconference.labour18 (accessed 6 June 2019).

125. Richard Jobson, *Nostalgia and the Post-War Labour Party: Prisoners of the Past* (Manchester: Manchester University Press, 2018), 151.

126. 'Toast remarks by the President and Prime Minister Blair', 5 Feb. 1998, http://www.clintonfoundation.org/legacy/020598-remarks-by-president-and-pm-blair-at-state-diner.htm (accessed 28 Feb. 2006).

127. Lance Price, *The Spin Doctor's Diary: Inside Number 10 with New Labour* (London: Hodder and Stoughton, 2005), 216.

128. Christopher Meyer, *DC Confidential* (London: Weidenfeld and Nicolson, 2005), 59.

129. Con Coughlin, *American Ally: Tony Blair and the War on Terror* (London: Politico's, 2006), 119.

130. This accusation was made in *The Mirror*'s gossip column, 'The Scurra', on 4 Aug. 2004.

131. 'President discusses European trip: Remarks by the president in acceptance of bust of Winston Churchill', 16 July 2001, archived at https://web.archive.org/web/20010919232938/http://www.whitehouse.gov/news/releases/2001/07/20010716-3.html (accessed 29 Dec. 2005).

132. George W. Bush, 'Address to a joint session of Congress and the American people', 20 Sept. 2001, http://www.whitehouse.gov/news/releases/2001/09/20010920-8.html (accessed 7 March 2006).

133. 'Secretary Rumsfeld at Camp Pendleton Town Hall Meeting', 27 Aug. 2002, http://www.defenselink.mil/transcripts/2002/t08282002_t0827thm.html (accessed 2 March 2006).

134. Ben Macintyre, 'Remember, Winston also knew when to jaw-jaw', *The Times*, 28 Sept. 2002.

135. John Campbell, *Roy Jenkins: A Well-Rounded Life* (London: Vintage, 2015), 731.

136. Nigel Knight made little counter-impression with his book *Churchill: The Greatest Britain Unmasked* (Newton Abbot: David & Charles Ltd, 2008).

137. 'President Bush discusses importance of democracy in Middle East', 4 Feb. 2004, http://www.whitehouse.gov/news/releases/2004/02/20040204-4.html (accessed 1 March 2007).

138. 'Remarks by the vice president at Westminster College', 26 Apr. 2004, http://www.whitehouse.gov/news/releases/2004/04/20040426-8.html (accessed 2 March 2006).

139. Patrick J. Buchanan, Churchill, Hitler, and 'The Unnecessary War': How Britain Lost Its Empire and the West Lost the World (New York: Crown Publishers, 2008), xix

140. Time, 30 July 2006.

141. Rory Carroll, 'Mbeki attacks "racist" Churchill', Guardian, 5 Jan. 2005.

142. See, for example, Benedict Brogan, 'It's time to celebrate the Empire says Brown', Daily Mail, 15 Jan. 2005.

143. Mona Chalabi, 'Fact-check: did Obama really remove a Churchill bust from the Oval Office?', Guardian, 22 Apr. 2016.

144. It was authorized by House Resolution 497 on 19 December 2011 and unveiled on 30 October 2013, after which the assembled dignitaries were serenaded by Roger Daltrey of The Who singing 'Stand By Me'.

145. Olive Burrows, 'London Mayor Slammed for Obama Anti-British Label Due to Kenyan Roots', Capital FM, 22 Apr. 2016, accessed via Nexis UK.

146. Sunday Times, 5 Feb. 1995.

147. Andrew Marr, 'Top Tory comes out for the Euro', Independent, 25 July 1996.

148. Margaret Thatcher, Statecraft (New York: HarperCollins, 2002), 362, n. 363. See also Andrew Roberts, 'Lies, damn lies and quoting Winston', The Sunday Times, 28 July 1996.

149. José Manuel Durão Barroso, 'From 1946 till today—a European success story. Why leadership matters', 8 Nov. 2013, http://europa.eu/rapid/press-release_SPEECH-13-900_en.htm (accessed 12 June 2019).

150. Bruno Waterfield, 'Barroso calls for Europe to show the Churchillian spirit', Daily Telegraph, 9 Nov. 2013.

151. Boris Johnson, The Churchill Factor (London: Hodder & Stoughton, 2014), ch. 20. Quotation at 308.

152. 'The eurozone should become the United States of Europe', said Viviane Reding, the vice president of the European Commission. 'Like Winston Churchill, I believe that the UK will not be part of this, but it should remain a close ally with the federated eurozone, with which it would continue to share a common market, a common trade policy and hopefully a common security agenda.' Sam Coates, 'Britain will get new deal from a "United States of Europe"', The Times, 18 Feb. 2014.

153. 'BNP claims on Churchill "absurd"', BBC, 20 March 2009, http://news.bbc.co.uk/1/hi/england/sussex/7955799.stm (accessed 11 June 2019).

154. James Turley, 'Too extreme for BNP?', *Weekly Worker*, 26 March 2009, https://weeklyworker.co.uk/worker/762/too-extreme-for-bnp/ (accessed 12 June 2019).

155. Stuart MacDonald, 'Churchill's family angry at UKIP hijack', *The Sunday Times*, 24 May 2009.

156. Denis MacShane, 'Reclaiming Churchill as the European campaigner', *New European*, 19 May 2019, https://www.theneweuropean.co.uk/top-stories/reclaiming-churchill-as-the-european-campaigner-1-6054446 (accessed 13 June 2019).

157. Felix Klos's pamphlet-length book, *Churchill on Europe: The Untold Story of Churchill's European Project* (London: I.B. Tauris, 2016), came with a cover-sticker which called it 'The Must-Read Book for the Referendum'. Andrew Roberts' review (21 June 2016, https://winstonchurchill.hillsdale.edu/churchill-europe-felix-klos/) observed that Klos had ignored Churchill's post-war premiership, a period in which Britain notably failed to engage with the European project. Klos's extended version, published as *Churchill's Last Stand: The Struggle to Unite Europe* (London: I.B. Tauris, 2017), makes good the deficit. It also provides evidence (83) that Churchill did (at least briefly) envisage British membership of the United States of Europe but did not advocate this in public for tactical reasons.

158. Jesse Norman and Peter Oborne, *Churchill's Legacy: The Conservative Case for the Human Rights Act* (London: Liberty, 2009), 6; Jon Danzig, 'Britain's human rights law: endorsed by Churchill, written by British lawyers, adopted by 47 European countries', British Influence, 24 May 2015, https://web.archive.org/web/20150527205710/www.britishinfluence.org/britain_s_human_rights_law (accessed 12 June 2019); Saxon Norgard, 'Churchill's Fight for Human Rights', RightsInfo, 30 Nov. 2017, https://rightsinfo.org/churchills-fight-human-rights/ (accessed 30 Nov. 2017).

159. Michael Heseltine, speech to the People's Vote rally, 23 March 2019, https://www.youtube.com/watch?v=Y8oWrF2CXF8 (accessed 13 June 2019).

160. Guy Verhofstadt, Facebook post of 7 Feb. 2017 (praising *Churchill On Europe* by Klos), https://www.facebook.com/GuyVerhofstadt/posts/churchill-was-a-federalist-he-led-the-battle-for-a-united-europe-in-this-fascina/10155422072900016/; Verhofstadt speech of 14 Feb. 2017, http://www.europarl.europa.eu/doceo/document/CRE-8-2017-02-14-INT-2-007-0000_EN.html (accessed 13 June 2019); James Crisp, 'Verhofstadt accuses Brexiteers of destroying Churchill's legacy, calls for "EU government"', 14 Feb. 2017, https://www.euractiv.com/section/future-eu/news/verhofstadt-accuses-brexiteers-of-destroying-churchills-legacy-calls-for-eu-government/; Kate McCann, 'EU negotiator sparks fury after claiming Sir Winston Churchill would have voted Remain', *Telegraph*, 15 Feb.

2017, https://www.telegraph.co.uk/news/2017/02/15/eu-negotiator-sparks-fury-claiming-sir-winston-churchill-would/ (all accessed 13 June 2019).

161. Tim Shipman, *All Out War: The Full Story of Brexit* (London: William Collins, 2017), 395–6.

162. Ben Riley-Smith, 'EU referendum: David Cameron invokes Churchill's battle against Hitler in BBC Question Time grilling', 20 June 2016, https://www.telegraph.co.uk/news/2016/06/19/eu-referendum-david-cameron-to-appear-on-bbc-question-time/ (accessed 13 June 2019).

163. Five years earlier, the *Sun* (10 Dec. 2011) had Photoshopped Cameron's face onto a picture of Churchill, alongside the headline 'UP EURS: Bulldog PM sticks up for Britain...but risks backlash'.

164. He is so-described in the Further Reading section of Sarah Gristwood and Margaret Gaskin, *Churchill: An Extraordinary Life* (London: National Trust Books, 2019).

165. Andrew Roberts, *Churchill: Walking With Destiny* (London: Allen Lane, 2018), 976, 980.

166. *Question Time*, BBC1 (14 Feb. 2019).

167. Ben Riley-Smith, '"Thatcher would have blocked Huawei"', *Daily Telegraph*, 9 May 2019.

168. Heath, *Course of My Life*, 473.

169. Lewis Goodall, 'In the Tories' darkest hour, they need a Churchill', Sky News, 3 June 2019, https://news.sky.com/story/in-the-tories-darkest-hour-they-need-a-churchill-11733780 (accessed 13 June 2019); Tom Richmond, 'Why Britain needs a Winston Churchill-like figure to see us through this dark hour', *Yorkshire Post*, 6 June 2019; cover image of the *New Statesman*, 14–20 June 2019.

170. Madhusree Mukerjee, *Churchill's Secret War: The British Empire and the Ravaging of India During World War II* (New York: Basic Books, 2010). See also the documentary *Bengal Shadows*, dir. Banerjee and Partho Bhattacharya 2017. Note that Andrew Roberts devotes considerable space to the issue, whereas a previous generation of biographers, including even Clive Ponting, had overlooked it entirely: *Churchill*, 785–9.

171. Andrew Pulver, 'Winston Churchill of *Darkest Hour* a rebuke to Trump, says film's director', *Guardian*, 28 Sept. 2017; '*Darkest Hour* movie inspires Trump to visit his war bunker: Report', *Press TV*, 11 Feb. 2018, accessed via Nexis UK. The visit took place in 2019.

172. The significance of what had happened did not instantly become clear with the opening of the relevant papers in 1971. The episode is not mentioned, for example, in Henry Pelling, *Winston Churchill* (London: Macmillan, 1974).

173. Winston S. Churchill, *The Second World War Vol. II: Their Finest Hour* (London: Reprint Society, 1951), 156. As Patrick Cosgrave noted in a letter to

the editor of *The Times*, published 23 Feb. 1974, this is an example of Churchill concealing something which was to his credit. See also Cosgrave's book *Churchill at War Vol. I: Alone 1939–40* (London: Collins, 1974), 217.

174. *Question Time*, BBC1 (14 Feb. 2019).

Chapter 3

1. Lucy Noakes and Juliette Pattinson (eds), *British Cultural Memory and the Second World War* (London: Bloomsbury, 2014), 2.

2. Marita Sturken, *Tangled Memories: The Vietnam War, the AIDS Epidemic, and the Politics of Remembering* (London: University of California Press, 1997), 1–2, 86.

3. 'Reflections of a Director' on the 2006 DVD version of *Young Winston*.

4. S.N. Lipkin, *Docudrama Performs the Past* (Cambridge: Cambridge University Press, 2011) and *Real Emotional Logic* (Carbondale and Edwardsville: Southern Illinois University Press, 2002); Andrew Butler et al., 'Using popular films to enhance class room learning', *Psychological Science*, 20/9 (2009).

5. As established in Stuart Hall, 'Cultural Studies: two paradigms', *Media, Culture and Society*, 2 (1980), 57–72.

6. S. Feldman and L. Sigelman, 'The politics of primetime television: The Day After', *The Journal of Politics*, 47/2 (1985), 559–60.

7. Emphasis added. The poem is quoted in full in Rodney J. Croft, *Churchill's Final Farewell* (Croft, 2014), 104–5.

8. Katherine Verdery, *The Political Lives of Dead Bodies. Reburial and Postsocialist Change* (New York: Columbia University Press, 1999).

9. See most notably Paul W. Kahn, *Political Theology. Four New Chapters on The Concept of Sovereignty* (New York: Columbia University Press, 2011), 26.

10. Kahn, *Theology*, 154–5.

11. Harald Wydra, *Politics and the Sacred* (Cambridge: Cambridge University Press, 2015), 2–5.

12. 'Birthday Presentations To Sir Winston Churchill' *The Times*, 1 December 1954. Emphasis added.

13. Winston S. Churchill, *The Second World War. Vol II. Their Finest Hour* (London: Cassell, 1949), 88.

14. Anthony Montague Browne (AMB) to Jack Le Vien (JLV), 7 December 1959, LEVN 2/1, John Douglas Le Vien papers, Churchill College Archives Centre.

15. For more on this, see David Reynolds, *In Command of History. Churchill Fighting and Writing the Second World War* (London: Penguin, 2005), 506.

16. *Daily Telegraph*, 19 July 1972.

17. *New York Times*, 5 December 1954.

18. Quoted in Jonathan Black, *Winston Churchill in British Art, 1900 to the Present Day: The Titan with Many Faces* (London: Bloomsbury, 2017), 157, 180.

19. Bryan Forbes to AMB, 20 February 1963, CHUR 4/448A-B, Winston Churchill papers, Churchill College Archives Centre.

20. *Daily Telegraph*, 2 December 1974; *New Statesman*, 6 December 1974.

21. *Observer*, 22 October 1967.

22. *New York Times*, November 24 1974.

23. Verdery, *Political Lives*, 5.

24. Verdery, *Political Lives*, 20.

25. For more on this see Richard Wightman Fox, *Lincoln's Body: A Cultural History* (New York: Norton, 2015).

26. https://www.nps.gov/linc/index.htm (accessed 5 June 2017). For more on the 'Lincoln cult', see David Donald, 'The Folklore Lincoln', *Journal of the Illinois State Historical Society (1908–1984)*, 40/4 (Dec., 1947), 377–96

27. John E. Washington quoted in Donald, 'Folklore', 380; more generally see Jeff Smith, *The Presidents We Imagine* (Madison, Wisconsin: University of Wisconsin, 2009), 84–96.

28. Peter Bogdanovich quoted in Joseph McBride, *Searching for John Ford* (London: St Martin's Press, 2003), 301.

29. 'Journey to Lincoln', *Lincoln* DVD (2013).

30. See Martin Pugh, *The Tories and the People* (London: Wiley-Blackwell, 1985) and Diana E. Sheets, 'British Conservatism and The Primrose League: The Changing Character of Popular Politics, 1883–1901', PhD thesis, Columbia University 1986.

31. For more on Disraeli see Steven Fielding, 'British Politics and Cinema's Historical Dramas, 1929–1938', *Historical Journal*, 56/2 (2013).

32. J. Fox, 'Winston Churchill and the "Men of Destiny": Leadership and the role of the Prime Minister in wartime feature films', in Richard Toye and Julie Gottlieb (eds), *Making Reputations. Power, Persuasion and the Individual in Modern British Politics* (London: Taurus, 2005), 97–8.

33. Reynolds, *Command of History*, 525.

34. Steven Fielding, 'What did "the people" want?: the meaning of the 1945 general election', *Historical Journal*, 35/2 (1992), 629.

35. Richard Toye, 'Winston Churchill's "Crazy Broadcast": Party, Nation, and the 1945 Gestapo Speech', *Journal of British Studies*, 49/3 (2010).

36. *The Times*, 1 December 1954; House of Commons Debates (HC Deb) 25 January 1965 vol. 705 col. 667.

37. Reynolds, *Command of History*, 523.

38. Ernest Simon papers, 'Party Manners, Personal Statement by Lord Simon of Wythenshawe', 23 October 1950 and 'Party Manners. Heading for Lord Simon's Speech, House of Lords, 7 November 1950', 5 November 1950, M11/6/8a, Manchester Archives.

39. For more on this incident, see https://howitreallywas.typepad.com/how_it_really_was/2009/09/operation-unthinkable.html (accessed 19 June 2019).

40. David Kynaston, *Family Britain, 1951–1957. Tales of a New Jerusalem* (London: Bloomsbury, 2010), 434.

41. Winston Churchill's 80th Birthday, Programme Files, BBC Written Archive (BBCWA).

42. Audience Research Report, 'Birthday greetings to Sir Winston Churchill from some of his friends', VR/54/630, BBCWA.

43. Details of the funeral are outlined in Croft, *Final Farewell*.

44. HC Deb 25 January 1965 vol. 705 col. 667.

45. *Observer*, 31 January 1965.

46. https://www.telegraph.co.uk/history/11377818/My-grandfather-Winston-Churchill-was-buried-fifty-years-ago-today.-It-wasnt-a-funeral-it-was-a-triumph.html (accessed 1 June 2019).

47. http://news.bbc.co.uk/1/hi/uk/89507.stm (accessed 3 June 2019).

48. Verdery, *Political Lives*, 5.

49. Quoted in Black, *Churchill in British Art*, 189–91, 195, 199.

50. *Guardian*, 2 December 1969.

51. *The Times*, 2 December 1969.

52. https://www.telegraph.co.uk/news/uknews/1512840/Touching-tribute-to-Churchill-stirs-fears.html (accessed 29 May 2019).

53. *Guardian*, 25 September 1969.

54. John Lahr, *Prick up your Ears* (London: Bloomsbury, 2002), 21.

55. Lahr, *Prick*, 113–14, 273.

56. *Guardian*, 6 March 1969; Chun-Yi Shih, 'Into the Blazing Light: Liminality in Joe Orton's What the Butler Saw', *Body, Space & Technology*, 1/1 (2000).

57. *The Times*, 6 March 1969.

58. *The Times*, 17 July 1969.

59. *Guardian*, 20 July 1969.

60. HC Deb 14 May 1968 vol. 764 col. 1030–2.

61. HC Deb 11 February 1969 vol. 777 col. 1115–16.

62. HL Deb 22 July 1969 vol. 304 col. 763–6.

63. For more on the process see Black, *Churchill in British Art*, 210–5.

64. *The Times*, 2 November 1973; https://www.telegraph.co.uk/news/uknews/1450683/Winston-Churchills-statue-had-a-look-of-Mussolini.html (accessed 19 May 2019).

65. *Time and Tide*, 24 February 1961; *Spectator*, 17 February 1961.

66. *Daily Worker*, 10 February 1961.

67. *Guardian*, 15 June 1961.

68. Edgar Peterson, Notes for Writers, CHUR 4/452A-B.

69. Reynolds, *Command of History*, 509.

70. *Sunday Telegraph*, 12 February 1961; *Sunday Times*, 5 March 1961.

71. *The Times*, 13 February 1961.
72. *Daily Mail*, 11 February 1961.
73. *Daily Worker*, 10 February 1961.
74. *Guardian*, 1 December 1961.
75. *Daily Mail*, 8 and 11 February 1961.
76. See comments of various IMDB users, https://www.imdb.com/title/tt0053548/ reviews?ref_=tt_urv (accessed 6 May 2019).
77. *Sunday Times*, 5 March 1961.
78. AMB to JLV, 2 June 1961, LEVN 2/1.
79. AMB to JLV, 21 January 1964, CHUR 4/455.
80. Jane Welby to AMB, 19 August 1962, CHUR4/454.
81. AMB-JLV, 26 July and 9 August 1963, 15 and 16 January 1964, LEVN 3/1.
82. Publicity for *The Finest Hours*, CHUR 4/455.
83. Letter to Churchill dated 11 July 1964, CHUR 4/456A-B.
84. *Evening News*, 29 April 1964; *Sunday Telegraph*, 3 June 1964.
85. *The Times*, 29 April 1964.
86. *Spectator*, 8 May 1964.
87. *Sunday Express*, 3 May 1964.
88. Clementine Churchill to Winston Churchill, 24 May 1945, Mission to Moscow, CHAR 20/197A/5.
89. Dore Schary to Churchill, 23 May 1956, CHUR4/447.
90. *Los Angeles Times*, 9 July 1941.
91. *Daily Telegraph*, 3 August 1945.
92. 'Notes on discussion with Sir Winston Churchill', Wright and Webb Solicitors to AMB, 30 June 1958, CHUR 4/448A-B. On the financial side of these discussions, see David Lough, *No More Champagne. Churchill and His Money* (London: Head of Zeus, 2015), chapters 25 and 26.
93. Marjorie Thorson to Nigel Balchin, 1 October 1958, CHUR 4/448A-B.
94. Thorson to Anthony Moir, 2 October 1958, CHUR 4/448A-B.
95. French to AMB, 14 February 1961, AMB to Moir, 3 November 1961 CHUR 4/450A-B.
96. French to AMB, 26 May 1961, CHUR 4/450A-B.
97. AMB to French, 23 and 26 October 1961, CHUR 4/450A-B.
98. French to AMB, 1 December 1961, 1 March 1962, CHUR 4/450A-B.
99. Quoted in Lough, *No More Champagne*, 303.
100. Bryan Forbes, 'The Churchill Story', 22 July 1962, CHUR 4/450A-B.
101. *Daily Express*, 19 October 1962.
102. Bryan Forbes, *A Divided Life* (1992), 111–14.
103. AMB to French, 28 February 1963, AMB to Churchill, 15 May 1963, CHUR 4/448A-B.
104. *Daily Mail*, 19 October 1971; *Guardian*, 30 October 1971.

105. Carl Foreman to AMB, 3 October 1963, AMB to Foreman, 4 October 1963, CHUR 4/448A-B.

106. *Daily Herald*, 6 December 1963.

107. 'Reflections of a Director' on the 2006 DVD version of *Young Winston*.

108. *Evening News*, 11 July 1972.

109. Carl Foreman, *Young Winston. His Greatest Screenplay* (London: Ballantine Books, 1972), 9.

110. *Daily Telegraph*, 19 July 1972.

111. *Morning Star*, 21 July 1972.

112. https://api.parliament.uk/historic-hansard/commons/1901/may/13/army-organisation#S4V0093P0_19010513_HOC_302, cols. 1563–79.

113. *Evening Standard*, 20 July 1972.

114. *New Statesman*, 28 July 1972.

115. James Brabazon to Cedric Messina, 28 January 1965; James Brabazon to Copyright Dept, 28 June 1965; and Gerald Savory to C.P. Tel., 7 July 1966, Writers Files, Dennis Potter, BBCWA.

116. John R. Cook, *Dennis Potter: A Life on Screen* (Manchester: Manchester University Press, 1995), 44–6.

117. *Observer*, 7 May 1967; *Sunday Telegraph*, 7 May 1967; *Guardian*, 4 May 1967; *The Times*, 4 May 1967.

118. *Sunday Times*, 7 May 1967.

119. Milton Schulman, Evening Standard, n.d. *Message to Posterity*, Programme Files, BBCWA.

120. Audience Research Report, *Message for Posterity*, VR/67/293, BBCWA.

121. For more on Days of Hope, see Steven Fielding, 'Socialist television drama and the construction of political meaning during the crisis of Britain's post-war settlement', *Twentieth Century British History* (forthcoming).

122. Unless otherwise stated, this account of the *Soldiers* controversy relies on Helen Freshwater, *Theatre Censorship in Britain* (London: Palgrave, 2009), ch. 4.

123. *New York Times*, 25 April 1967.

124. *Observer*, 15 October 1967; *New York Times*, 19 November 1967.

125. *Observer*, 15 December 1968.

126. Quoted in John Bull, *New British Political Dramatists* (London: MacMillan, 1983), 43.

127. Richard Johnstone, 'Television Drama and the People's War: David Hare's Licking Hitler, Ian McEwan's *The Imitation Game*, and Trevor Griffiths's Country', *Modern Drama*, 28/2 (1985), 189–90.

128. *The Times*, 22 August 1978.

129. *Daily Telegraph*, 5 October 1981.

130. Weekly Review Meetings, 4 December 1974, BBCWA; *Daily Telegraph*, 2 December 1974.

131. *New Statesman*, 6 December 1974; *Listener*, 12 December 1974.

132. https://www.cinemablend.com/news/1731500/did-that-pivotal-darkest-hour-scene-really-happen-joe-wright-fills-us-in (accessed 17 July 2019).

133. *Daily Mail*, 20 January 1981.

134. Thomas Carlyle, *On Heroes, Hero-Worship, and the Heroic in History* (London: Fraser, 1841), 1.

135. Alan Shelton (ed.), *Thomas Carlyle: Selected Writings* (Harmondsworth: Penguin, 1971), 189.

136. Thomas Carlyle, 'Shooting Niagara—And After?', *Macmillan's Magazine*, 26/4 (1867).

137. Winston Churchill, *Savrola: A Tale of The Revolution in Laurania* (London: Longman, 1900), 85–6.

138. Alex von Tunzelmann, interview with the author, 5 August 2019.

139. https://winstonchurchill.org/publications/finest-hour/finest-hour-176/books-arts-curiosities-brian-cox/ (accessed 5 August 2019).

140. *Guardian*, 20 December 1980.

141. See Steven Fielding, 'The heart of a heartless political world: screening Queen Victoria', in M. Merck (ed), *The British Monarchy on Screen* (Manchester: Manchester University Press, 2016), 64–85.

142. https://yougov.co.uk/topics/politics/articles-reports/2018/05/18/who-are-mon archists (accessed 17 July 2019).

143. *New Statesman*, 25 August 1937 and 2 October 1938.

144. See for example, David Cannadine, 'Churchill and the monarchy', in David Cannadine and Ronald Quinault (eds), *Winston Churchill in the Twenty First Century* (Cambridge: Cambridge University Press, 2004).

145. http://www.guardian.co.uk/commentisfree/2013/mar/22/theatre-queen-worry-democracy-politicians (accessed 8 May 2013).

146. Despite this, a Conservative councillor who had clearly seen the episode regarded it in upbeat terms, telling the BBC's '5 Live Breakfast' show on 19 September 2019 the then-embattled Boris Johnson could be as great a prime minister as Churchill, citing the apparent fact that despite having a 'terrible time' during the London smog he got 'the people on his side'. Remarkably, and suggesting the power but also the limitations of the small screen to shape perceptions, she did not refer to Churchill's wartime role!

147. Wydra, *Sacred*, 2–5.

148. https://www.newstatesman.com/politics/brexit/2017/07/nigel-farages-love-dunkirk-shows-how-brexiteers-learned-wrong-lessons-wwii (accessed 4 July 2019).

149. 'Reflections of a Director'.

150. The comment of Internet Movie Data Base user tonybu1, https://www.imdb.com/review/rw2258019/?ref_=tt_urv (accessed 27 June 2019).

151. Verdery, *Political Lives*, 5.

152. https://www.theguardian.com/uk/2000/may/08/mayday.world (accessed 16 July 2019).

153. https://www.dailymail.co.uk/news/article-1337315/TUITION-FEES-VOTE-PROTEST-Thugs-deface-Cenotaph-urinate-Churchill.html (accessed 18 July 2019).

154. https://www.independent.ie/world-news/and-finally/churchill-fitted-with-strait jacket-26877663.html (accessed 18 July 2019).

155. https://www.telegraph.co.uk/news/politics/margaret-thatcher/11684868/Margaret-Thatcher-papers-BBC-assisted-the-enemy-during-the-Falklands-War.html (accessed 21 June 2019); *Sun*, 12 May 1983; *Observer*, 21 February 1993.

156. https://www.express.co.uk/news/history/553982/Naval-veteran-Jim-Sweeney-Winston-Churchill-funeral (accessed 2 June 2019).

157. Arthur Matthews email to the author, 22 June 2019.

158. Although the movie *Viceroy's House* (2017) does highlight Churchill's role in the bloody partition of India.

159. https://tardis.fandom.com/wiki/Winston_Churchill (accessed 17 July 2019).

160. Notably, on the big screen in 2012, Abraham Lincoln battled Dracula's offspring in *Abraham Lincoln: Vampire Hunter* and waged war on the undead in *Abraham Lincoln vs Zombies*. Despite their bizarre narratives both films reinforced Lincoln's iconic status.

161. https://www.telegraph.co.uk/comment/personal-view/3602776/BBC-gets-the-historical-drama-of-Dunkirk-absolutely-right.html (accessed 24 July 2019).

162. See for example https://www.theguardian.com/stage/2011/nov/03/three-days-in-may-review (accessed 24 July 2019).

Epilogue

1. Speech of 24 July 2019, https://www.gov.uk/government/speeches/boris-johnsons-first-speech-as-prime-minister-24-july-2019 (accessed 25 July 2019).

2. Speech of 25 July 2019, https://hansard.parliament.uk/commons/2019-07-25/debates/D0290128-96D8-4AF9-ACFD-21D5D9CF328E/PrioritiesFor23Government (accessed 23 December 2019).

3. Natasha Clark, 'Boris' Darkest Hour', 21 June 2019, https://www.thesun.co.uk/news/9343411/boris-vote-of-confidence-election-leadership-race/ (accessed 26 June 2019).

4. https://www.telegraph.co.uk/news/2016/05/14/boris-johnson-interview-we-can-be-the-heroes-of-europe-by-voting/ (accessed 13 December 2019).

5. https://yougov.co.uk/topics/politics/articles-reports/2019/06/18/four-more-discoveries-our-conservative-member-surv (accessed 25 July 2019).

6. Anthony King (ed.), *British Political Opinion 1937–2000: The Gallup Polls* (London: Politico's, 2001), 185–5.

7. https://www.independent.co.uk/news/uk/politics/tory-leadership-boris-johnson-poll-uk-prime-minister-jeremy-hunt-brexit-a9003486.html (accessed 25 July 2019).

8. https://www.telegraph.co.uk/politics/2019/06/29/churchill-moment-boris-have-takes/ (accessed 13 December 2019).

9. https://www.theguardian.com/commentisfree/2019/jun/24/boris-johnson-prime-minister-tory-party-britain (accessed 25 July 2019).

10. https://www.theguardian.com/politics/2019/jun/22/boris-johnson-steve-bannon-texts-foreign-secretary-resignation-speech (accessed 25 July 2019).

11. Mandy Rhodes, '"We're the ones on the right side of history": interview with Steve Bannon', 5 Dec. 2018, https://www.holyrood.com/articles/inside-politics/we%E2%80%99re-ones-right-side-history-interview-steve-bannon (accessed 25 July 2018).

12. Duncan Bell, 'Cyborg Imperium, c.1900', in Anne Chapman and Natalie Chowe (eds), *Coding and Representation from the Nineteenth Century to the Present: Scrambled Messages* (Routledge, forthcoming).

13. Speech of 6 Sept. 1943, in Robert Rhodes James ed., *Winston S. Churchill: His Complete Speeches 1897–1963, Vol. VII: 1943–1949* (London: Chelsea House Publishers, 1974), 6823–27.

Index

For the benefit of digital users, indexed terms that span two pages (e.g., 52–53) may, on occasion, appear on only one of those pages.